CENTRAL ASIA

A New Horizon of Political Culture and People Participation

Dr Sumant Swain

KNOWLEDGE WORLD

KW Publishers Pvt Ltd
New Delhi

ISBN 978-93-93649-34-1

Published in India by Kalpana Shukla

KNOWLEDGE WORLD
KW Publishers Pvt Ltd
4676/21, First Floor, Ansari Road, Daryaganj, New Delhi 110002
Phone: +91 11 23263498/43528107
Email: knowledgeworld@vsnl.net • www.kwpub.com

Printed and Bound in India

2011 FPBA BEST PUBLISHERS AWARD (ENGLISH)

Contents

Dedicated to

Parents,
Bandita and Samarjeet

Acknowledgements

This book about *Central Asia: A New Horizon of Political Culture and People Participation* has been greatly influenced by teachers, family, colleagues and friends. I feel privileged to have been inspired and nurtured by my outstanding teacher and mentor *Prof Ajay Patnaik* who deserves the lion's share of the credit of this book. His deep insight of the subject, sustained guidance, continuous encouragement, warm affection and flexible approach throughout the preparation of this book enabled me to accomplish this work successfully. He went through the entire work with painstaking thoroughness. For me he is a friend, philosopher and guide. My words are insufficient to express my feelings for him. I shall forever remain indebted to him for his guidance and suggestion. I am pleased to help spread the knowledge he has given me to the next generation of researchers.

I also offer my gratefulness to *Prof. Arun Mohanty* without whose scholarly guidance, academic and insightful suggestions, constructive remarks, constant and continuous encouragement and psychological and emotional support, this book would not have seen the light of the day.

I am highly indebted to *Mrs Namita Mohanty* for constantly inspiring and stimulating me to keep on working on this book. The motherly affection that she has bestowed on me has acted as a stimulus injecting in me the inexhaustible energy to accomplish this book.

My sincere gratitude is also due with Prof. Sudhansu Pattnaik, Prof. Tulsi Ram, Prof. Anuradha Chenoy, Prof. Sanjay Pandey, Prof. Gulshan Sachdeva, Dr. Phool Badan, Dr. Tahir Asghar, and Dr. Nalin

Mohapatra for their insightful interaction during the preparation of this book.

I am also extremely indebted to the Indian Council of Social Science Research (ICSSR) for providing me financial assistance and sending me to the Russian Academy of Sciences, Moscow, Russia through the Indo-Russian cultural exchange programme for collection of reference materials and interaction with experts which has enhanced the quality of this book.

I am grateful to Prof. Bakhtiyar Mirkasymov, Prof. Grozin Andrey Valentinovich, Prof. Aleksei Malashenko, Prof. Alexandrov Dmitriy Alexandrovich, Prof. Vyacheslav Ya. Belokreitsky, Prof. Irine Zvyagelskaya, Prof. Sergey Lounev, Prof. Usmanov Abdulkhakovich Mumtaz, Prof. Habibullo Rajabov Rajobovich, Prof. Mikhail S. Meyer, and Prof. Tatyana L. Shaumian for helping me put different perspectives into this book.

I wish to thank the Centre for Russian and Central Asian Studies of Jawaharlal Nehru University, which provided me a very hospitable and stimulating intellectual environment throughout the preparation of this book.

I am also thankful to the staff of Jawaharlal Nehru University Library, Institute of Defence Studies and Analysis Library, the Nehru Memorial Library at Teen Murti House, Indian Council of World Affairs Library, Indian Council of Social Science Research Library, the Russian State Library, Oriental Institute Library, Onion Library, Carnegie Moscow Centre Library, Institute of Ethnography Library, Institute of CIS Studies Library, Foreign Literature Library for their courtesy and cooperation and for helping me in tracing out some of the primary and secondary source materials.

I am grateful to my parents, wife Bandita, son Samarjeet, younger brother and sisters, uncles and aunts, grandmother and other relatives for bearing with my long absence at home and constantly encouraging me keep up the tempo during these strenuous and hectic days.

I am also thankful to my elders Dr Nihar Ranjan Das, Mr Nishikanta Mohapatra, Dr Amar Prusty, and Dr Mahesh Ranjan

Debta, who have always been a source of inspiration and strength while preparing this book at Jawaharlal Nehru University.

I really feel glad to express my utmost gratitude from the deepest corner of my heart to my bosom friends Dr Santosh Rout, Dr Sibasankar Mohanty, Dr Ramakrushna Pradhan, Mr Prasant Sahoo, Dr Gyana Ranjan Panda, Mr Pradosh Satapathy, Dr Birendra Suna, Mr Aurobind Rout, Dr Shakti Pradaynee Jena, Dr Gatikrushna Mahanta, Dr Angira Sen Sharma, Dr Priyabrata Majhi, Dr Nibedita Rout, Mr Santosh Das, Dr Gayatri Panda, Dr Bratati Barik, and for exerting their utmost selves to help me in every possible way during such a crucial period of my preparation of the book. I must express my gratitude and love to them, whose names could not be mentioned in this limited space, but to whom I owe much for whatever little I have accomplished in the academic field.

I am very much grateful to KW Publications specially Ms Kalpana Shukla and Mr Jose Mathew for agreeing and guiding the publication process so competently and quickly.

Last but not the least, though the ideas have been borrowed from various sources, all errors of omission and commission are, however, entirely my own.

Sumant Kumar Swain

Preface

The Central Asian political culture is shaped by its unique history, culture, tradition and social formations. From the earliest to the present day of its civilisational growth, Central Asian political cultures are characterised by unified political system. This unified political system has the peculiar characteristic of having the minimal participation of its citizens. Before the October revolution of 1917, there was an autocratic political system in the Central Asian region as it was part of Tsarist Russia. During those years there was no mass participation in political process. But soon after the successful Socialist revolution, the Bolshevik government adopted the Marxist–Leninist model for the development of the Soviet society. However, though the people got their right to participate in the political affairs of their countries, but in reality, there were no free and fair elections conducted and there was very less participation by them. The voter participation figures were often manipulated only to show the world that a true democratic form of government exists there. In the Soviet political system, people did not have the right to freedom of expression; the media, both print and electronic, was under the control of the state. In this system, social organisations and civil society groups like trade unions, cooperatives, cultural societies etc. played a very limited role. The political system was absolutely dominated by the Communist Party and the opposition political parties were not allowed to play any role in the political process of the country.

After assuming leadership in March 1985, Gorbachev introduced some constructive and radical reform measures for overcoming the stagnation in the economy and reshaping the Soviet political system in order to give a humane face to Soviet Communism through his policy of Perestroika (restructuring) and Glasnost (openness). The main goals of Gorbachev's radical reform were to restructure the Soviet economy and speedier democratisation of the Soviet political system. After the declaration of Gorbachev's reform policy the former Central Asian republics also experienced the momentous changes that took place in the Soviet Union.

The subsequent collapse of the Soviet Union radically altered the social, economic and political systems of the newly independent states of Central Asia i.e. Kazakhstan, Kyrgyzstan, Tajikistan, Turkmenistan and Uzbekistan. Following the Western model, they tried to rebuild their political system. A close look at the constitutions of the five Central Asian republics shows that all of them guarantee equality of rights and freedom to their citizens, irrespective of race, nationality, religion, sex, language or social origin. The other requirements of constitutional democracy are bi-cameral legislature, multiparty system and periodic elections which the respective constitutions have incorporated. The constitutions of all the republics also profess sovereignty, democracy, secularism, republicanism and separation of powers as their underlying principles. However, their state structure can be characterised as 'unitary' rather than 'federal' despite of the fact that in some cases a federal system has been guaranteed under their constitutions. The constitutional system of the five Central Asian republics gives an impression that liberal democracy has triumphed there. But in practical sense, the conditions required for a liberal democratic system are completely absent in these states. As ethnic cleavages and cultural divergence are deep rooted, and civil society is considerably weak, the political culture is also influenced by these forces. In the post-Soviet phase the major features of political culture in these republics are strong executives, intolerance, mistrust and clientism, which hinder the development of democratic culture. However, after the 9/11 incident with more external engagement in this region, the political regimes of the five republics are making some attempts to democratise their political system.

This book is aimed at highlighting the development of political culture in the Central Asian region and the role of political parties, other non-political formations like the opposition, media, civil society and ethnic minority groups who are also augmenting the process of democratisation. This book consists of five chapters. The first chapter analyses the concept, definition and various theories of political culture and participation and in the end of this chapter it discusses the relationship between political culture and participation. The second chapter deals with the political culture and participation during the Soviet period and it analyses the Soviet political system and the prospects of political participation in that period. The third chapter focuses on the country-wise institutional developments like the growth and functioning of the executive and legislature and its constitutional provisions, functions and relevance in post-Soviet Central Asia. The fourth chapter discusses the formation and role of political parties, minorities, media and civil society in augmenting the process of democratisation in Central Asia. The fifth chapter summarises the whole topic and gives concluding remarks based on the above analysis and the findings of the field study that was undertaken for this purpose. The book concludes with some way forward that can be considered as steps—and if implemented—can improve the quality of the political process and stimulate the democratisation process in the five republics of the Central Asian region.

This book has drawn its essence from various sources. It has effectively used some primary sources like government documents, constitutions, draft of the state laws and speeches of various leaders of the Central Asian republics etc. Apart from this, the book has also extensively used secondary sources that comprise books and articles from academic journals and newspapers etc. Interview with experts from some authoritative Russian and Indian scholars have also been added to the texts which were specially undertaken for the purpose of this book.

Students, academicians, researchers, policy makers, businessmen and diplomats would be enormously benefited by this book. I sincerely believe that this book would make its humble contribution to enriching knowledge about the newly politically formed five Central Asian countries' constitutional provisions and political practices for India's Central Asia connect policy.

Map of Central Asian Countries

Abbreviations

RSDLP	Russian Social Democratic Labour Party
RSFSR	Russian Soviet Federated Socialist Republic
USSR	Union of Soviet Socialist Republics
TSSR	Turkmen Soviet Socialist Republic
UCC	Uzbek Central Committee
CPSU	Communist Party of the Soviet Union
YCL	Young Communist League
TSSPW	Turkic School of Soviet and Party Work
CALPA	Chief Administration of Literary and Publishing Affairs
TASS	Telegraphic Agency of the Soviet Union
CPK	Communist Party of Kazakhstan
DDK	Democratic Kyrgyzstan Movement
MVD	Ministerstvo Vnutrennikh Del (Ministry of Internal Affairs)
CIS	Commonwealth of Independent States
OSCE	Organization for Security and Co-operation in Europe
UTO	United Tajik Opposition
PDPT	People's Democratic Party of Tajikistan
CPT	Communist Party of Tajikistan
DPT	Democratic Party of Turkmenistan
PDP	People's Democratic Party
NGO	Non-Governmental Organization
IRP	Islamic Renaissance Party
RPPK	Republican People's Party of Kazakhstan
SDP	Social Democratic Party
UPDP	Uzbekistan People's Democratic Party
ULDP	Uzbekistan Liberal Democratic Party

SNDP	Self-Sacrifice National Democratic Party
UNRDP	Uzbekistan National Revival Democratic Party
JSDP	Justice Social Democratic Party
LDP	Liberal Democratic Party
NIDHR	National Institute of Democracy and Human Rights
PCDS	Public Council of Democratic Security
TNURM	Tajikistan National Unity and Revival Movement
ICSR	Institute for Civil Society Research

1
Theoretical Perspectives

Every political system of the world is studied on the basis of political culture and participation. The tradition of political culture and participation not only gives impetus to know the entire political system of a country but also provides knowledge about the establishment of an ideal political system with effective political participation. In the modern world, people are so informed and active in every sphere that on the one hand they try to establish a political system which gives optimum benefit to the common people and provide national security, and on the other a culture of active citizen participation. Without active participation, the country may fail to provide good governance and prosperity as is evident of many newly independent states.

1.1 Political Culture

Political system of a country is shaped by its history, culture, tradition and pattern of social formations and these elements play a major role in developing the political culture of a country. The notion of political culture assumes that the attitudes, sentiments and cognitions that inform and govern political behaviour in any society are representing coherent patterns together and are mutually reinforcing. In spite of the great potentialities for diversity in political orientations, in any particular community, there is a limited and distinct political culture which gives meaning, predictability, and form to the political process.[1] Also, each individual must, in his or her own historical context, learn and incorporate into his or her own personality, the knowledge and feelings about the politics of his or her people and community.[2]

The political culture of a society is limited but is given a firm structure by the basic factors of dynamic psychology. Therefore, a generation must receive its politics from the previous one; each must react against that process to find its own politics and the total process must follow the laws that govern the development of the individual personality and the general culture of a society.

The functioning of a political system is to be seen with reference to a nation's political culture because the citizens' attitude to the political system clearly affects the kind of demands made, the way they are expressed and organised, the reaction of the political system and the nature of the popular support etc.[3] For this reason, it is necessary to study the history, social structures and cleavages which affect the politics of a country. It has also been seen that the society is the source of conflict and sometimes of violence, which the political unit must resolve or regulate. Nearly every political unit has faced the task of confronting social crisis that has tested its ability to survive. Political values of the society have been connected with an interest in the conditions of the social order and the political stability of regimes. These regimes have also been maintained by a mixture of incentives including force, legitimacy, tradition and the distribution of material benefits.[4] The contemporary political system has faced lots of challenges like ethnic conflict, religious extremism, vast economic disparities, inequalities and conflicting value systems that make the functioning of a stable political process difficult. Even with all these social and economic differences, society presents a political system that tries to resolve disputes and maintain political stability. Society also provides a support that helps to maintain the stability of the political system through economic and social structures, established pattern of interpersonal relations and consensus on the goals of social life.

Wildavasky points out that each nation is a mix of cultures that requires a realistic understanding of political culture in actual political practice. For him, political culture is not a static conceptual frame for classifying nations but living principles that constantly interact with daily political life. In a country, or the international system, the motivations generated by the political subcultures are the very product of politics. The peculiarities of a nation's politics will vary according to the type of political culture held by those in the government, those acting as opposition and by the several competing groups seeking access to elite positions.[5] So, people's political ideas, attitudes, values etc. normally passing down from one generation to the next, imply that the attitudes and values of the past tend to be conveyed into the present. However, the individual's political ideas change throughout life in response to political experiences, with basic orientations often remaining the same. Thus, the attitudes of previous generations based on the political events of their lifetimes may indirectly influence the political conduct of contemporary citizens. Political culture provides a set of 'resources' in terms of images, symbols, myths and traditions enabling people to make sense of their position, and generate a kind of need that influences the selection and interpretation of the available cultural resources.[6]

A nation's political culture includes its citizens' orientations towards three levels: the political system, the political and policymaking process, and policy output and outcomes. The political system is the governance of its political institutions involving both input and output functions. The principal inputs are political parties, interest groups and the mass media. The main outputs are legislatures, executives, bureaucracies, courts and the nation itself. The policymaking process includes the actions, conflicts, alliances, behavioural styles of parties, interest groups, movements and individuals involving citizens' and leaders' policy expectations from the government.[7]

Political culture was originated as an analytical tool for political scientists using quantitative behaviouralist methods. So, the theory of political culture was developed in response to the need to bridge a growing gap in the behavioural approach in political science between the level of microanalysis with psychological interpretations of the individual's political behaviour and the level of macroanalysis with the variables common to political sociology.[8] It constitutes an attempt to integrate psychology and sociology in political analysis for mapping attitudes in mass societies. This theory is associated with modernisation theories and the behaviouralist revolution of the 1950s and 1960s.

1.1.1 Concept of Political Culture

The 'word political culture' is the combination of two words—political and culture. Politics simple means the study of state, government and relating to public affairs. But the culture is a historically created system. It is a system of beliefs and practices, in terms of which a group of human beings understand, regulate and structure their individual and collective lives.[9] In that connection a classical anthropological definition states that "culture is that complex whole which includes knowledge, beliefs, art, morals, law, custom and any other capabilities and habits acquired by man as a member of society".[10] So, the culture is the main source of political power and legitimacy. A political organisation is an arrangement for maintaining order, resolving disputes, selecting authoritative leaders and thus promoting community among two or more moral forces.[11] A political culture is a part of the larger culture of a society. It abstracts from the larger culture those orientations relating to political objects. Within the political system subculture has also played a major role. Subculture means societal groups who possess a particular identity. A political subculture is a group of the population that possesses a distinct and consistent set of attitudes, beliefs and orientations to political objects. So the culture and politics are inextricably linked in a reciprocal relationship. Sometimes governmental decisions affect the culture of a country and vice versa. The concept of political culture was popularised through the writings of Gabriel A. Almond, Sidney Verba and Lucian W. Pye though many of the political thinkers also stressed upon the political culture before these thinkers. Rousseau conceived political culture in terms of the morality, customs and public opinion of a particular people.[12] Tocqueville argued that political culture was 'the habits of heart', that lead to the whole moral and intellectual condition of people.[13] Burke argued that a nation is not merely a territory of landmass, but more importantly an embodiment of history, morals, and culture, extending to time, values, and telling a way of life that grows out of "the peculiar circumstances, occasions, tempers, dispositions and moral, civil, and social habitudes of the people". For him it is an invention of ages and generations, an idea of continuity or tradition.[14]

In the behavioural revolution of politics, many scholars relate people's fundamental and deep sentiments towards politics, public opinion, and political ideology. Almond and Powell define political culture "as the pattern of individual attitudes and orientations towards politics among the members of a political system".[15] Almond's political culture theory gives some importance to political attitudes, beliefs, values, and emotions in the explanation of political, structural and behavioural phenomena—national cohesion, patterns of political cleavage, modes of dealing with political conflict, the extent and the character of participation in politics, and compliance with authority.[16] He also analysed that orientations are predispositions to political action. These orientations are also determined by such factors as traditions, historical memories, motives, norms, emotions and symbols.[17] The political objects of the orientations include such institutions as the executive, legislature and judiciary, the political parties, pressure groups, a person's view of himself or herself as a political actor, and his or her view of other citizens.[18] Georgi Shaknazanov who was the President of the Soviet Political Science Association, has explained political culture as the participation of diverse social opinions in politics; the political culture of the people and political culture training, as the regulation of social-political attitudes.[19] At the same level, Lucian Pye defined political culture as the set of attitudes, beliefs and sentiments, which give order and meaning to a political process, providing the underlying assumptions and rules that govern behaviour in the political system. In this sense, political culture includes both the political ideals and the operating norms of a polity. This is the manifestation in aggregate form of the psychological and subjective dimensions of politics including 'public opinion, political ideology, national ethos and the basic consensus, values and constitutional integrating sentiments of a people'.[20]

Another famous definition was given by the American political scientists Gabriel Almond and Sidney Verba that political culture is the pattern of orientations to political objects among the members of the nation. By 'political objects', they meant parliaments and political parties, as well as less tangible aspects of a nation's political life such as the conventional account of its history. So, political culture can also be understood in terms of the political practices and rituals of a given community.[21] Almond and Verba seemed to imply that political culture never changed and never varied internally. Marxists objected that Almond and Verba's major book *Civic Culture* ignored class and power relations, and many detractors raised the red flag of normative bias.[22]

The other perspective on political culture is that of Daniel Elazar, who focused on patterns of political culture prevalent in each state and not on the specific distributions of political orientations held by individuals. For him political culture comprised the habits, perspectives and attitudes that exist to influence political life; regional variations in political forms resulted directly from differences in political culture among the states.[23] To Elazar, political culture is the particular pattern of orientation to political action in which each political system evolves. He argues that each state has certain dominant traditions about what constitutes proper government action. Three aspects of political culture are influential in structuring the nature of a state's political systems. These are:

- The set of perceptions of what politics is and what can be expected from government, held both by the general public and the politicians

- The kinds of people who become active in government and politics, as holders of elective office, members of the bureaucracy and active political workers
- The actual way in which the art of government is practised by citizens, politicians and public officials with their perceptions[24]

The concept of political culture today is more comprehensive than that of earlier ones. David Robertson describes it as "the totality of ideas and attitudes towards authority, discipline, governmental responsibilities and entitlements."[25] Likewise, Richard Rose writes of the 'values, beliefs and emotions', which 'constitute' the culture and give meaning to politics.[26] Despite their new broad explanations, many of these extended definitions retain elements of the old behaviouralism. Thus, Dennis Kavanagh, acknowledging that a political system is embedded in a political culture goes on to say that culture disposes its members to regard certain forms of political behaviour and institutions as normal and others as abnormal.[27]

Brian Girvin considered that political culture works at three levels: the macro, mesco and micro.

- The macro level of political culture refers to those symbols and values which define the collective enterprises, typically the nation-state, and which are normally unchallenged. The rules about how this collectivity organises itself inhabit the mesco level.
- In mesco level values and assumptions may be the object of political struggle.

At the micro level, it is to be found as 'normal politics'.

- Each level of political culture is seen as constituent forms of identity and sets of values. Political culture does not describe a pre-given set of psychological state, but supplies a language of politics.[28]

For Macridis, a political culture constitutes of commonly shared goals and commonly accepted rules of individual and group interaction in terms of which authoritative decision and choice will be made by all the 'actors' within a political system.[29] He also mentioned that political culture determines the pattern of leadership, its mode of legitimisation, the instruments it employs with manipulation, persuasion, coercion and its transformation as new values and beliefs that are injected in the system.[30]

More recently Stephen Chilton has proposed nine criteria for defining the concept of political culture:

i. ***Supramembership***
Political culture is not a mere aggregate of individual subjective orientations but it is a superorganic and collective phenomenon that goes beyond the particularistic existence of any given individual or an aggregate of individuals considered in isolation.

ii. ***Sharedness***
Political culture must be capable of being shared providing "a common framework of mutual orientation." An arbitrary collection of people (e.g. travellers in the desert) with an equal distribution of characteristics (e.g. all thirsty) does not necessarily make a culture.

iii. ***Inequality***
The influence on political culture varies according to the political influence of individuals or classes of individuals. This difference in influence, between the elite and the populace, is instrumental in facilitating an adequate understanding of the scope and depth of political change.

iv. ***Behavioural Property***
Political culture is not only a collection of abstract ideas and beliefs but it must be capable of being observed in social behaviour.

v. ***Post-behavioural Property***

Although political culture is observable in social behaviours, it should be distinguished from mere regularities of behaviour. Behavioural regularities can be used by factors other than culture. This distinction allows us to probe into embedded cultural meanings and define culture by these meanings rather than by mere regularities.

vi. ***Unrestricted Applicability***

The concept of political culture must be capable of being applied on different levels of social organisation and across a board of societies. A narrow definition specially designed for a particular research purpose would limit the scope of the applicability of this concept.

vii. ***Non Reductionisms***

While a universally applicable concept is crucial for broadening the scope of cultural studies, attention should also be paid to "the uniqueness of any culture's approach to politics". Reducing diverse criteria to some lowest common denominator for cross-cultural studies is unsatisfactory, giving insufficient attention to the richness and uniqueness of different cultures.

viii. ***Comparability***

A well-defined political culture concept must permit not only meaningful comparisons between cultures but also meaningful comparisons between different aspects of a single culture. Intra-cultural comparisons are as important as intercultural ones, because such comparisons allow one to see and understand the role of internal dynamics of a society that play in effecting political change.

ix. ***Objective Testability***

The concept of political culture must be capable of generating hypotheses that can be tested for validity in terms of some objective standards against empirical data—but such objective standards are currently lacking in the study of political culture.

After mentioning these criteria, Chilton argues that a definition of political culture must meet these requirements and those which fail the test are not conceptually acceptable.[31] He also defines political culture as the shared way of relating among a group or groups of people.

Political culture theory defines political culture in this fourfold way:

- It consists of the set of subjective orientations to politics in a national population or subset of a national population.
- It has cognitive, affective and evaluative components. It includes knowledge and beliefs about political reality, feelings with respect to politics, and commitments to political values.
- The content of political culture is the result of childhood socialisation, education, media exposure and adult experiences with governmental, social and economic performance.
- Political culture affects political and governmental structure and performance. The causal arrows between culture and structure and performance go both ways.[32]

1.1.2 Dimensions of Political Culture

Gabriel Almond constitutes political culture in terms of three dimensions—the cognitive, the affective and the evaluative.

- The cognitive dimension refers to people's knowledge about the political system, its role and the incumbents of these rules, its inputs, and its outputs.
- The affective orientation attempts to grasp the feelings about the political system, its role, personnel, and performance.
- The evaluative orientation refers the judgements and opinions about political objects that typically involve the combination of value standards and criteria with information and feelings.[33]

Among all three dimensions, evaluations may change because of empirical experiences, and norms and values are deeply embedded in long lasting, durable orientations towards political actions and the political system. After Almond, Sidney Verba also advanced a four-fold classification for understanding political culture, including national identity, identification with one's fellow citizens, beliefs about government policy and beliefs about decision-making process.[34]

1.1.3 Types of Political Culture

Almond and Verba identified three ideal types of individual and collective political culture. These are: parochial, subject and participant.

- A parochial political culture was characterised by general ignorance about political objects, leading to absence of involvement in political objects leading to absence of involvement in political activity.
- A subject political culture was characterised by widespread knowledge about political processes, but a disinclination to participate in political activity, often because of feelings of powerlessness.
- Participant political cultures combined knowledge about politics with a willingness to participate in the political process.[35]

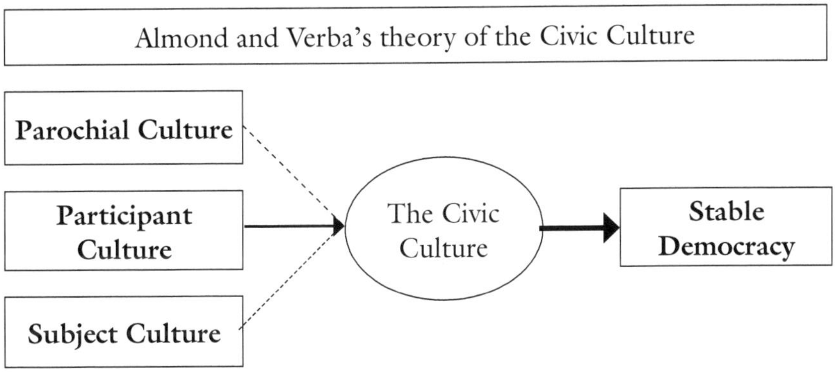

They regarded these types of political culture as the properties of both individuals and political systems. They also argued that the best type of political culture for a stable democratic system should involve a mix of subject and participant elements. They labelled this mixture as civic culture where citizens would possess high levels of knowledge about the political process by participating as political actors.

Apart from that, Elazar also describes three basic types of political culture:

- 'The traditionalist culture' takes an ambivalent position towards the market place and becomes paternalistic and an elitist commonwealth. Even if the government has a positive role, it is limited only to maintaining the status quo because the political power is closely held by a self-perpetuating group where social and family ties are most important and the non-elite refrains from any political activity.
- 'The individualistic political culture', by emphasising utilitarian motives for the organisation and operation of government—with the political system serving the private market place or the private concern (not a common good)—remains personalistic, professionalised and anti-bureaucratic.
- The third type is 'moralistic', emphasising the commonwealth conception of the political system and is considered to be oriented toward achieving the public good by advancing the public interest. Most importantly, communal orientation and concern with issues, through political participation and an active government, are valued and encouraged.[36]

Lucian W. Pye also mentioned that in all political systems at least two political cultures exist—an elite political culture and mass political culture:

- The elite political culture involves the attitudes, sentiments and behaviour patterns of those who function through the operation of the political recruitment. They have been brought to active roles within the political system and have a direct effect on the outputs of the system. The elite political culture, thus, involves primarily those in the authoritative structures but also the leadership elements of the non-authoritative structures and processes.

- The mass political culture is formed by the attitudes and orientations of the population as a whole towards politics. It includes the participating citizens and the rank-and-file members of both the authoritative and non-authoritative structures who do not have significant control over outputs of the system. The mass political culture led to the political development that the sentiments and values of the common mass make it possible for people to work together effectively in seeking collective goals.[37]

In the changing era of multi-faceted political system, citizens are sharply divided on both the legitimacy of the regime and solutions to major problems.[38] The political culture of the world is also divided into many political processes in which independent nation states adopt political systems according to the will of their citizens. However, sometimes political systems are also adopted under the influence of international political forces. Sometimes, the objective of the political culture connotes the authoritative standards that define the range of acceptable behaviour for actors within any political system. With this system people are less interested in an individual's objective state of mind than in any particular features of the system which shape a person's conduct. In Communist societies the Marxist–Leninist ideology constitutes a set of goals or ideals for the population.[39]

In the early twentieth century a variety of political systems arose that divided the world. When Fascism was on the rise in Europe, Communism was establishing itself in the Soviet Union, colonial administrations governed large parts of the world and monarchial or authoritarian governments ruled other parts of the world. During this period, Western Europe and North America strained to maintain democracy in this sea of conflicting currents.[40] Today, many of these forms of governance are no longer widely accepted. Communism still has strongholds in China and Cuba, but it has lost its image as a progressive force for global change. Some nations of the world still accept autocratic or religiously based systems of government. However, the global wave of democratisation in the 1990s has raised democratic principles to a position of preeminence. Most of the people in the world today seem to favour democratic principles even if they differ in how those principles should be applied.

But in Socialist societies, the elites are monolithic, ruthless and unrepresentative. In these societies, the unified elite have absolute and unbounded power. All intermediate bodies, all individual groupings and particularly professional groups are in fact controlled by delegates of the elite. A classless society leaves the mass of the population without any possible means of defence against the elite. In that society, there exist a determined and ruthless body of rulers on the one hand and a vast mass of unorganised and unarticulated people on the other. By contrast, the liberal democracies operate by means of democratic and responsive elites drawn from a wide area and these rulers are continuously kept in check by the operation of the political process. These 'pluralistic elites' operate through a political machinery which has been accepted as 'legitimate'.

Marxists argue that political culture itself is derivative of economics and determines political interests and political action (an individual's class position). The proletariat does not possess the means of production that can manifest political sentiments unlike capitalists who own the means of production. Because economic power derives from political outcomes, the laws governing the political system reflect the class interests of the capitalists. Therefore, law as well as political culture largely can be understood as part of the 'superstructure', shaped by 'the economic base' of particular societies.

Political observers have seen that political culture is very important in influencing not only politics but economic life as well. Alexis de Tocqueville argued that Islam is incompatible with democratic ideals, while Christianity sustains them. Likewise, Max Weber suggested that the particular values fostered by Protestantism were the key to capitalist development in the West. In a similar vein, Tu Wei-ming has put forward the important point that particular cultural values explain the rise of East Asia as an economic power giant in the last few decades of the twentieth century.[41] In the same direction, Lucian Pye's study of political culture in Asia shows how Confucianism, Hinduism and Islam contribute to paternalistic, familistic, consensual and clientelistic political patterns throughout East, Southeast and South Asia. He argued that the Asian countries may have their own patterns of modernisation and education and economic growth need not necessarily lead to democratisation. The unanticipated reversal of modernisation and the emergence of populistic Islamic fundamentalism in Iran and in the Middle East shows the strength of traditional political culture and socialisation process.[42]

Many scholars view the relationship between political culture and other parts of the social system as a matter of interaction effects. The importance of culture in a polity does not imply that other political and economic factors are not important. In this regard, Samuel Huntington's analysis that twenty-first century world politics will largely be determined by cultural factors, with the 'clash of civilizations'—rather than ideological and economic factors—depends on a particular interpretation of the collapse of Communism in the early 1990s. To Huntington, culture emerges as the most important factor in world politics precisely because ideological and economic problems have been 'settled'.[43] In the ideological point of view, Liberalist study of political culture was pointless since all the indicators pointed to the rise of educated, civically oriented participant societies. In the Marxian point of view, political culture is the historical process in dialectic terms. Marx put his thought pressing forward material and political moral progress in a benign sequence—material improvement produces three subcultures: an exploitative and ever-concentrating capitalistic class; an exploited, propagandised and coerced working class; and an enlightened organisation of revolutionaries. The end result is a universal enlightenment culture and society of mass welfare, rationality and creativity.[44]

Citizens' attitudes and beliefs are shaped by personal experiences and by the agents of political socialisation. Also, in any historical period there may be change in the culture of many nations. Modernity, secularism, post-material values, fundamental and ethnic awareness, democratisation, and marketisation all reflect both general societal developments and specific historic events. In the contemporary world, the most significant changes in the political socialisation process are the emergence of the electronic and print media. The major impact of mass media on attitudes and behaviour was mediated by elites like think tanks, political leaders, analysts and other intellectuals etc. The messages transmitted by the media were interpreted by these peoples and it was presumed that ordinary people were protected from mass manipulation. Sidney Verba and his collaborators demonstrate that the various groups of politicians, bureaucrats, business leaders, labour leaders and the like describe the media as being at the very highest level of political influence.[45]

Criticism

Like many other theories, political culture has been criticised from four different perspectives. These are discussed below:-

- The criticism that is advanced by Brian Barry and Carole Pateman that political socialisation produces political attitudes, which in turn cause political behaviour and underlie political structure. They also make the case that causality can and does work the other way—institutions and performance influence attitudes. The early advocates of political culture explanation also recognised that causality worked both ways—attitudes influence structure and behaviour and that structure and performance in turn influence attitudes.

- The second criticism is reflected in the works of Jerzy Wiatr, who argues that attitude change results from economic and social-structural change.
- The third line of criticism is mainly reflected in the writings of Stephen White and others arguing that it is inadmissible to separate political attitudes from behaviour.
- The fourth criticism was advanced by Ronald Rogowski and Samuel Popkin, who underline that political structure and behaviour can be explained by the short-term material interest calculations of political actors. There is no place for values, norms, feelings and more complex cognitive components. History, memory and cultural context have no explanatory power.[46]

In spite of that criticism, the political culture theory has great value in the present plural sociopolitical system of the world. In a multicultural society, it needs a broadly shared culture to sustain it. Since it involves several cultures, the shared culture only grows out of their interaction and should both respect and nurture their diversity and unite them around a common way of life.[47] The main central problems faced by political groups are integrating diverse peoples having different norms and interests into a cohesive organisational framework. Due to globalisation and the changing nature of modern technology, no society today can insulate itself against external influences. Capital, technology, peoples, ideas and so on move more freely across territorial boundaries and introduce new forms of thought and life.[48]

Modernisation has been the major cultural trend that has transformed the world and public values. The secularising influences of science and control over nature have altered economic and social systems thereby shaping political cultures, expanding throughout the world from the West. This trend towards cultural modernisation continues to have powerful effects as it has the power to penetrate any society. Exposure to modernity through work, education and the media shapes an individual's personal experiences and sends messages about modernity in other societies by encouraging citizen participation, individual equality, improved living standards and increased life expectancy, and government legitimacy based on policy performance.

Post-material values have given rise to new citizen groups, like the environmental movement, the women's movements and other public interest associations. These changing values have also reshaped the policy agenda of industrial democracies and more citizens are asking government to restore the environment, expand social and political freedoms and emphasise policies to ensure social equality. Politicians in these democracies are struggling to balance these new policy demands against the continuing policy needs of the past.

Due to economic globalisation, modernisation and technological innovation, the cultures of countries will grow closer together exchanging ideas, values, habits, and performance—eventually leading to a fusion of cultures.

The premise of political cultures was the diversity among the community, within nations and other political groups. In a wider context, political culture referred to an integrated contestation of ideas not only about government but about political life as a whole, from the meaning of social existence, to social priorities and to actual policies. The theory of political culture would connect cultural values to political attitudes, political attitudes to individual political behaviour, individual behaviour to social choices, social choices to political policies and institutions, policies and institutions to social changes; which in turn would affect cultural attitudes and create a new cultural cycle.[49] The present modern welfare state gradually replaced the earlier laissez–faire state at least partly and the new political history looked at social groups and patterns of action focusing on voting patterns, ethnicity, religion and class. So, political culture is not static in that it transforms from one generation to another. It maintains the corelation between continuity and change within the political system in terms of socioeconomic and political developments of a state that facilitate future political stability.

1.2 Political Participation

The development of an effective political system of a country depends to a large extent on its citizens' active participation in the political process. Opening up opportunities to a large number of citizens engaging in politics, political participation refers to those voluntary activities by which members of a society share in the selection of rulers directly or indirectly, and in the formation of public policy. In a democratic form of government, citizens take part in public life both through direct forms of political participation such as voting, party work, organising for a cause, demonstrating, lobbying and more indirect forms of participation such as membership in civic groups and voluntary associations influencing the quality of programmes and politics of government. Democracy, literally meaning rule by the people, implies that all citizens should play a role in the governing process.[50] Citizen participation in the political affairs of the country is greatly influenced by the norms that are established by the political cultures which entail duties of citizens and their political rights and enhance participation in the process of elections. The range of political participation depends on four factors: the types of offices that are directly elected; the level of government; the frequency of elections and the number of votes that ballot gives the voter at any election.[51] So, political participations are representing a general value in our society.

Political participation directly provides feedback to policymakers, and it helps to improve their planning. It is also essential to establish in a responsive government that responsiveness is necessary to legitimise authority, and that legitimacy is a precondition to a stable and orderly government.[52]

Political scientists often stress upon political participation over a period for an effective and stable political system. To Aristotle, man is a political animal whose highest potential is to participate in a shared public life among friends. He analysed political participation as a self-sufficient and natural end in itself for the good life. Therefore, institutions should be judged in their capacity to nurture a public and participatory way of life.[53] He classified political systems according to two principles; the number of people who participated in making political decisions and whether the system was guided by good or perverted ends."[54]

Rousseau also mentioned that freedom and legitimate authority became possible in a setting where people made their own laws and participated directly as citizens in exercising sovereignty. So "participation" appeared to be a more powerful agent than "consent" for justifying rights and obligations in a political society. It was the continuous participation where the citizens judged and deliberated over public affairs as a public member rather than as a private individual. He put forward the point that sovereignty could not be "represented," and it had to be assumed that citizenship was necessarily coterminous with participation. For him, participation was not just an expression of sovereignty, but it was also society's means for political education. Without it, the public knowledge and outlook of the citizen disappears, to be replaced eventually by the "rational egoism" of Lockean individuals.[55]

Political participation concerns the manner in which citizens interact with government and through active participation in government; citizens attempt to inform their needs to public officials. Legislators, chief executives, and judges are all participants in the policy process and political participation is not only limited to those elected and appointed officials. Most people participate in government and politics to extend and expand their capacity and understanding.

Political scientists distinguish between conventional and unconventional modes of participation. For them, conventional means of participation are those that are more common and accepted whereas unconventional ones are less ordinary and are sometimes viewed as less acceptable. The conventional manner of participation is for citizens to initiate contact with government officials. This type of participation can take many forms. Citizens may make phone call, write, fax, sign a petition, or send a telegram to their elected representatives or other government officials. This contact could be about a pending piece of legislation affecting many people or a problem specific to the individual making the contact. Because government officials, especially the elected ones, would like to keep their constituents happy—this kind of participation can be very effective.

On the other hand, government invites comments from the public on a variety of matters and one of them is public hearings. A public hearing is frequently held prior to a legislative body's taking action on an issue. Passage of a local government's budget, the rezoning of a piece of property and a decision regarding a public utility's rate hike request are examples of situations often subject to public hearings. At these proceedings, citizens may give the decision-making body their views concerning the pending action. In addition to formal public hearings, many local governments set aside time during their meetings for public comments.

Comments are sought not only by legislative bodies but also executive agencies charged with implementing legislation frequently seek public inputs regarding proposed rules and regulations.[56] The participation strategy or technique, and the kinds of participation skills which are needed in the development of a policy are often quite different from those needed while a policy is being implemented. In democratic countries, political involvement is genuinely spontaneous or voluntary, and depends upon the citizen's sense of civic duty. For most citizens, the only political activity is voting, and even this is sometimes difficult to promote.

In addition to individual political activities, citizens can also participate in the political process through interest groups and political parties. Interest groups and parties are important means of organising political power, either to influence the government decision making or to assure the effective implementation of policy decisions. They can also effectively link the general public to the political process to the extent that the political organisations crystallise and represent popular demands within the political decision-making process.[57]

As a nation develops politically and economically, the formal interest groups tend to grow in power and importance relative to the informal groups. Consequently, workers, farmers, and even ethnic minorities organise formally to influence politics and in some cases governments create formal interest groups as a means of controlling society.

Therefore, social status, organisational involvement, gender, education etc. consistently affect the rate of political participation. Ideology or values provide a second basis for long-term predispositions. Ideology can be expressed in terms of the voters' position on a single left-or-right value dimension.

1.1.2 Concept of Political Participation

The word political participation comprises two words—political and participation. Participation means involvement in certain affairs. It is the act of taking part or having a share with others in some action.[58] There is a close connection between participation and the very idea of the political. Politics itself implies action in common for a certain purpose and it presupposes some degree of participation. So, participation is defined briefly as taking part and political participation as taking part in the formulation, passage or implementation of public policies.[59]

Political participation denotes the actions by which individuals take part in the political process. It is the voluntary action by which people seek to influence the making of public policy. Participation refers to those acts that are not formally empowered to make decisions and they only influence the behaviour of those who have such decisional power and successful participation refers to those acts that have the intended effects.[60] It may also refer to a set of attitudes such as a person's sense of political competence, or high levels of interest in and information about politics.[61] Political participation may increase when state provides opportunities to its citizens. The establishment of universal adult suffrage provides right to form associations and free speech, and maintaining a free press provides an incentive to individuals and social groups to enter the political process.[62] Apart from that political participation also increases in relation to other types of changes. It includes the development of the institutional framework; the growth of central authority in relation to politically autonomous local authority; the expansion of bureaucratic system, its autonomy, and the degree of its penetration into the society and economy and the growth of a sense of national identification.[63] So, political participation is likely to be greater in an open democratic society than in authoritarian one.

Political participation consists of taking part in the process of formulation, passage, and implementation of public policies by citizens, aiming at influencing decisions which are taken by public representatives and officials.[64] In that context, democratic participation refers to the process by which citizens influence or control those who make major decisions affecting them. People seek to participate in a partial process in a variety of ways. Some individuals are highly active in politics and they may join political parties, and canvass on behalf of particular candidates in elections or engage in administrative work in the cause of a local party organisation. Other may join single-issue pressure groups with the aim of advancing particular causes or demands and some may become career politicians by successfully standing for public office. In complete contrast, other people would appear to abstain completely from political activity, refusing even to vote.

J.S. Mill has advocated an extension of popular participation that it is only possible in certain areas like in policy formulation rather than in its implementation.[65] The Report of the Skeffington Committee on Public Participation in Planning distinguishes between those stages of the planning process which require expertise and those in which the layman may play a role. Participation involves doing as well as talking and there will be full participation only where the public is able to take an active part throughout the plan-making process. The report also enumerates the four stages of the planning process at which it is realistic for the public to participate:at the announcement of the plan, in opinion surveys leading to the identification of the choices open and finally the discussion of the favoured proposals.[66] Milbrath analysed political participation in the broadest terms—from spectator activities including exposing oneself to political stimuli, voting, and political discussion to campaign activities and to gladiatorial activities such as soliciting political funds, being a candidate for office, and actually holding public or party office.[67] He also pointed out that a society in which most adults are intensely interested and involved in politics means that political considerations determine a person's opportunities for education, for a job, for advancement on the job, for a place to live and for goods to enjoy.[68]

Verba and Nie define political participation as behaviour designed to affect the choice of governmental personnel and policies. They exclude passive forms, civil disobedience and political violence, efforts to change or maintain the form of government, behaviour outside the sphere of government, behaviour mobilised by the government and unintended political outcomes.[69] They argue political participation as "all voluntary activities by individual citizens intended to influence either directly or indirectly political choices at various levels of the political system."

Political participation may also be defined as individual or collective action at the national or local level that supports or opposes state structures, authorities and decisions regarding allocation of public goods. Three aspects of the definition should be emphasised. First, the action can be verbal or written. Second, it can be violent or nonviolent; and thirdly it can be of any intensity.

Individuals' interest in politics may be active or passive. The active action can be verbal or written and inaction refers to passive forms. These interests involve political attitudes and sentiments such as feelings of patriotism, political alienation, apathy, and indifference, and political awareness, such as attention to politics in the media.

Both action and inaction can be related or unrelated to the electoral process, aggressive or nonaggressive in nature, directed toward structural or non-structural objects, related to phenomena outside the sphere of government, and mobilised or voluntary (for instance, the communication of various orientations toward aggressive and nonaggressive actions by political authorities is "mobilised inaction").[70]

Political participation combines an element of manipulation by others with some degree of independent choice and judgement. This is particularly true with respect to the poor, dependent and insecure. Moreover, while participation by the poor through patrons, within ethnic groups, through special interest groups, or through parties allows them to bring pressure on the government, it also permits governments to communicate and bargain with the poor; to threaten them; to exercise loose or tight control; and to coopt the most vigorous and ambitious among the poor. Control and cooption can be channelled through patrons and brokers, from higher to lower strata within ethnic groups, through special-interest associations and through parties. Thus, the poor access to government carries with it accessibility to manipulation.

Political participation in democratic countries relates to not only bargaining by the citizens with the government but also cooperation with the political system. Booth and Seligson define it as "behaviour influencing or attempting to influence the distribution of public goods."[71] One important facet of this definition is that their notion of public goods is commonly used to refer to roads, schools, health centres and other services provided by governments and, once supplied, more or less open to all members of society.

The degree of individual participation varies according to their socioeconomic conditions, education, and willingness among citizens in a political system. Verba, Nie and Kim argued that the universal tendency for citizens with higher levels of 'socioeconomic resources' was to be more willing to participate in politics. Socioeconomic resources primarily constitute education and income and these resources provide the skills, the stimulation and the capability to participate in many kinds of political activity.[72]

There are three 'modes' or kinds of political participation—voting, electoral campaigning and non-partisan lobbying.

These three kinds of participation differ in terms of the degree of institutional conflict implied, and the amount of individual initiative and effort required. These three kinds of participation discussed by Verba, Nie and Kim have been termed as conventional or elite—directed to distinguish them from unconventional, protest or elite-challenging modes of participation such as demonstrations, strikes, damage to property or violence against people. But citizens tend to see at least some of these options as supplements rather than alternatives to voting, campaigning and lobbying. However, few express support for outright violence. So, the concept of political participation stresses the idea of public membership, of citizens sharing justice and orienting their actions toward a public or common good. By being closely associated with a view of politics as the set of activities and relationships concerned with maintaining community, fostering cooperation among individuals and groups, and encouraging settlement of disputes through public communication, participation is seen as based upon the individuals' identification with the common interests of the community, which may of course be descriptively correct or incorrect. In any case, it stresses freedom to act with others in order to promote a shared purpose. This notion of political participation appears to be identified with a particular combination of individual and group functions performed through increasing political knowledge, promoting self-realisation and developing political virtues.

Politics is understood as a struggle over scarce power resources. In Lasswell's phrase, "the political process is the shaping, distribution, and exercise of power—freedom is directed towards protection of private advantage, and political participation becomes instrumental to that end". Here it is clear that participation functions to ensure citizens' interests and is not overlooked by elites. And it functions to provide legitimacy for elite decisions in the system in which decisions are made.

John Stuart Mill goes further and argues that democratic political economic institutions shape the character and political efficacy of individuals in a way that leads them to greater political participation. In "De Tocqueville on Democracy in America," *Consideration on Representative Government,* and *Political Economy*, Mill argues that active participation in local and representative political institutions diffuses intelligence and sharpens the mental and judgemental abilities of the citizen. Democratic politics encourages individuals to become familiar with the current issues and it applies to moral principles of everyday living. Furthermore, active political participation brings individuals out of their self-regarding private lives and develops their moral capacity to be concerned with the welfare of others.[73]

G.D.H. Cole extended Mill's argument that a democratic workplace would transform society. Cole saw the democratic organisation of the workplace as the key element in not only providing the individual worker with the attitudes, skills, knowledge and incentives to participate in the political process in and beyond the workplace, but also in transforming the existing political system from more oligarchic to more democratic. The transformation of the worker from a person who is poor, not free, submissive, and politically inefficacious to one who has developed natural capacities for self-government, freedom, and self-assertion can come about only by moving away from an autocratic and towards a democratic workplace.[74]

Both Nie and Burstein assume that the relationship between mass-media use and political participation is recursive, with media use leading to increased political activity and no effect of participation on media use. The assumption is that contact with political information and societal institutions through the mass media produces an inclination to participate actively in political life.[75]

1.1.3 Theories of Political Participation

There are mainly five models identified by various scholars for political participation which are: Socioeconomic Status, Psychological

Resources, Social Connectedness, Group Identity or Consciousness, and Group Conflict. These are discussed below:-

a. Socioeconomic Status

The socioeconomic status model of political participation is mainly developed by Almond, Verba and Nie. In this model, participation is primarily driven by individuals' resources i.e., time, money and skills and civic orientations—attitudes which individuals hold towards themselves or the political system which predisposes them towards political action. Because high-status individuals are located in social environments which encourage and enforce positive attitudinal and participatory norms as well as civic skills, they are more likely to participate in politics than are low-status individuals.[76] Though Verba and Nie claim no causal priority for social class over other social characteristics, empirical studies of political participation rely almost exclusively on this model. Individuals with high level of education are more likely to participate in politics than individuals with low levels of education. The evidence is almost as persuasive for the relationship between income and participation though the effect of income on participation is typically less than that for education.

In recent times, theorists have mainly stressed on the economic model of political participation. Citizens will participate in politics according to an economic perspective if their expected benefits from doing it exceed their expected costs. This axiom will hold under all conditions provided citizens possess sufficient resources to expand at least some of them in political activity. A minimal level of education may be conceptualised as a source which citizens can use in dealing with public officials, even if this only involves going to the polls to vote for or against political candidates every year or so. So, this approach takes two forms.

In one form, attempts are made to examine the economic rationality with which voters choose at election time on the basis of their own perceptions of the policy stands of the candidates or parties.[77] The second form that the economic approach to political participation takes is to examine the extent to which various voting rules and electoral arrangements precisely aggregate voter preferences from collective-consumption goods.[78]

In an Economic Theory of Democracy, the American political scientist Anthony Downs presented a ground-breaking application of microeconomic models to the study of politics on general and voting in particular. The analysis of Downs is built around the axiom that individuals base their electoral choice upon a calculation of costs and benefits. So the choice of whether or not to participate in political activities depends on whether the individual concerned feels that the act imposes costs or yields benefits. The whole approach is built around the idea that the individual is rational and calculative and that as a rule individuals seek to minimise personal costs. A favourite metaphor is talks of politics as a supermarket. As Iain McLean puts it, "when I go to vote I am doing something similar but not identical to what I do when I go shopping. In both cases I 'buy' what I 'want'". Therefore, should an individual decide that her or his vote will make no difference to the outcome of an election, then that individual will not vote. Moreover, it is also possible that the benefits associated with a particular electoral outcome might accrue to the individual whether or not she/he votes.[79]

b. Psychological Resources

This theory gives importance to the individual's psychological orientations such as political interest, political efficacy, trust in government and civic body etc. This theory also focuses on one minority group that uses group-orientation, rather than system orientation, as psychological indicators. This theory would stand by identifying psychological states that might motivate individuals to participate and states which can be usefully characterised as instrumental. Instrumental participation is goal-oriented participation. This is intended by the citizen to get government to implement public policies or to solve political problems that concern him. Instrumental participation would be based on what Easton calls demands, subjectively meaningful attitudes about what government should or should not do.[80]

Expressive participation, on the other hand, is participation for its own sake. Here participation is itself seen as inherently rewarding or pleasant. It has two dimensions. First, participation can be inherently pleasant because politics is dramatic, exciting, offering opportunities for social interaction and self expression. Secondly, participation can be inherently rewarding because it fulfils a subjectively felt obligation to participate.[81]

Verba and Nie argued that neither demands nor interests nor civic duty should cause a high level of efficacy, nor should efficacy itself cause participation rather, efficacy is a necessary condition for instrumental participation.[82] This theory also mentioned that three factors are conducive for effective political participation i.e., political goals, engagement of politics and sense of obligation.

c. Social Connectedness

Sociologists, social psychologists and political scientists have theorised at great length about the nature of the individual's relationship to the larger society and sometimes negative, isolating consequences of life for individuals as they struggle to make their way in mass society.

Putnam, Teixeira, and Uslaner argue that the decline in political participation over the past 20 years is directly related to the lack of connectedness between individual citizens and the larger political and social community. These contemporary scholars use structural or behavioural factors such as organisational involvement, church attendance, home ownership and marital status as indicators of social connectedness in contrast to the earlier scholars who emphasised the psychological aspects of social connectedness.[83]

d. Group Identity or Consciousness

This theory demonstrated that importance of group identity is a factor influencing individual political behaviour. The group-consciousness model of political participation is more relevant as an explanation of minority behaviour in the present world order. For example, in America, participation levels of Blacks and Whites, shows that Blacks participate more than Whites controlling for socioeconomic status, because of their heightened levels of group consciousness.

Miller et al find that group consciousness is associated with participation for Blacks, women, and the poor, while Wilcox and Gomez conclude that group identity significantly increases Black participation. However, group identity is not consistently related to participation when estimated separately for other ethnic groups. This theory looks at two dimensions of group consciousness—group closeness and out-group distance.[84]

e. Group Conflict

This theory emphasises that individuals, and the groups with whom they identify, have real historical and present-day relations with other groups. These inter-group interactions may be or have been conflictual, either over the division of scarce (real or symbolic) resources and the application of political power, or fundamental cultural values like religion. Several themes are central to group conflict theory, particularly competition for limited resources, in-group identification, and out-group hostility—all of which are reflected in the individual's social, political and economic behaviours.[85]

Political efficacy is important for political participation. It encompasses a wide variety of sentiments, feelings and aspects of human psychology. It is about the extent to which a person senses that he/she can make a difference politically as well as the degree to which that person feels politically literate or politically competent. Moreover, political efficiency is the way a person feels about the ability of the social groups with which she/he identifies to orchestrate change or achieve aims. The development of group consciousness represents a process through which dissatisfactions are aggregated across individuals and then politicised. It also incorporates the notion of shared interests and the recognition that the individual's welfare is inseparable from that of the group.

Politicised group consciousness is further delineated through the realisation that the inability to gain valued resources in a society is not a consequence of personal failing, but rather results from inequities in the decision-making and reward distribution process. Politicised group consciousness acts to promote electoral participation among highly identified members of subordinate groups at rates higher than expected on the basis of socioeconomic characteristics alone. Participation is not simply a reflection of the social conditions that people experience. How people perceive and evaluate their positions is an important link between the experience of certain social situations and political participation.

Robert. A. Dahl, for example, hypothesises that some citizens have to be socialised into such an acceptance on pain of the survival of the "democratic" game itself.[86] Duncan Black assumes that individual preferences are ordered on an underlying dimension (such as the Liberal–Conservative dimension of political issues) and shows that if the preferences of each individual are single-peaked or bell-shaped on the dimension, then majority rule can produce a non-imposed collective decision. Anthony Downs adds competing political parties to a variety of preference distributions on the dimension of issue space and shows that citizen irrationality can actually be fostered by the parties.[87] Finally, a third set of theorists imply that majority rule and other voting rules are merely alternatives to the rule of unanimous consent, the rule under which economic (private market) exchange takes place. As a consequence, unanimity should be used as a benchmark (or constitutional rule) for evaluating other (operational) voting rules since it, and it alone, is the rule whereby any voter can ensure that he will not have to accept the imposed choice of others

Today, the typical individual in nearly all states is aware of and clearly affected by the government. He or she is generally encouraged to participate in some way in the political process. So widespread is the norm of mass political participation that it is regarded as one of the features of the modern political unit, in contrast to the non-participatory traditional or primitive state.

Popular sovereignty is the basis of legitimate political power. It is the doctrine that the right to rule belongs to the people and that those who govern derive their authority from the people. If political power is derived from the people, the people should be involved in politics to exercise their sovereignty.

Mass political involvement does not necessarily mean that citizens participate in a democratic way by choosing their leaders or setting polity. Authoritarian regimes often have other motives for promoting mass participation. Some traditional authoritarian regimes and some conservative military regimes try to stifle political participation. However, most such regimes, especially those eager to promote social and economic change, find it useful to stimulate mass citizen involvement. Elections can promote social and economic change finding it useful to stimulate mass citizen involvement. Elections can promote the sense of participation even if there is only one candidate for each office or the results are rigged. By means of rigged elections and other forms of controlled participation, authoritarian regimes try to enhance their own legitimacy in the eyes of the citizens and outsiders. By channelling popular participation into activities that it can control, the regime can satisfy those who want to be politically active and give the masses the feeling of being part of the political process. In addition, authoritarian regimes may encourage voluntary civic action as a means of mobilising the talents and energies of the masses in the pursuit of goals determined by the elite.

The forms of individual political action can vary from reading about political developments in the newspaper to voting, to petitioning an elected official or a bureaucrat for a favour to active participation as a campaign worker or party propagandist. Even apparently nonpolitical civic volunteer action is a form of political participation in the sense that it gives the individual a sense of involvement and an administrative part to play in the political system.

In democratic countries, political involvement is genuinely spontaneous or voluntary, and depends upon the citizens' sense of civic body. For most citizens, the only political activity is voting, and even this sometimes is difficult to promote.

In a Communist political system, the primary tasks of the Communist Party—the only party with any meaningful existence—were to assure political, social and economic control over the society and to oversee the implementation of the wishes of the party elite at the grassroots. In this society, people participate only through the hierarchical structure of the party system and everything that is controlled by party.

Nowadays, the problems of social inequality, environmental degradation, ethnic problems and other social issues provide an impetus to citizens' participation both in the policy formulation and implementation of public policy. Implementation of government policies and decisions largely depends on the active participation of masses. Most of the interest groups are demanding direct participation in decision-making process against many existing institutions, government, and political parties, by operating outside and seemingly in defiance of politics. In the present situation as modernisation proceeds, political systems have become institutionalised and politics professionalised, technocratic and non-partisan and as a result the level of participation has declined. For more participation in the political process, the government decentralised the political process but still the level of participation is very low. In that context, Elena C. Varn Meter suggests that effective citizen participation can be the bottomline for government.[88]

Verba and Nie's model of political participation views life circumstances as influencing voter registration and other forms of political participation, both directly and indirectly through civic attitudes. In this model life circumstances create the conditions that establish, modify and reinforce relevant civic orientations and the skills necessary for political activism.[89] In the present world this represents a very mature political system though not with stable institutions. Institutional change, reform and decay have been infectious and voters have responded to it. In that context,

Verba highlighted the following necessary conditions for effective political participation:

f. Resources

For Verba and Nie, resources are most important for political participation. These include:

Intellectual resources: There are a number of intellectual resources that increase the likelihood that an individual will attempt some participatory act which will be successful. They are:

- information about politics, issues, channels of communications, and the rules of political participation
- skills in manipulating these channels of access. Skills in written and oral expression, in reasoning, and in manipulating others are important.

Material resources: These include all those material possessions that can be used to increase one's political effectiveness: money, control over jobs, land, or other resources.

Social resources: These include the people or organisations that one can manipulate and can get to support in a political act. People who have friends, who belong to organisations, or who work in places where it is possible to organise one's fellows are more likely to participate successfully. If the individuals who possess one resource are likely to possess all the others, and those who are missing the same are likely to have none. This way the distribution of participation in a society is likely to be badly skewed. As Dahl has pointed out, there is a wider distribution of political power if resources are dispersed.

g. Costs of Participation

The notion that resources will be useful for political participation implies the opposite side of the coin. It means that the participation will cost something in the way of resources and participation takes time, money, and effort.

h. Motivations to Participate

An individual will attempt to participate not only due to the resources he or she possesses, but on the motivation to do so. Those who have had no experience of successful participation—either in relation to politics or elsewhere—are likely not to believe in the efficacy of their acts. This makes clear the extent to which political participation depends upon a learning process—both in relation to politics and in relation to other social situations.

Everyone has a wide range of subjectively defined needs, but not all are perceived as having anything to do with decision makers. The more an individual perceives governmental activity as relevant to his own needs, the more likely he is to attempt political participation.

As the government becomes active in a particular field—culture or health, for example—it makes it more likely that individuals will define problems within that realm as having some political content and as needing governmental action.

Participation is conceptualised as a goal-directed activity, but this does not rule out the possibility that participation may represent a satisfaction in and of itself. Through participation in political activities the individual can meet other people and satisfy social needs.

i. Structural Conduciveness

An individual or group will participate upon the degree to which there are available channels for such participation. If the structures of politics are not conducive to participation, it will take place less frequently.

The formal participatory structure is an important set of structures that are relevant to the formal and legal structures. Most such legal rules are permissive as far as the individual participant is concerned. They allow him to participate, but he must do so voluntarily. Free speech and other civil liberties allow individuals to speak their minds about politics and they do not require them to do so. Though some nations have laws requiring voting, the United States permits it without requiring it.

In nongovernmental organisations, participation through voluntary associations, unions, and like takes place. These organisations may be both direct providers of benefits for citizens and means to attain further benefits for them from the government. In general, the unorganised populace in any society will be more likely to be exploited and less likely to participate effectively. Since the density of organisational membership varies from one social group to the other, this channel of participation will vary in its availability to different groups.

j. Cultural Conduciveness

Just as the structural setting within which an individual finds himself would affect his likelihood to participate and in that way cultural conduciveness is necessary for political participation. If the general beliefs of the culture or of his own relevant subculture are such as to foster participation, the individual is more likely to take part. There are many such general beliefs that are relevant and in which one finds variations from group to group. These include general beliefs in the manipulability of the environment, the responsiveness and trustworthiness of government, the trustworthiness of one's fellow citizens (in so far as one wants to collaborate with them) and the legitimacy of political activism.[90] These are the necessary conditions for political participation but for the effective political participation it needs the proper social capital. Putnam defines social capital as "features of social organisations such as networks, norms and social trust that facilitate coordination and cooperation for mutual benefit."[91] Social engineering of the society is necessary for better participation in the political process.

The relationship between political culture and political participation are complementary to each other. The political system of any country can't function without effective political participation. In any form of government in the world whether Liberal or Marxist, as adopted by the nation state, the need is to facilitate citizens' active participation in that country. It may be restrictive according to the established political system. In the Liberal Democratic state, the political system always tries to engage its citizens in every level from policy formulation to the policy-implementation level. The established political culture sometimes changes according to the wish of the citizens of the country. The purpose of participation in contemporary democracy is not to involve directly the majority of citizens in the process of public policy formation. Rather, the purpose of citizen participation properly is viewed as a means of achieving and maintaining the stability of the political system through the popular selection of political leaders or elites. The governmental elites are the persons who do and should make public policy decisions. They are far better equipped in terms of education, information, interest, time and others to make such decisions.[92] On the other hand, effective participation requires information, discussion and involvement in the political process. Now, these things are easier due to the internet revolution, social media, availability and accessibility of electronic and print media, state concern about citizens, active citizenship and people's willingness for voluntary participation to politics. So, political participation is always important in any political system. Good government could be created by the active involvement of citizens.

Notes

1. Pye, Lucian W. (1967), "Political Culture and Political Development", in Lucian W. Pye and Sidney Verba (eds.), *Political Culture and Political Development (p.7)*. New Jersey: Princeton University Press.
2. Ibid.
3. Pramanick, Swapan Kumar (1981), "Political Culture or Class Culture", in L.S. Rathore (ed.), *Political Sociology (p.176)*. New Delhi: Meenakshi Prakashan.
4. Kavanagh, Dennish (1983), *Political Science and Political Behaviour.* London: George Allen and Unwin Publishers Ltd. p. 66.
5. Lane, Ruth (1992), "Political Culture: Residual Category or General Theory", *Comparative Political Studies,* vol. 25., no.3., October. p. 375.
6. Street, John (1994), "Political Culture: From Civil Culture to Mass Culture", *British Journal of Political Science,* vol. 24., no.1.. January. p. 101.
7. Haynes, Jeffrey (2005), *Comparative Politics in a Globalizing World,* Cambridge: Polity Press. Pp. 183-184.
8. Pye, Lucian W. (1967), "Political Culture and Political Development", in Lucian W. Pye and Sidney Verba (eds.), op.cit. p.8.

9. Parekh, Bhikhu (2006), *Rethinking Multiculturalism: Cultural Diversity and Political Theory*. New York: Palgrave Macmillan (Second Edition). p.143.
10. Meisel, Joh. (1974), "Political Culture and the Politics of Culture", *Canadian Journal of Political Science*, vol.7,. no.4, December. p.602.
11. Huntington, Samuel P. (1968), *Political Order in Changing Societies*, USA: Yale University Press. p.8.
12. Hua, Shiping (2004), "Political Cultures", in Mary Hawkesworth and Maurice Kogan (eds.), *Encyclopedia of Government and Politics*, vol. 1., 2nd Edition, London: Routledge. p. 493.
13. Ibid.
14. Zhou, Zhenghuan (2005), *Liberal Rights and Political Culture: Envisioning Democracy in China*, New York and London: Routledge. p. 27.
15. Pramanick, Swapan Kumar (1981), "Political Culture or Class Culture" ,in L.S. Rathore (ed.), op. cit., p. 176.
16. Almond, Gabriel A. (1983), "Communism and Political Culture Theory", *Comparative Politics*. vol. 15., no. 2., January. p. 127.
17. Kavanagh, Dennis (1983), op.cit., p.50.
18. Almond, Gabriel A. (1983), "Communism and Political Culture Theory", op.cit., p.129.
19. Ibid.
20. Hua, Shiping (2004), "Political Cultures",in Mary Hawkesworth and Maurice Kogan (eds.), op. cit., p. 493.
21. Barrie Axford, Gary K., Browning, Richard Huggins, Ben Rosamond, John Turner, and Alan Grant, (1997), "*Politics: An Introduction*",London and New York: Routledge. p. 78.
22. Pateman, Carole (1971), "Political Culture, Political Structure, and Political Change", *British Journal of Political Science*, vol.I. p.291.
23. Gendzel, Glan (1997), "Political Culture: Genealogy of a Concept", *Journal of Interdisciplinary History*, vol.28, no.2, Autumn.p.231.
24. Conway, M. Margaret (1989), "The Political Context of Political Behaviour", *The Journal of Politics*, vol. 51., no. 1., February. p.4.
25. Street, John (1994), op. cit., p.102.
26. Ibid.
27. Ibid.
28. Ibid. p. 103.
29. Kim, Young C. (1964), "The Concept of Political Culture in Comparative Politics", *The Journal of Politics*, vol. 26., no. 2., May. p. 331.
30. Ibid. p. 332.
31. Zhou, Zhenghuan (2005). op.cit. Pp. 51-52.
32. Almond, Gabriel A. (2000), "The Study of Political Culture", in Lane Crothers and Charles Lockhart (eds.), *Culture and Politics: A Reader*, New York: St. Martin's Press. p.10
33. Almond, Gabriel A. and Verba, Sidney (1963), *The Civic Culture: Political Attitudes and Democracy in Five Nations*, Princeton & NJ: Princeton University Press. p. 15.
34. Verba, Sydney (1967), "Comparative Political Culture", in Lucian W. Pye and Sidney Verba (eds.), *Political Culture and Political Development*, Princeton & NJ: Princeton University Press. p. 526.

35. Barrie Axford, et al, op.cit., p.81.
36. Conway, M. Margaret, op. cit., p.5
37. Pye, Lucian W. (1971), "Identity and the Political Culture", in Leonard Binder, James S. Coleman, Joseph La Palombara, Lucian W. Pye, Sidney Verba, and Myron Weiner (eds.), *Crises and Sequences in Political Development*, Princeton: Princeton University Press. Pp.102-103.
38. Gabriel A. Almond, G. Bingham Powell, Kaare Strom, Jr. and Russell J. Dalton (2004). *Comparative Politics Today: A World View* (8th Edition), Singapore: Pearson Education. p. 52.
39. Kavanagh, Dennis, op.cit., p.50.
40. Gabriel A. Almond,et al, p. 48.
41. Hawkesworth, Mary and Kogan, Maurice, op.cit., p. 498.
42. Almond, Gabriel A., "The Study of Political Culture", in Lane Crothers and Charles Lockhart (eds.), op.cit, Pp 14-15.
43. Hawkesworth, Mary and Kogan, Maurice, op.cit., p. 498.
44. Almond, Gabriel A., "The Study of Political Culture" in Lane Crothers and Charles Lockhart (eds.), op.cit., p.8.
45. Ibid. p.16.
46. Ibid. Pp10-11.
47. Parekh, Bhikhu, op.cit., p.219
48. Ibid. p.171.
49. Lane, Ruth (1992), "Political Culture: Residual Category or General Theory", *Comparative Political Studies*, vol. 25., no.3., October. p.381.
50. Osbun, Lee Ann (1985), *The Problem of Participation*, New York: University Press of America. p.v
51. Lipsest, Seymour Martin (1995), *The Encyclopedia of Democracy*, vol. III, London: Rutledge. p.915.
52. Weiner, Myron, "Political Participation: Crisis of the Political Process", in Leonard Binder, James S. Coleman, Joseph La Palombara, Lucian W. Pye, Sidney Verba, and Myron Weiner (eds.), op.cit., p.160.
53. Schwartz, Joel D. (1984), "Participation and Multi Subjective Understanding: An Interpretivist Approach to the Study of Political Participation", *The Journal of Politics*, vol. 46., no.4., November. p.1121.
54. Lipset, Seymour Martin, op.cit., p. 913.
55. Scaff, Lawrence A. (1975), "Two Concepts of Political Participation", *The Western Political Quarterly*, vol. 28., no.3., September. p. 452.
56. Magill, Frank N. (1996), *International Encyclopedia of Government and Politics*, vol. II., London: Salem Press. 1996. p. 1016.
57. Theen, Rolf H.W. and Wilson, Frank L. (1996), *Comparative Politics* (3rd Edition), New Jersey: Prentice-Hall. p. 16.
58. Parry, Geraint (1972), "The Idea of Political Participation", in Geraint Parry (ed.), *Participation in Politics*, Manchester: Manchester University Press. p.3.
59. Ibid. p.5.
60. Verba, Sidney (1967), "Democratic Participation", *Annals of the American Academy of Political and Social Science*, vol. 373., Social Goals and Indicators for American Society, vol. 2. ,September. p. 55.
61. Kavanagh, Dennish, op.cit., p.181.
62. Weiner, Myron, "Political Participation: Crisis in the Political Process", in

Leonard Binder, James S. Coleman, Joseph La Palombara, Lucian W. Pye, Sidney Verba, and Myron Weiner (eds.), op.cit., p.174.
63. Ibid. p.175.
64. Barrie Axford, Browning, Gary K., Huggins, Richard, Rosamond, Ben, Turner, John and Grant, Alan, op.cit., p. 110.
65. Parry, Geraint, "The Idea of Political Participation", in Geraint Parry (ed.), op.cit., p.10.
66. Ibid.
67. Asher, Herbert B., Richardson, Bradley M. and Weisberg, Herbert F. (1984), *Political Participation: An ISSC Workbook in Comparative Analysis*, New York: Campus Verlag Publisher. p.48.
68. Kavanagh, Dennis,"Political Behaviour and Political Participation", in Geraint Parry (ed.), op.cit., p.111.
69. Conge, Patrick J. (1988), "The Concept of Political Participation: Towards a Definition", *Comparative Politics*, vol. 20., no. 2., January. p. 242.
70. Ibid. p. 246.
71. Ibid. p. 244.
72. Miller, W.L. (2004), "Political Participation and Voting Behaviour", in Mary Hawkesworth and Maurice Kogan (eds.), *Encyclopedia of Government and Politics*, London: Routledge. p. 413.
73. Schweizer, Steven L. (1995), "Participation, Workplace Democracy, and the Problem of Representative Government, *Polity*, vol. 27., no. 3., Spring. p. 362.
74. Ibid. p. 863.
75. Smith-Louis, Lynn (1979), "Individual Political Participation: the Effects of Social Structures and Communication Behaviour", *The Pacific Sociological Review*, vol. 22., no-1., January. p. 28.
76. Leighley, Jan E. (1995), "Attitudes, Opportunities and Incentives: A Field Essay on Political Participation", *Political Research Quarterly*, vol. 48., no. 1., March. p.183
77. Sproule-Jones, Mark and Hart, Kenneth D. (1976), "A Public-Choice Model of Political Participation", *Canadian Journal of Political Science*, vol. 6., no.2., June. p. 176.
78. Ibid. p. 176.
79. Barrie Axford, Browning, Gary K., Huggins, Richard, Rosamond, Ben, Turner, John and Grant, Alan, op. cit., p. 130.
80. Lawrence, David G. (1981), "Towards an Attitudinal Theory of Political Participation", *Polity*, vol. 14., no-2, Winter. p.334.
81. Ibid. p. 335.
82. Ibid. p.337.
83. Leighley, Jan E. and Vedlite, Arnold (1999), "Race, Ethnicity, and Political Participation: Competing Models and Contrasting Explanations", *The Journal of Politics*,Vol. 61., no. 4., November. p. 1095.
84. Ibid. p. 1096.
85. Ibid.
86. Sproule-Jones, Mark and Hart, Kenneth D., op.cit., p.176.
87. Ibid.
88. Rosenr, Judy B. (1978), "Citizen Participation: Can We Measure Its Effectiveness?", *Public Administration Review*, vol. 38, no 5, September-October. p. 462.

89. Conway, M. Margrate, op. cit., p. 6.
90. Verba, Sidney, op. cit., pp. 63-66.
91. Krishna, Anirudh (2002), "Enhancing Political Participation in Democracies: What is the Role of Social Capital?", *Comparative Political Studies*, vol. 35., no-4., May. p.439.
92. Osbun, Lee Ann (1985), "*The Problem of Participation*, New York: University Press of America. p.87.

2
Soviet Legacies

The present Central Asian States—namely, Uzbekistan, Turkmenistan, Kyrgyzstan, Tajikistan and Kazakhstan—emerged as national republics during the Soviet period. But in these five Central Asian countries, political, social and economic developments were different from each other. Ethnic composition, political culture, political participation and economic development were distinctive even before the conquest by Russia in the 19th century, since all these countries experienced a wide variety of civilisational, cultural and social contacts. Prior to the Russian conquest, Central Asia was an area of historical settlement and numerical preponderance of the Uzbek, Tajik, Kyrgyz and Turkmen peoples. It shares borders with China's Sinkiang Province with hundreds of miles in the east and it had reached to the Caspian Sea opposite Baku. The northern limit of Central Asia extends almost to the Trans-Siberian Railroad and intersects that line in the vicinity of the city of Petropavlovsk in the Kazakh Republic. Within these territorial limits, these regions have different and distinct historical backgrounds regarding the evolution and formation of the state system.

2.1 Origin of Civilisations

The origin of the Central Asian civilisations is traced back from the ancient period. In Uzbekistan, the earliest recorded inhabitants of the region were Persian-speakers, who settled in the valleys of the *Syr-Darya* and *Amu-Darya* rivers. Scythians, Persian-speakers, and smaller group of nomads largely populated the plains to the north of the *Syr-Darya.*[1] In the seventh century, Arabs gained control over important parts of this region and spread Islamic culture and Arabic script. This resulted in the new cultural patterns spreading over the existing Persian and Turic Cultures. Then, they came under the Mongol influence. In 1219, the Mongol rule weakened, particularly after the reign of *Timur* or *Tamerlane*, establishing *Samarkand* as the capital of a revived empire, and thereby, the name Uzbek first emerged on an important political level. Early in the 16th century, *Transoxiana* (the area between the two great rivers of the Oxus and Jakartes) came under the control of Uzbek tribes moving from the steppe regions of the north and led by Muhammad Shaibani Khan. During this period, their nomadic life-style gradually gave way to sedentary life, settling in cities and towns of the region as they began to mix with the local inhabitants, including other Turkic peoples and Persian speakers. However, without giving up their tribal identification, the Uzbeks simultaneously associated with other sedentary peoples under the general name of '*Sart*'. Elite-level bilingualism occupied key parts of the region's identity, where Turkic language was used for political life and the high culture was largely a form of Persian. In the 17th century, the highly autonomous kingdoms or Khanates namely Bukhara and Khiva were established.[2]

The origin of *Khanate* was mainly based on elements of nomadic society. The nomadic society was united from top to bottom by kinship. This society in form was a series of concentric circles. The nomadic village was composed of a series of extended families. This village in turn combined with related villages into a large unit, the clan—all the members of which had descended from a single ancestor many generations back. The clan combined with other clans into a confederation, all related by ties of descent in common from a single founder, traced from father to son. This clan confederation was the basis of a political unit, the state or principality, which was called the Khanate.[3]

The Turkmen are widely believed to have descended from the *Ogur* tribes migrating from the Altai region north of Mongolia in the latter part of the 10th century. They founded the Seljuk dynasty, with Merv being the capital. The largely nomadic Turkmen tribes had not formed any national state and lordship was divided between the Persian Empire, the Khivan Khanate and the Bukharan Emirate.[4]

Likewise, the origin of the Tajiks as a settled people is traced back to as early as 3000 B.C. But the first historical record of the eastern Iranian kingdom dates from the last millennium B.C.[5] In the upper Oxus was Bactria, the home of Zoroaster and of Roxanne, who married Alexander the Great. Sogd (Sogdiana) extended along the middle Oxus.[6] Alexander, by conquering both Sogd and Bactria in 329 B.C., left a legacy of Greek culture and legend, which survives even to this day. He also left new cities as strong and visible evidence of his rule, among them Khodzhent and Kulyab.

The Greco-Bactrian Kingdom of Alexander's successors fell in the second century B.C. at the onslaught of a Tatar Tribe, the nomadic Tokhari, who founded the Great Kushana Empire. The Kushanas ruled Central Asia for the next five hundred years and its conquest by the White Huns (Ephtalidas) in the third century A.D. marked the beginning of political fragmentation of the area which was exacerbated by a new invasion of nomadic Turks three hundred years later.

The Arab conquest in the seventh century A.D. was a milestone in the history of Central Asia. The dynamic religion of Islam replaced other existing faiths such as Zoroastrianism, Buddhism and Nestorian Christianity and remained the dominant cultural and social force in the area until modern times.[7] It moulded diverse peoples into a uniform social community.

The conquest restored old cultural ties with the Middle East and the Mediterranean basin sparking the growth of a splendid civilisation. There was high resistance to the Arabs initially, requiring several campaigns leading to the suppression of many local rebellions and the most important of them was the revolt of A.D. 776-83.[8] Mukanna is enshrined in the Soviet Tajik pantheon as a fighter for popular freedom. As the authority of the Baghdad Caliphate in Central Asia declined, powerful local families held the political power. The local dynasties of the Takharid (821-73) and the Saffarids (873-903) were followed by that of the Samanids (903-99).[9] The Samanid rule brought a period of unprecedented economic prosperity and cultural development, which are still considered the highest achievements of Persian culture.

The Samanid Empire had an efficient and highly centralised government. In that time, trade was highly visible among other things. However, arts developed rapidly and the Samanid capital of Bukhara became a great centre of learning in the Muslim world. A sophisticated Farsi language, the language of the great medieval Persian literature of the ninth and tenth centuries represented by poets like Rudaki and Firdousi, was formed by the impact of Arabic on the Iranian Dari Language.[10]

By the end of the tenth century, internal unrest and the growth of religious heresies had undermined the power of the Samanids. The dynasty saw another Turkic invasion of the Karakhanids, who were followed in the twelfth century by the Seljuk Turks.[11] Both tribes got assimilated and adopted Islam. Political fragmentation resulted but economic prosperity was not seriously affected, and learning and culture continued to flourish under the impact of new religious movements. Islamism originated as a resistance movement against the Seljik rulers and Sufism, a rebellion against orthodoxy, injected into Islam a strong mystical element manifesting itself in the court literature of the period.[12]

The thirteenth century Mongol invasion of Chingiz Khan was the second milestone in the history of Central Asia. But in that period, instead of developments, it went downwards. The splendid civilisation that fell was never to recover, despite subsequent periods of prosperity and cultural growth. The people of eastern Iran mixed with the Turks and the blended cultures that emerged differed from that on the Iranian plateau across the Oxus. The pan-Iranian unity of the Samanid Empire was irretrievably lost.

After the death of Chingiz Khan his heirs divided the empire, and some measure of prosperity returned to Central Asia. Timur, the great conqueror of the fourteenth century, enriched his capital of Samarkand with the spoils of war. He developed all the communication facilities and irrigation facilities, and also developed trade and encouraged the work of artisans, artists and scientists. There was a revival of literature, this time written in the Turkic language. The last major invasion before the coming of the Russians occurred in the fifteenth century when the Uzbeks, the Turkic nomads who were a part of the Golden Horde, swept through Central Asia.[13] They established a decentralised Khanate and supplied the last ethnic element to the people who now bear their name. But the mid-eighteenth century Khanate was again broken up into independent principalities: Bukhara, Khiva, Kokand, Gissar and Badakhsan. These engaged in continuous wars that led to population losses, destruction of the irrigation networks, and a general social and economic upheaval.[14]

Historians describe that the ancestors of the Kyrgyz who are mixed with Turkic, Mongol and Kipchak descent originated from the area around the upper reaches of the Yenisei.[15] They were gradually forced to emigrate southwards under pressure from various tribal confederations and then form the Mongol advances towards the Tien Shan mountain range. Settling in the Tien Shan region, they could not escape Mongol domination, and during the 13th century found themselves in the territory of Chingiz Khan's second son Chagatai. As imperial power declined during the 15th century, the various Kyrgyz tribes appear to have created the first independent Khanate with some degree of autonomy from nominal Mongol overlords.[16] Soviet historians argued that it was during this period that the Kyrgyz developed their distinctive language, and acquired a sense of nationhood though the social organisation remained centred around tribal and kinship ties. At various times they were ruled by the Turkic and Chinese empires, before coming under the authority of the Khanate of Kokand at the beginning of the 19th century.[17]

Like the other four republics, the Kazakhs are a Turkic people, descendants of nomadic tribes who settled probably on the territory of present-day Kazakhstan in the south and north of this region and nomadic postoralism remained the dominant way of life of this region.[18] In the early 13th century Kazakhstan was conquered by the Mongols and the cities of the south. The 14th and 15th centuries were marked by power struggles, most of which were centred on the southern part. Mongol princes from the Golden and White Hordes fought among themselves making way for Uzbek and Nogai contenders to control this region. By the end of the 16th century, ethnic Kazakh people dominated all the areas of the modern Kazakhstan, parts of Western Siberia and some northern parts of modern Uzbekistan. By the beginning of the 17th century, three major groups had emerged among the Kazakhs—each under the leadership of its own Khan (leaders). They were the Great Horde, the Middle Horde and the Little Horde.[19] These Hordes were further divided into tribes and clans.

The origin and development of all these five Central Asian countries passed through and evolved through various stages in terms of socioeconomic and political development by the beginning of the 17th century. There was no verified power in Central Asia and frontiers were not clearly defined. The various Khans and other rulers were at almost constant war with each other creating constant instability. In most of the region the political structure was less oppressive because the people were not seen as slaves to the land and the rulers did not enjoy arbitrary and absolute rule.[20] Like other areas, the Khan of the Kazakh horde was elected at a meeting of various local rulers, nobles and clan elders.

In addition to this aristocracy of Khans, on a more local level the elders met to choose a leader to represent them in negotiating disputes among families and regulating migration.[21] A Khan had to prove his military power to remain a ruler. The government was tyrannical and oppressive giving cruel punishment to its opponents. The clergy enjoyed a high status and respect in a society where illiteracy and superstitions were widespread.[22] The people of the region had no right to participate in political process even if they were aware of various activities of the governments.

The 19th century Central Asia consisted of three Khanates—Kokand, Bukhara and Khiva. At the beginning of the 19th century, among the three Khanates, the most populous was the Khanate of Bukhara having a population of around three million; Kokand and Khiva had around 1.5 million each. A major portion of the population was settled in the Oasis and river valleys especially of the Amu-Darya, Syr-Darya, Kashka-Darya and Surkhan-Darya and lived in big cities such as Tashkent, Bukhara, Kokand and Samarkand.[23]

Although prosperous in earlier times, by the middle of the 19th century the region was in a state of decay, isolated from the modern world; its population was static and economy was depressed.[24] The Tsarist Empire of Russia after its defeat in the Crimean war diverted its interest towards Central Asia. The main objective of the Tsarist Empire was to exploit the economic resources of the Central Asian region. Tsarist Russia annexed the Khanates of Kokand and reduced the size of the other two Khanates of Bukhara and Khiva which were later reduced as vassal states of the Tsarist Empire. The annexed territories remained under the Governor General of Turkistan.[25] The Tsar's taxes on the population of Russian Turkestan were between fifty to one hundred per cent higher than those levelled upon the liberally treated people of European Russia. [26] The Russian officers appointed lower level officials, who were highest bidders in the terms of revenue generation and the native officials who won in these clandestine auctions made sure to get back their investment and a sizable profit from the peasantry. In addition to that there was dividing up of the territory of Central Asia into native states and Russian Turkestan; the native peoples were split by every local nationality into a number of groups, each with a different type of government to face. The Uzbeks, who were the bulk of the population in Khiva and Bukhara, were split further by the organisation of Samarkand and Ferghana and Syr-Darya Oblasts in Turkestan. The Tajiks were divided between the Emirate of Bukhara and Ferghana Oblast in Turkestan. The Kyrgyz were divided between the Ferghana and Semirechi Oblasts. The Turkestan contained numbers of Uzbeks, Kazakhs, and Kara-Kalpaks.[27]

In each of these areas, existing and artificially fostered enmities among the various peoples resulted in the creation of a communal problem. Despite that, the social structure of Central Asian region did not witness much change. The Tsarist Empire supported the traditional rulers like the Khans and Emirs with its troops and helped the despotic rulers of these feudal states to exploit the general masses. These three Khanates were economically backward feudal states with many strong remnants of the much older slave-owning society.[28]

During this period the position of women was miserable. Women in Central Asia were like human puppets, who were visible on the streets of Central Asia not as human beings but as moving bundles whose feet were only visible to the passersby.[29] They had no intellectual culture and they were not even sent to schools, being considered unequal to men. Several married groups, spanning at least two generations, would form a single entity, living, working and, in the case of the nomads, migrating together. Marriages were arranged by close relatives in accordance with the rules of Islamic and customary law. Neither the bride nor the bridegroom had any say in the choice of their future partner. There was frequently a considerable difference in age between husband and wife, since the financial obligations incurred by the male were very heavy, especially the payment of the bride price; only young men from the wealthiest families could afford this.[30] The minimum age set by Islamic law at which a girl could be given in marriage was nine years. Female members of the family made an important contribution to family economy, producing foodstuffs, clothing and furnishings. Female mortality was very high. Medical help was minimal. In nomad and semi-nomad communities, and possibly in remote settled areas, women were not veiled, although they did wear some form of headgear which also covered part of their upper body. There was a strict division of labour which served to mark out the boundaries of male and female space. It is generally supposed that women in nomad communities enjoyed a greater degree of freedom. By the early twentieth century, there were some facilities for the education of girls. For the most part, these took the form of elementary religious schools run by the wives of the local mullah. In middle and upper-class circles women received a fuller education and a few became accomplished literary figures in their own right. [31]

In the colonial period, Central Asia was highly underdeveloped and only a few strategic roads and railways were built and some cotton industries were established. The percentage of literacy at that time was not more than two to three percent. On the other hand, the Russians interfered very little with established tradition.[32] The people were allowed to pursue their own way of life and enjoyed religious and cultural freedom.

The administration of Turkestan was under the charge of the War Ministry. The Governor General appointed by the Tsar enjoyed wide powers both for military and civil administration of the territory. He had also great power in matters relating to Bukhara and Khiva. He appointed from among the representatives of Russian nobility, military officers, and the administrative officers.[33]

In the administrative hierarchy, the Military Governor stood at the apex of the administration and all the powers were concentrated in his office. Military officers were heads of *Uyezd* (region) and city administration. Besides the above two levels, the Tsarist government also made use of the so-called popularly elected lower village administration. The post of *Volost* (lowest administration unit consisting of a few villages) administration and village officials were filled through election. Their appointments were confirmed by the Military Governor of the *Oblast* (province). These elected officials worked under the control of the *Uyezd* administrations.[34] But in actual practice, the process of election was merely a farce. Those who were well-connected with the Russian administration and loyal got elected to this post. The Russians monopolised both the election and selection process.

During the Tsarist period, revolutionary circles began to develop in a number of Central Asian cities due to underdevelopment and exploitative character of the Tsarist rule. Under extremely poor socioeconomic conditions, the Socialist movement took its roots at the beginning of 20th century. Initially, the movement faced numerous difficulties. Along with the Socialist movement, two other important movements also appeared on the political scene in Central Asia. They were conservative traditionalists and the liberal modernists, respectively called *Quadimists* and *Jadidist.*[35] The Quadimists were defenders of the sanctified traditions and exercised exclusive control over the native economic, socio-cultural and educational institutions. These were used as an instrument to deter the penetration of modernising influences. The Quadimists went up against the alien, aggressive and arrogant culture of Russian intruders. The most important tool in the hands of Quadimists was the native educational system, financed and regulated by religious endowments drawing its strength from *Wakf* (religious institution owned) land.[36]

As opposed to the Quadimist movement, the Jadidists believed that the imperative of socioeconomic change could be met not just through a puritanical revival of what they called the "Golden Age of Early Islam" but with acceptance of elements of modernisation. Socialism, however appeared repulsive to them on account of its political and economic philosophy. Renowned Jadid intellectual Bek-Buchi said, "it basically violated the spirit of Islam and ran counter to the law of Shariat".[37]

In this chaotic situation Socialism appeared in Central Asia. The Socialist movement was spearheaded by Socialist workers as well by those who had been banished from Russia on political grounds and had sought refuge in Central Asia. By 1902, a small group had already started functioning among them. After the second Congress of Russian Socialist Democratic Liberal Party (RSDLP) held in 1903, Social Democratic groups were formed in Tashkent, Samarkand, Kyzl Arvat and Ashkabad by 1904. Among these groups, the Samarkand group was prominent which came under the direct control of

Bolsheviks as early as 1905. At the Tashkent and Samarkand centre, prominent members of the native workers and native intelligentsia were A.G. Rasheed, V.T. Bakarje, M.V. Muratov, A.V. Khudash and A.R. Bakhisov.[38] Towards the end of 1906, in the first Turkestan Conference of the RSDLP, it was decided to establish a union of Turkestan organisations of the RSDLP.[39] This organisation became part of the RSDLP and participated in the Party conferences, while the Bolshevik faction within it worked independently.

In the year 1905-1906, the Socialist movement gained momentum following the large-scale participation of the local people. Apart from participation, many political parties were established in various areas. In Turkestan, the Turkestan Jadidists formed a political party in 1909. At that time Central Asian people had helped the process of the overthrow of the Tsar through the rebellion of 1916, and expected the taking of power by the Soviets. Due to this anticipation the Tashkent Soviet had declared itself the sole rightful organ of government on September 12, 1917—nearly two months before the revolution in the capital. Suppressed by troops under the control of the Provincial Government, the Soviets took power again in a bitter four-day street battle during the week after Lenin's government was established. The battle was decided by the support of the Uzbeks and Kyrgyz from the old city and surrounding villages. On the other hand, the Khiva and the Bukhara Emirates continued to exist for another three years.[40]

In April 1917 this group convened the Congress of the Muslims of Turkestan in Tashkent appointing a National Committee and, during the October Revolution, it endeavoured to seize power and form a Muslim government. This local party supported the establishment of a national territorial federal system to create two autonomous republics—Turkestan and Kazakhstan. Also, groups calling themselves the Young Bukharans and the Young Khivans were set up in the respective protectorates, taking their inspiration from the Young Turk movement with similar objectives as the progressive Jadid movement.[41]

In Kazakhstan, there also formed a national group called the *Alash Orda* (horde of Alash, after the mythical ancestor of the Kazakh tribes) and by 1917 the *Alash Orda* had become a political party. This group was nationalist and secular in outlook and by July 1917 it was demanding an autonomous Kazakh republic with the separation of Church and State. It was also opposed to pan-Islamism describing the movement as 'oriental utopia'. Two other main political parties existed in Kazakhstan such as the *Ush Zhuz* which was formed in Tashkent in 1914, being both Socialist and very pan-Islamic in outlook, and the Islamic *Brilik Tuuy*.[42]

The struggle for popular support in Central Asia was three-sided. There were the Bolsheviks, the feudal reactionaries and the nationalist bourgeoisie. The Bolsheviks' chief weapon was their policy of national equality. The feudalists had the power of tradition and religion. The bourgeois nationalists had the native people's hatred of all things Russian. The latter two groups also had in varying degrees, the military backing of the Russian restorationist forces and of foreign interventionists. Later, there was a measure of unity between them against the common enemy, the Soviets.

The making of Bolshevik nationality policy is intimately bound up with the name of Joseph Stalin, himself a member of an oppressed nation, coming from the Caucasus—an area which probably has one of the most complex mixtures of nationalities and religions. From 1912 onwards, he was the recognised Bolshevik authority and its chief policy-maker on the problems of national minorities. The nationality policy was first defined as granting to each nation the right to full self-determination.

For the proper establishment of law and order of the country, the first Russian Soviet Constitution was adopted at the fifth All-Russian Congress of Soviets, more than eight months after the establishment of Soviet rule. This constitution became the model for other Soviet Republics. Under this constitution the highest agency was the All-Russian Congress of Soviets. This was to be elected by Town Soviets on the basis of one deputy for every 25,000 workers and by Regional

Congresses of Rural Soviets on the basis of one deputy for 125,000 inhabitants.[43] Thus, two characteristic features of Soviet constitutions up to 1936, weighted representation of the proletariat and indirect elections, were established. The former device was defended on the ground that the proletariat was the leading class in the revolution, although numerically weaker than the peasantry. The main purpose of the indirect election to the non-local Soviets was that it made easier to hold Congresses of Soviets; the entire apparatus less costly, more flexible, more accessible to the workers and peasants and at the time of urgency it would necessarily be able quickly to recall a deputy or to elect him to the General Congress of Soviets. The All-Russian Congress of Soviets held Supreme Soviet state power but legislative and executive powers were shared by the Central Executive Committee. This Committee was supposed to exercise legislative power when the Congress was not in session. The administrative agency *Sovnarkom* also acted as legislature, although its legislation consisted of decisions and orders and not of decrees or statutes.[44] Thus, this first constitution was record of a clear development of the Soviet state structure.

The new governments in Bukhara and Khiva were unique in that they constituted themselves as Soviet Republics, not Socialist Soviet Republics, as was the case everywhere else where the Soviets came to power. In both cases, the Council of People's Commissars consisted almost entirely of natives, and the independence of these states in internal affairs was complete. On March 4, 1921, the close relations existing between the new Bukharan state and the Russian Soviet Federated Socialist Republic (RSFSR) were formalised in an agreement in which the latter recognised "without reservation, the self-government and complete independence of the Bukharan Soviet Republic, with all the consequences deriving therefrom".[45]

The richest merchants, mullahs and ex-officials of the Emirs were not allowed to vote or stand for election to the first All-Bukhara Congress of Soviets. Other steps included the confiscation of the property of the Emir and his highest officials and the abolition of the old taxes. During the revolutionary times in Central Asia, a nationalist rebel movement, the so-called *Basmach* that operated under local warlords. The growth of this movement was due to two reasons. Firstly, a struggle for national independence sprang up following the destruction by the Soviets of the Kokand Muslim government and subsequent outrages; and secondly, the economic crisis stemming from the ruin of cotton crops in the Ferghana Valley, with its attendant famine.[46] The Basmachis claimed to be fighting a 'holy war' in defence of Islam against the Red Army. These groups in the latter times were suppressed under the Soviet rule.[47]

2.2 Formation of Statehood

While the economy improved, the advancement in education and the gradual involvement of the Central Asian people in public life led to an increasing national consciousness. Each nationality began to demand its own national unification. The existing state boundaries carried over in part from the heterogeneous native states formed by conquest, and in part from the gerrymandered Tsarist Oblasts, created friction. In 1923 Kirghiz, Kazakh and Turkmen Congresses were composed of delegates from these minority nationalities living within the Bukharan Republic, inhabited mainly by Uzbeks. These Congresses were held in Turkestan, alongwith other similar meetings making the native peoples explicit in their desire for their own state.

In 1924, the Soviet Union agreed that the state boundaries shall be determined by the will of the people themselves. The nationality policy of Soviet Union was Soviet in form and Socialist in content. This delimitation was made possible by the fact that the advances in economic and political organisation and social consciousness in Khiva and Bukhara Republics led the people of these areas to choose a Socialist course of development and thereby become eligible for incorporation into the newly-formed USSR.[48]

The economic progress of the previous years and the demand for the formation of national states led the All-Bukhara Congress of September 1924 to declare Bukhara a Socialist republic. The

Congress also went for the unification of its predominantly Uzbek portions with the Uzbek areas of Turkestan in a single Uzbek Soviet Socialist Republic and put forward the demand that the Pamir mountain area in the south be established as a Tajik Autonomous Republic within Uzbekistan. It also agreed to the separation of the predominantly Turkmen areas for unification with the Trans-Caspian area into the Turkmen Soviet Socialist Republic. Thus, the Bukhara and Khorezm (Khiva) multi-national Republics disappeared, and in their place were organised the first two constituent republics of the Union and Central Asia—Uzbekistan and Turkmenistan, including large parts of what had been the Autonomous Turkestan republic of the RSFSR.[49] Two years later Turkestan was dissolved into the Kazakh and Kyrgyz Autonomous republics. In 1931, the Tajiks, who had formed an autonomous republic within Uzbekistan, were raised to equal status as the seventh Union Republic, but it was not until 1936 after the nomad Kazakhs and Kirghiz had been won over to a settled mode of life, that they attained equal statehood.

Under the Soviet political system, Central Asian Countries were governed by the single political party i.e., Communist Party with the Marxist–Leninist principles. All the issues were decided by the Soviet Communist Party in the name of 'democratic centralism'. This governed four principles. Firstly, the leaders of each echelon in the Party were to be elected by the membership they served. Secondly, policy options were to be freely debated by the membership prior to decisions. Thirdly, Party members were obliged to exhibit unquestioned obedience to their superiors. Fourthly, through debate on an issue was supposed to be open to all Party members, the decisions were to be made by the leadership. Once the decision was made, it was to be followed without dissent.[50] Article 3 of the 1977 Constitution of the Soviet Union mentioned that the Soviet state is organised and functions on the principle of democratic centralism, namely the election of all bodies of state authority from the lowest to the highest, their accountability to the people, and the obligation of lower bodies to observe the decisions of higher ones. Democratic centralism combines central leadership with local initiative and creative activity, and with the responsibility of each state body and official for the work interested to them.[51] The Soviet authorities abolished the court of *Qazi* and introduced the centralised judicial system all over the region.

The political culture was an elite political culture in the sense that an indoctrinated Communist Party made "an objective revolutionary situation", very broadly defined, to be the necessary and sufficient condition of a Communist revolution.[52] The USSR Constitution of 1977 mentioned that the Communist Party of the Soviet Union and other political parties, as well as trade unions, youth and other social organisations and mass movements, participate in the formulation of the policy of the Soviet state and in the administration of the state and social affairs through their representatives elected to the Soviets of People's Deputies and in other ways.[53]

Article 51 of the 1977 Constitution of the USSR mentioned that citizens of the USSR have the right to form political parties and social organisations and to participate in mass movements that promote the development of political activeness and independent activity and the satisfaction of their various interests. Social organisations were guaranteed conditions for the successful performance of their statutory tasks.[54] The political organisation of Soviet society, i.e. the system of state organs and mass public organisations, was guided by the Communist Party constitutionally; all the powers residing in rural and urban Soviets officially known as Soviets of Working People's Deputies: these formed the political basis of the state. Activities in the Soviets were based on democratic centralism. This was a process that included the electivity of the Soviet at all levels and the control and subordination of lower organs by higher organs. The administrative organs were controlled by the people and the granting of initiative to local Soviets in state and local practical matters.

The Constitution of the USSR established a federal system. The Constitution provided that the autonomous regions as sovereign Soviet Socialist states were guaranteed the right to freely secede from the USSR. Their territorial integrity was assured and each was left to own territory.[55] In reality, none of these provisions and rights was to be taken seriously. The Soviet government was federal in form and unitary in spirit. Article 1 of the Soviet Constitution 1977 mentioned that the Union of Soviet Socialist Republics was a Socialist state of the whole people, expressing the will and interests of the workers, peasants, intelligentia and the working people of all the nations and nationalities of the country. Article 2 of the same constitution elaborated that all power in the USSR belonged to the people. The people exercised state power through Soviets of People's Deputies, which constituted the political foundation of the USSR. All the state bodies were under the control of and accountable to the Soviets of People's Deputies.

In the Federal system, the Soviet Union was supreme and controlled all units or republics. All the republics had their own constitution, though finally controlled by the Centre. In the Central Asian case, the first or second secretary was always a Russian, who was in the charge of military or security areas. This secretary was more powerful than others. On the other hand, the other officials were appointed from the titular peoples.[56]

According to the constitutions of the respective states, the election of Deputies varied from state to state like one deputy for every 8000 inhabitants in Kyrgyzstan and one deputy for every 27,000 inhabitants in Kazakhstan.[57] Between sessions of the Supreme Soviet, the highest body of the state power was the Presidium of the Supreme Soviets of the respective states. The Supreme Soviet, the highest legislative organ, appointed the government of the republic, i.e. the Council of Ministers. The local bodies of state power were the Soviets of Working People's Deputies of the *oblasts*, *raions*, *cities*, *settlements*, and the *aul* and *sela* (villages), which were elected for two year terms by the population. Each of the republics sent their deputies to the Supreme Soviet of the USSR.

Despite the creation of nascent national and territorial administrations for Central Asia in the mid-1920s, Soviet rule remained largely nominal in many areas and there were few ideologically committed personnel to carry out basic administrative tasks, and to actualise grandiose plans of social transformation. Party organisations remained weak—many of them not formally established until the early 1920s, and they often lacked people from the indigenous communities or cadres who had the comprehensive understanding of the peculiarities of the region. In Kazakhstan the Party had around 26,000 members in 1922, of whom around a third were Kazakhs, but most of the latter were semi-literate and had little idea about Marxist doctrine. In many areas Party organisations and later local Soviets served to institutionalise traditional clan and tribal rivalries. In Turkestan recruitment drives sought to attract members of the Muslim community whether intellectuals 'infected' with Jadidism or ordinary people who saw no incompatibility between Party membership and the maintenance of old religious traditions, and who resisted strongly when the Party elite attacked Islam.[58] Therefore, at successive Party Congresses, resolutions emphasised the necessity to include indigenous cadres and to use national languages in education, the courts, media and administration.

In Kazakhstan, indigenous membership grew slowly, rising from 8 per cent in 1924 to 38 per cent in 1928 and in Uzbekistan it reached to about 40 per cent by 1927. In April 1928 the Uzbek Central Committee adopted a resolution on the 'Uzbekistan' government apparatus, to make this to 100 per cent by 1930, but the target achieved was in fact 22.6 per cent.[59] Problems in finding indigenous cadres were due to the low levels of literacy and education that persisted until 1930s. Even in the middle of 1930s more than 90 per cent of city Soviet chairmen in Uzbekistan had only a primary education. The aim of collectivisation programme in Central Asia as Rakowska-Harmstone has suggested, was Korenizatsiya or nativisation that was based upon the assumption that drawing Muslims into the power structure would eventually lead to class loyalties overriding older emotional and traditional ties to group and religion.[60]

Central Asian participation in modern sectors was limited by cultural and historical conditions. These included: first, a tradition of looking to other Turkic peoples primarily Tatars for cultural leadership; secondly, a Muslim cultural heritage which inclined Central Asian intellectuals towards humanistic careers rather than scientific and technical ones and which severely restricted the participation of women in public and social life; thirdly, an instinctive chauvinism of the Europeans—primarily Russians—who dominated the political system and especially of those Europeans settled in Central Asia itself and fourthly, the generally low levels of education and training among Central Asian nationalities.[61]

Since 1917, Soviet policy had been to modernise the occupational structure of Central Asian society and to promote the participation of Central Asians in Soviet organisations. They promoted native cardres into responsible positions in the state and Party apparatuses.

In the mid-1930s the Soviet leadership was less willing to sacrifice efficiency to ethnicity in making key appointments. Nevertheless, sizable numbers of young Central Asians acquired some training and entered the modern sector of Central Asian society during this period, bringing them into direct contact with skilled European cadres for the first time.[62]

In 1932, Kazakh first Secretary F.I. Goloshchekin was removed for failures that had 'fed' nationalism. In 1937-39 most of the leading nationalists were arrested and executed, alongside the remaining old Communists. The centerpiece was the trial of Uzbek first secretary Akhkmal Ikramov and Faizulla Khojaev alongside Nikolai Bukharin in 1938. Khojaev confessed that he had sought to undermine the fulfillment of cotton production targets and that he had hoped to create an independent Uzbek economy.[63] Within a very short period the native elites of the region had been decimated, and a new generation began to take its place; a younger generation with a technical rather than humanitarian education, schooled to the hard realities of Soviet rule.

The representation of the titular nationalities in Republican Party organisations grew rapidly in three of the Central Asian republics. In 1945-70 it was seen rising from 42.7 per cent to 54.9 per cent in Uzbekistan, rising from 39.7 per cent to 55.3 per cent in Turkmenistan, and rising from 42.1 per cent to 47.9 per cent in Tajikistan. In Kazakhstan and Kyrgyzstan, where there were a larger number of Russians, indigenous membership remained below 40 per cent until well into the 1970s. [64]

Despite all the changes, Slavs occupied dominant control positions in administrative, security and industrial sectors. In the other spheres it was found that there was shortage of trained personnel rather than any policy to favour Slavs. Decrees issued by the Central Committee in the 1950s and 1960s continued to complain about the failure of Central Asian party organisations to find young, competent officials from the local population, and noted the failure of these organisations to adapt their work to the needs of the local situation. Yet the same documents also attacked the fact that even when put forward local cadres often failed to break with negative aspects of ancient traditions—for example, maintaining an ambiguous attitude towards 'religious survivals'.[65]

In the late 1920s, there were many complaints that the efficiency of local cadres was undermined by the impact of tribalism and family connections which led to the dominance of 'groupism' and cronyism in public life. Due to these complaints, CPSU eliminated much of the previous elite —not only Central Asia's nobility but also its few industrialists. In the Stalin period, there was a pervasive atmosphere of purge and terror in both the Communist Party and administration. Moscow earlier attempted to maintain some degree of ethnic representation in Party and administrative organisations. But in the early 1930s, Stalin sought to ensure central control over the republics, and considerations of efficiency and loyalty took priority over affirmative action.

The Russians who occupied the key positions were closely tied to the Central Party apparatus in Moscow and used their positions in the non-Russian areas to implement central policies. This pattern was strongest in Uzbekistan and Kazakhstan, but somewhat weaker elsewhere in Central Asia. Important positions like Chairmanship of KGB and others were held exclusively by non-indigenous cadres in Uzbekistan, Tajikistan and Turkmenistan, and only a small proportion of incumbents in Kazakhstan and Kirgizia were indigenous. Thus, the Russian organisational secretaries were charged with carrying out the regime's policy of promoting Central Asians into responsible positions at the upper and middle levels of the state and Party bureaucracies and the Russian chairmen of the KGB were charged with supervising, controlling and removing native cadres so promoted.[66]

By 1960s, the apparatus of the Communist Party had been merged with the state apparatus, creating a party-state. During the final decades of the USSR, the party-state was the only actor in Soviet society that no one could legitimately contest and its authority was supreme.[67]

The Soviet society did not allow a civil society to emerge in the Western sense. Marx argued that civil society is the sphere in which a man is regarded as a private, egoistic, atomised individual with inalienable rights (equality, liberty, security, property). The state is the illusory 'community', the ideal universal sphere in which a man is seen as a social member of the community with duties as a citizen of the state.[68] It lacked a level of social organisation above family and friends—a level of voluntary organisations and private clubs that scholars regard as a major foundation of a democratic society. The party-state controlled all organisations linking individuals who were neither family members nor close personal friends. Private individuals were not allowed to meet and form associations, even those intended to foster private and personal goals. Various trade unions, women's organisations, Komsomol and other social organisations were working under the strong hold of the Communist Party.

Among the social organisations, Komsomol was playing a leading role in Soviet political affairs. The role of the Komsomol was very vital in the participation of the Soviet political system. This Young Communist League was founded in 1918. From the early years the

Komsomol was an idealistic and radical organisation devoted to doing its part to lead the Soviet people to Communism.[69] The task of the Komsomol was to organise the most politically minded and active of the country's youth into a centralised disciplined community second only to the Communist Party itself.[70] Komsomol members were not necessarily members of the Communist Party. Technically it was not a Party agency, although it was certainly controlled by the CPSU. It was founded on a base in military units, factories, apartments, offices, schools and collective farms. The most important Komsomol leaders were members of the central committee of the CPSU. Composed of young people between the ages of fifteen and twenty-eight, the Komsomol included only about half of the Soviet youth who met its age requirement. Those applying for membership were required to enjoy a good reputation in their neighbourhoods, schools and work places.[71] Pioneer was also an important organisation, in which almost every school child was a member. This organisation was the effective instrument for spreading Communist Party influence throughout the land.[72]

In the political field, trade unions were clearly the agents of the state and the Party. They served as the major link between the workers and the political leaders. As such they were charged with mobilising the labour force, assisting and encouraging it to increase the productivity to satisfy the economic goals set by the central planners.[73] The Unions were a major communicator between state and people. The government and Party frequently interrupted production to give ideological, political and economic matters. At the same time, the trade unions afforded the Soviet people one of the few forums for effectively expressing their concerns.[74]

March 1953 marked the beginning of a new era in the whole Soviet society due to the death of Stalin. Under the leadership of Khrushchev far-reaching changes began to be felt in all facets of Soviet development. In the political sphere, the Party played the crucial role of guiding and controlling the state apparatus. However, centralisation in Party management began to be balanced by decentralisation and the extra-legal activities of various organs of control were curbed like that of the secret police established during the Stalin period. The 20th Party Congress of 1956 paved the way for the enforcement of the 1936 Constitution both in theory and practice. This Constitution clearly distinguished the role of the Party and the state organs, with emphasis on the leading role of the Party. Political institutions like the Supreme Soviet, Council of Ministers and above all Procurator's office and local Soviets were encouraged to function as the Constitution had empowered them. It also emphasised the principles of collective responsibility and observance of democratic norms within the Party and government. By the mid-1950s the rights of the Union Republics in economic management were extended and by the early 1960s they acquired a wider character.[75] The 22nd Party Congress of the CPSU had given special importance for the better relationship between centre and state.

After this reform process, Khrushchev tried to facilitate for common mass participation in the policy making process and administration level with the introduction of "all people's states". He advocated the gradual transfer of functions from state to public organisations and to that effect millions of citizens were attracted to part-time work in the Soviets, the other governmental agencies and the public organisations. All this policy reflected his populism.

In the Brezhnev era new organisations were not designed or created to draw the citizens into public life (e.g., the *druzhiny*). There had been a number of actions taken that did facilitate the access of at least some citizens into the decision-making process. For example, in 1969 a *Kolhhoz* Council was created at the centre and at the *raion*, *oblast*, and *republic* levels as well. These councils were headed by the top agricultural administrator at each level and at the all-Union level at least. The Council's membership was over-whelmingly administrative or professional in occupation. The 125 members in 1969 included 25 regional, republican, or central administrators, 56 kolkhoz chairmen, 18 middle-level kolkhoz administrators, 11 kolkhoz professionals, 6 link-leaders and senior shepherds, and only 8 rank-and-file Kolkhozniki.[76]

The granting of the right of control to the Party organisations of educational and scientific institutions probably resulted primarily in the admission of less elite elements into the decision-making processes of these bodies. In the higher educational institutions, the heads were advised by a scholarly council composed of the institute or university administrators and leading professors. To a large extent, this council was a committee of Party members. However, the Party organisation was as a whole much less elite in nature, containing, on the average, 42% of the institution's faculty. Even the Party Bureau included not only full professors and administrators, but also students, graduate students and junior faculty as well. Moreover, the Party committee unlike the scholarly council, did not have to wait for the Head of the Institution to initiate an issue, and, in case of disagreement with the Head, it could take the dispute to the district Party committee. If the Party committee had become a more important centre of discussion and decision, it could well have been that younger viewpoints were then better heard and represented.[77]

Council of Kolkhozy, the granting of the *Pravo Kontrolya* to the Party organisations of scientific-educational institutions, and the increased emphasis upon scientific information might have been primarily to benefit potential participants from the 'middle class', but the trend towards greater worker–peasant participation which began in the Khrushchev period continued after his removal in 1964. Ethnic significance also became attached to processes at lower levels of the Party and state bureaucracies. In the rural and primary Party organisations, as per the 1961 results, Muslims already constituted 81.9 per cent of the deputies in the *raion* and *oblast* level Soviets of Uzbekistan—over 80 per cent of the deputies at the village and urban village level and even 45.8 per cent of the deputies at the city or urban level.[78]

"Popular participation" in the Soviet Union was vastly different in nature from that in liberal democratic countries, and indeed in many respects a total inversion. Western observers have commented on political participation of the Soviet Union using the terms as support participation, pseudo-participation, and ritual participation or have eschewed participation in favour of mobilisation. But the Soviet political participation provided more opportunities for effective popular influence.[79] In the words of Brzezinski and Huntington, "the Soviet regime increasingly uses political participation to control its people and the control produced by political participation flow in one direction only".[80] Marx was also opposed to any kind of political participation which was conditional on the ownership of property, or of a certain kind of property. At this point in the development of Marx's views the attainment of universal suffrage might well have seemed sufficient to prevent the domination of political life by private relationships. That is, Marx saw universal suffrage as the means by which men are liberated from status and property differences as determinants of citizen status. [81]

For better participation, the third constitution of USSR adopted in 1977 mentioned both the policy making and administrative functions. Below the level of the Supreme Soviet of the USSR there were Supreme Soviets in each of the fifteen republics which were federated in the USSR. Each such Supreme Soviet had its own presidium and its own council of ministers. Below the republic level there was a Soviet in each province. At the low level of province there were Soviets in cities and in rural counties. Each had its executive committee. The various Soviets in the republics were elected, formally and directly by the people, in every five years, while deputies to the lesser Soviets were named in direct election for two and half year terms.[82] In these elections, all adult citizens of the geographical area defined as under the jurisdiction of the Soviet could vote and be represented, regardless of their place of work. There was no system of indirect elections, such as in the Communist Party conferences functioning at the level of the country, the big city, the province, the republic and the union according to which delegates to higher levels of the Party system came from the Party conference immediately below. [83] In the Party-dominated Soviet political system, all the elites were participating within the ideological parameters of the political arena. So the Party was more powerful than the elites, but was not omnipotent. Party-specialist elite interdependence, not party dominance, characterised party-elite relations.[84]

Letters to the editor or the publication of articles in journals, personal appeals to governmental or political officials, membership in many types of committees (e.g. various types of student committees, house or street committees, parent committees in the school, various committees at the place of work), participation in various city-wide councils or commissions—so far as could be observed by an outsider, these activities made relatively little difference on the surface from their counterparts in the West.

2.3. Women's Emancipation

Women's emancipation and empowerment was of great importance to the Soviet Union. Specifically, Kremlin attempted to utilise the emancipation of women as a strategy to mitigate the influence of Islam in the Central Asian region. In this respect, programmes for female emancipation were perceived by Moscow as an essential component of its ambition to create a secular and unified Soviet state. Women's emancipation was the strategic priority due to three reasons. Firstly, there was genuine horror and disgust at the social injustice in the Russian eyes that the treatment of Central Asian women in traditional society seemed tantamount to slavery. Secondly, there was a political imperative to create a surrogate proletariat to engage in the class war and also the related war against religion. Thirdly, there was an economic necessity to draw women into socialised production.[85]

The commitment to the development of state institutions was designed to promote work and education for women. This special programme was organised and monitored by the central organs of the Communist Party in Moscow. In 1918, the Central Committee created commissions for propaganda and agitation among women.

During 1919, female rights assumed a high priority when they were directed by the 'Department for Work among Women'—the *Zhentodel*. The *Zhentodel* had three sections: agitation, the press and work among women of the East. This group was defined as women in the Central Asian republics. The *Zhentodel* as an organisation had two main aims—to expand the influence of the Party among working-class women and to liaise with other organisations to promote the construction of nurseries, because these were understood as essential for the liberation of women.[86]

At the ideological level the campaign for the emancipation of Central Asian women emerged out of Russian 'feminism' drawing inspiration from Inessa Armand and Aleksandra Kollantai. These feminists argued that women should be equal members of society with full participation in the public sphere. The *Zhentodel* was activated to supervise the liberation of women in the Muslim republics. But there were problems. In 1917, just 2 percent of women in Central Asia were literate and it was believed that it was this illiteracy that at least in part preserved the patriarchal religious structures of the region. In 1920, Party activists were sent to Central Asia to inspect the situation of women.[87]

It was believed by the Kremlin that this situation could be used to its advantage and therefore, they would seek to replace traditionally 'oppressed' woman by the new 'Soviet' woman. Women in Central Asia became a key to state-building. Throughout the 1920s, Central Asian women were used by the centre in an attempt to exert control in this peripheral part of the empire. They became, in Massell's splendid and telling phrase, 'a surrogate proletariat'. Gender was used as a tactic to demolish existing structures and to implant new social and political norms. In addition to class and family the third burden was nationality.[88] The Bolsheviks believed that women could be educated out of their class, distanced from patriarchal domestic structures and also weaned off from adherence to national identities. This would also have the additional benefit of providing a new pool of educated labour. The mix of motives discussed above raises the question of whether the Soviet programme was one of genuine emancipation or was merely pragmatic.

The Russian Soviet Federal Socialist Republic Criminal Code also attempted to legislate for female rights. Under this Code, certain traditions were banned. In particular, *kalym* (the paying of a bride price), marriage without consent and polygamy were outlawed. A number of women's rights were spelt out. These included the right to initiate divorce, the right to equal succession, the right to equal witness in court, the right to participation in public life and the right to vote. Women's clubs were set up throughout the region to educate women. The first such club was established in the old quarter of remote rural areas. The clubs offered a range of medical, legal circles, amateur dramatics devoted mainly to the performance of playlets on contemporary themes, consultations on nutrition, hygiene and child care, and also lectures, film shows and concerts.[89]

Soviet authorities regarded education as an essential component of political and economic mobilisation. In Central Asia, in the early 1920s, the level of literacy amongst the indigenous peoples ranged from an average seven per cent amongst the Kazakhs, to just over two per cent amongst the Turkmen and one per cent in Tajiks. One of the first priorities of the new state was to remedy this situation. Special ABC courses were set up in railway coaches, tents, factories and every other conceivable venue. Great efforts were made to reach the female population. The women's sections were especially active in this field, but the trade union, Young Communist League and other socio-political organisations also contributed to the campaign. By 1927, the entire educational system had been Sovietised. Primary schooling was made compulsory for boys and girls by 1930. This was later expanded to an eight-year course. Schools were not only the place where a general educational programme was provided but also the channel through which the values and goals of Communism could be inculcated in the younger generation.[90] The educational process was also used to challenge inherited conventions regarding the role of women in society.

The first steps to incorporate women into what Shirin Akiner has described as a 'socialised' workforce included the establishment of women's cooperatives. In 1927, a Central Committee resolution 'concerning the tasks of women's clubs in the Soviet East' called upon regional Party organisations to establish clubs in areas where tradition prevented women from joining the labour force. [91]

The Central Committee later decreed that as a matter of urgency women's clubs should encourage women into the workforce. By 1930, the *Zhentodel* was declared a success and the women question resolved. The Komsomol girls' brigades were regarded as effective in combating Islam. In Turkmenistan, for example, girls' clubs concentrated on ideological work which centred on rural schools. By 1937, women had advanced in public life to the point where they numbered six out of Central Asia's thirty four members of the Council of the Union, and twenty five of its hundred members at the Council of Nationalities in the Supreme Soviets at Moscow.[92]

After the educational development, energetic efforts were made to involve Central Asian Women in the political–administrative process. Female delegates were elected to represent their communities in public meetings at local and republican level. Activists were sent for training to the Communist University, the Turkic School of Soviet and Party Work and other such institutions. In the early 1920s, Central Asian women began to join the Party. In percentage terms participation remained low but the actual numbers were quiet high, given their lack of previous political experience. For example, in Uzbekistan, there were over one thousand Uzbek women Party members by early 1929.

In response to Lenin's injunction that more women should be elected to the Soviets, Central Asian women gradually came forward to stand as candidates. However, the progress was very slow due to two reasons—women were reluctant to take part in elections and there was much opposition from the male members of the community. Positive discrimination was used to accelerate promotion and a quota system was introduced whereby women were allocated approximately a third of the posts in government and in Party administrative organs.[93]

By the early 1980s, roughly half of the official working population in Central Asia was woman, whereas before the revolution hardly any female were employed in the region at all. By the late 1990s, nearly 100 percent of women had become literate, whereas 80 years ago only 2 per cent were. At the end of the Soviet period women participated in nearly all aspects of public life. In Uzbekistan, for example, women accounted for 50 percent of those employed by the government, while 45 percent of local deputies to the Soviet were women.[94]

In the Soviet state, the link between participation and elite recruitment was highly formalised as the Communist Party took pains to recruit the population into a variety of officially sponsored organisations such as the Communist Party, youth leagues, trade unions and women's associations. Through such organisations, the regime identified potential leaders and gave them experience in organising group activity. The party reserved the right to approve appointments to any position which carried high administrative responsibility or which was likely to affect the formation of public attitudes. The system for recruiting, training and appointing individuals for positions of leadership and responsibility in the regime was called the *nomenklatura* system and those individuals who were approved for the positions on *nomenklatura* lists were informally called "the *nomenklatura*". Many citizens regarded them as the ruling class in Soviet society.

During the Soviet period, elections and the electoral system on which they were based played a crucial political role. They served as vehicles for both limited contestation among political elites to achieve consensus and fully mobilised participation among the population to popularly legitimise decisions made undemocratically. Elections were one of the primary mechanisms though which the Soviet government distributed political rewards to loyal elite as well as checked their performance. The elected officials were essentially handpicked by the Soviet leadership and incumbents at all levels were expected to "bring out the vote" or lose their positions. The electoral law allocated responsibility for both supervising the nomination of candidates and conducting the elections, and therefore, determined a crucial basis of power relations among the political elite. Moreover, under Soviet rule the republic-level legislature in each Central Asian republic served as an instrument for regional leaders to exert influence on republican affairs.[95]

2.4. Media

Media groups were working in the purview of the government. Article 48 of the USSR Constitution mentioned that citizens of the USSR had the right to take part in the management and administration of state and public affairs and in the discussion and adoption of laws and measures of All-Union and local significance.[96] Soviet authorities used censorship as a major tool to control information. No official publication or broadcast was free of the censor's blue pencil. Every book, article, journal, radio and television script as a must, before publication, had to be submitted to the scrutiny of *Glavlit* (the Chief Administration of Literary and Publishing Affairs), the official censorship agency. Soviet writers and broadcasters as a must, had to familiarise themselves with a list of thousands upon thousands of forbidden topics that were to be published only with special permission. The Ministry of Culture even had a department of jokes, through which Soviet comics as a must had to clear their materials.[97] In spite of that the Soviet press was among the most extensive in the world. The political role the Soviet newspapers played was that of the propagandist and agitator, disseminator of political information and weapon of Communist building. But on the other hand the media provided the Soviet citizens with a public forum, a means of publicising complaints, criticisms, suggestions and seeking redress for grievances. The chief mechanism available to the citizen was a letter to the editor of a Soviet newspaper, expressing his criticism etc. [98] The two news services, *TASS* (Telegraphic Agency of the

Soviet Union) and *Novosti* (news), had correspondents throughout the world. *TASS*, a government agency, was the more authoritative news service. *Novosti* was ostensibly not a government agency, but it was clearly subject to the same checks and constraints as *TASS* or any other Soviet publication. The Soviet press depended neither on consumer demand nor on a commitment to the people's right to know. It established the bridge between the authorities (Party and government) and the people. The press was simply another instrument for shaping public attitudes and motivating the masses to accomplish the goals set by the nation's leaders. *Pravda* was the party paper and *Izvestia* was also an important source of news about the latest government policies. *Trud* (Labour) by trade union, *Krasnaya Zevda* (Red Star) by the military and *Komsomolskaya Pravda* (Komsomol Truth) by the Komsomol were the national newspapers.[99] One of the most important newspapers published in that time from Turkmen Soviet Socialist Republic was *Turkmenskaya Iskra* with wide publication.[100]

2.5 Gorbachev Period

At the time of Gorbachev, the Party guidance was relaxed. Stagnation among the leadership and the violation of the natural process of change were described as factors responsible for the poor performance of the Politburo, entire central committee and the Party apparatus.[101] Many Party members in leading posts stood beyond control and criticism, which led to failure in work and to serious malpractices. In the administrative levels, there emerged massive corruption, disrespect for the law, bribery, servility and glorification. Gorbachev pointed out that the country was verging on crisis.[102]

After coming to power, Gorbachev introduced far-reaching reforms of the political system through his policies of Glasnost and Perestroika, which ushered in a new era of press freedom, political democratisation and decentralisation of decision-making process. It brought about a radical change in Soviet politics and had a profound impact upon social, political and economic system of the country. During this period Soviet society faced many problems like corruption, inefficient economic system and backwardness; clan dominated political system and there was heavy bureaucratisation etc.

Gorbachev introduced his programme of reforming the Soviet political system in the 27th Congress of the Communist Party of Soviet Union through the policies of Perestroika (restructuring the economy and society) and Glasnost (for greater openness and transparency). Perestroika meant overcoming the stagnation process, breaking down the braking mechanism, creating a dependable and effective mechanism for the acceleration of social and economic progress and giving it greater dynamism. Perestroika also meant mass initiative. It was the comprehensive development of democracy, Socialist self-government, encouragement of initiative and creative endeavour, improved order and discipline, more glasnost, criticism and self-criticism in all spheres of society.[103] The essence of perestroika was in the fact that it united Socialism with democracy and revived the Leninist concept of Socialist construction both in theory and practice. [104] Although the programme was primarily introduced to reorient the government and economic apparatus which had become obsolete, it also brought major changes in social and cultural aspects of Soviet political system.

Glasnost led to the development of new forms of political mobilisation and creation of new socio-political movements among various nationalities. In an effort to revitalise Soviet society, Gorbachev's reforms, according to Lapidus, initiated what was, in effect, a major regime transformation—a transition, however limited and fragile from post-totalitarianism towards liberalisation and incipient democratisation of the Soviet system.[105] In the 27th Congress of the Communist Party of Soviet Union, Gorbachev emphasised on the Party programme. He said "our Party programme aims at the most effective exercise of all forms of direct democracy, of direct participation by the popular masses in the elaboration, adoption and execution of governmental and other decisions".[106] He also emphasised that for the better participation in the Soviet Union, the

Constitution also provided nation-wide discussions and referendums on major issues of country's life and for discussions on decisions to be passed by local Soviets. These channels for the promotion of direct democracy included citizens' meetings, constituents' mandates, letters from people, the press, radio, TV and all other means of eliciting public opinion and of quickly and sensitively responding to the people's needs and mood.[107]

The first politicised grassroots organisations stimulated by perestroika and glasnost, appeared in the Central Asian republics. With the mounting socioeconomic crisis and the weakening of party control, 'dissident' intellectuals began to openly express their opinions on the situation and on ways to improve it, diverging increasingly from the official line. Sensing a threat in such discussions, the authorities tried to contain political tempers and control the activity of the clubs by planting agents within them and by creating their own discussion clubs under the aegis of the Komsomol, especially among students. These 'domesticated' clubs made their own contribution to the development of political consciousness and soon overstepped the limits initially set for them.

The Ru ba Ru club in Tajikistan provided an example of these early youth clubs. It was formed at the end of 1988 by a group of young people headed by Jumahon Isoev, a lecturer at Dushanbe University.[108] The club organised meetings with Deputies of the republican Supreme Soviet, members of the government and state officials, with whom they conducted dialogues. Formally, the club was not a political organisation, but these exchanges of opinion inevitably acquired a political colouring.

In spring 1987, the Demos discussion club in the Kyrgyz capital of Frunze was created under the aegis of the editorial board of *Komsomolets Kirgizii*, the Komsomol newspaper. It was the first so-called informal organisation in Kyrgyzstan and consisted of about 40 people, mostly young Russian-speaking intellectuals of various ethnic origins. The newspaper published reviews of the discussions held at the club. The club members were criticised by the authorities for their attempts to discuss the idea of a Kyrgyzstan Popular Front. In 1989 the club split up. About the same time, another student political grouping, Zamandash, functioned under the aegis of the Chair of Philosophy at the Kyrgyz State University in Frunze.[109]

This first stage of development continued for nearly two years. In the second stage these clubs were replaced by openly politicised organizations, such as the Memorial Society created in Moscow in August 1988. The Memorial Society's goals were to rehabilitate the victims of the Stalinist repression, to render aid to the survivors and relatives of those who perished and to fight against the remnants of totalitarianism in Soviet society.[110] The first Memorial groups in Central Asia were created in Kazakhstan in Tselinograd (now Astana) and Alma-Ata in December 1988. The authorities tried to split the organisation by creating a parallel formation, Adilet, with the same proclaimed goals. Their aim was to sow discord among the members of Memorial, which comprised mostly of politicised intellectuals of European origin, and those of Adilet who were mainly representatives of the titular nation.

While the political activity of the Russian and Russophone population manifested itself initially in the formation of political clubs, the younger generation of the titular nationality expressed its protest through mass demonstrations or by seizure of land. At the beginning of 1990 the apparatus of the still-ruling Communist Party of Kazakhstan initiated the creation of the Kazakh Tili (language) society with branches throughout the entire territory of the republic; within a number of months many national youth movements arose under its aegis. The largest such organisation outside Alma-Ata was the Union of Independent Kazakh Youth in Shymkent (Chimkent). In summer 1990, young Kazakhs who had begun mass seizures of land for settlement in Alma-Ata, formed the Shanyrak, Daryn and Altyn Besik societies.[111]

Mass land seizures by Kyrgyz youth also took place in Kyrgyzstan's capital, Frunze in the beginning of 1989. The Ashar association was created, whose goal was to render aid to these squatters; it consisted of more than 5,000 families and became an all-republican organisation. The politicised wing of this association that lasted spawned the Ashar movement and Democratic Kyrgyzstan Movement (the DDK), both of which had a national revivalist orientation. In March-April 1990, two new national democratic associations, Asaba and Atuulduk Demilge (Civil Imitative), appeared and a 'democratic union' was created in Jalalabad. Numerous organisations of national democratic orientation began to appear throughout the republic.[112]

During this period, the Communist Party tried to seek support from various social forces, which were previously excluded from any role in social, political and economic sphere in order to legitimise its position in a changed context. It altered the relationship between state and society, legitimised new forms of expression and activity, expanding the resources at the disposal of new groups and altered the perceptions associated with political activism.[113] The main aim of Gorbachev's democratisation process was to use it as a means to get rid of those bureaucrats and Communist Party members, who were corrupt and had old ideas and opposed the reform programme. Another thing was, he hoped that democratisation would unlock popular energies and initiative and give people a stake in the system. The process of democratisation in Soviet society after glasnost led to the formation of "popular front". The main objectives of these popular fronts were to create a nationwide popular movement that would not only challenge the single party regime, but also support the Party reformers led by Gorbachev against the old guards in the Party and state apparatus.[114] These 'popular fronts' championed a number of causes and their typology included social, democratic and green movements.

The policy of glasnost in Central Asia provided the opportunity to the indigenous intelligentsia to reflect on their native history and culture which was a taboo subject during the earlier period. The relative free flow of information and growth of free press led to the rethinking of general people's interest in their past history and culture.

One of the important issues that confronted the Central Asian region during this period was rampant corruption and involvement of political elites in it. After coming to power, Gorbachev tried to probe the corruption charges levelled against the political leaders. In Kyrgyzstan, issues relating to corruption first surfaced during the 1980 cotton harvest. This led to the removal and punishment of Party officials and Soviet executives.[115]

In Turkmenistan Republic, revelation about clan, corruption and crime nexus came out on a large scale in the Tashauz province in 1984 and continued till 1986. The Thaelmann collective farm in the Leninisk district of the province fell short by more than 2,20,000 roubles. Farm chairman, Piriyev, concealed the shortfall by manipulating and falsifying financial documents, including so-called "advances" of some 2,44,000 roubles paid to the collective farmers for cotton which the state never received.[116]

Under Gorbachev this new trend focused on combating what was described as 'corruption' amongst the elite and reducing its measured flirtation with nationalism and other 'survivals of the past' such as Islam. Alongside this came a call for a 'renewal of cadres' and an attempt to involve the region in the general restructuring and reform of the Soviet economy.

Turkmen First Secretary S. Niyazov singled out the Tashauz oblast elite for basing personnel selection on kin or regional basis, and sacked many key officials. This campaign continued throughout Central Asia in the mid-1980s, with the public denigration of numerous officials and the replacement of hundreds. Yet many of those sacked soon reappeared in other posts. In Uzbekistan, I. Usmankhodzhaev, former party chief Rashidov's replacement and Moscow's ostensible scourge of corruption, was himself removed in early 1988, alongwith other key officials, and later imprisoned for his own role in the 'cotton affair'.[117]

Donald Carlisle notes that from Rashidov's death in late 1983 to January 1985, some 40 out of 65 oblast secretaries were replaced in Uzbekistan, including 10 out of 13 first secretaries. In January

1986, only 34 of 177 Central Committee Party Congress members were retained whilst only 2 Bureau members survived from 1981. In 1983-86 all five Republican Party first secretaries in Central Asia were replaced, though the last change involving Kazakhstan was to provoke the first signs of substantial resistance within the region. This new policy was given shape at the 27th Party Congress in February 1986, when Yegor Ligachev suggested that the time had come to rethink aspects of personnel policy.[118]

Kazakh party boss D. Kunaev was replaced by G. Kolbin, a Slav who had previously worked as a regional party boss within the Russian federation. Within hours of the announcement there were demonstrators on the streets of the Kazakh capital Alma-Ata and in the following days violent clashes left at least three people dead and many injured. Unrest appears to have affected many other parts of Kazakhstan in the following days, and in subsequent months hundreds of students lost their places in educational establishments, many party members were expelled and hundreds of those allegedly involved were subjected to administrative or criminal penalties. Official sources blamed events on hooligans lured by money and drinks or on corrupt supporters of Kunaev. However, a report produced by a Kazakh parliamentary commission in 1989 saw the events of December as the culmination of Kazakhstan's long history of socioeconomic exploitation and political domination by Moscow which had rendered the centre insensitive to local needs. In this version such violence as did occur was the product of an overreaction by the authorities and occurred despite the efforts of local leaders such as Nazarbaev to slam the situation.[119] The longer term effect of this first major sign of ethnic unrest in Gorbachev's Soviet Union was the end of the policy of inter-republican exchange of cadres and in practice the curtailment of Moscow's efforts to restore control in the region through the personnel policy.

During perestroika, economic growth in most of the Central Asian Republics declined and the population rose. For example, in Uzbekistan official figures recorded that economic growth had fallen from 8.6 percent in 1971-75 to 3.0 percent in 1981-85, yet the population had risen by 15.4 percent in 1979-85. Various regional organisations were already flourishing and the religious groups were active.[120]

Due to openness in Central Asian society, free expression of nationalism led to many ethnic conflicts in the region. Uzbek and Kyrgyz groups were involved in the violent clashes over land disputed in Uzbekistan's Andizhan oblast in 1989. Again in 1990, competing claims made by new ethnically based associations in the Osh region of Kyrgyzstan led to violence between the above two groups. Unemployment and land hunger were more acute in this region and local politicians were willing to support nationalism openly. Similarly, a dispute over claims to irrigation water and farm land led to violence between Tajiks and Kyrgyz villagers on the border of the two republics in 1989.[121]

Due to unemployment, population growth, economic crises, spread of literacy and civic consciousness, local nationalities showed ultranationalist tendencies and targeted non-titular groups. As a result, thousands of Russians left Central Asia since late 1989. Although there was very little direct threat to the Russians, the psychological atmosphere of uncertainty and the adoption of new language laws prompted a large number of Russians and other European populations to leave Central Asia in the wake of ethnic riots in Ferghana (1989), in Dushanbe (1990), and in Osh (1990). Out-migration of non-indigenous specialists from Central Asia was estimated to be more than 200,000 in 1990.[122]

In the late 1980s of Gorbachev period, anti-Russian mobilisation spread in various parts of the former USSR and most of the republics demanded independence. But in the Central Asian region there were no such demands for independence. Most of the local intellectuals and social organisations were more concerned about the environmental, ethnic, language and religious issues rather than the political one. Ajay Patnaik argued that the dissent during the glasnost years did not go beyond the realm of culture or environmental issues like attempts by the local intellectuals to rehabilitate the writers belonging to the Jadid tradition or to extensively focus on the issue of the shrinking of the Aral sea.[123] Decreasing soil fertility and health problems resulting from excessive use of fertilisers and pesticides were other issues to be raised by the emerging nationalists. In Kazakhstan, the *Nevada-Semipalatinsk* movement raised the issue of banning nuclear testing in the republic that had proved ruinous to the environment and health. Apart from that language issue got maximum support from nationalist groups in that time. However, between 1989 and 1990, the ruling republican leadership appropriated the issue and introduced language laws that made their titular language the state-language. Some of the cultural and religious traditions received state support and patronage, e.g. celebration of *Nawriz*, allowing opening of new mosques and electing the Central Asian Mufti, Muhammad Sadik, to the USSR Congress of People's Deputies in 1989 etc. As a result, groups such as Birlik in Uzbekistan, Agzy-Birlik in Turkmenistan and Zeltoksan, Azat and Alash in Kazakhstan could not make much headway.[124]

In March 1991, a referendum was conducted all over the Soviet Union. But in Central Asia, all the republics overwhelmingly supported the existence of Soviet Union. This was a free and fair referendum and the republics like Georgia and the Baltic Republics boycotted it. In some republics, like Ukraine, 60 per cent of the voters opted for preserving the USSR, whereas in Central Asian republics, nearly 90 per cent or more voted positively. The degree of the result varied from the state to state like 94 per cent in Kazakhstan, 87.7 per cent in Kyrgyzstan, 90.2 per cent in Tajikistan, and 95.7 per cent in Turkmenistan.[125]

The August 1991 coup in Moscow came as a shock to Central Asia. The leaders of the Central Asian republics watched quietly, counselling their populations to observe restraint. Only Kyrgyzstan's Akaev immediately attacked the illegality of the actions of Soviet Vice President Gennadiy Yanayev and his co-conspirators, and he mobilised the local Ministry of Internal Affairs (Ministerstvo Vnutrennikh Del–MVD) to protect him from an attempted power grab by Kyrgyzstan's Communist party.[126]

The coup's failure had dramatic consequences throughout the region. The collapse of the Communist Party of the Soviet Union (CPSU) meant that Central Asia's leaders had to dissolve their own Communist parties or have their political credibility called into question. The one leader, who chose not to do so, President and First Secretary Khallkar Makhkamov of Tajikistan, was driven from office by popular protest within weeks of the coup.[127]

Central Asia's leaders turned over the Communist Party's property to the governments that they headed. Largely without property and lacking well-developed ideological programmes, the instant post-coup successor parties, like Uzbekistan's National Democratic Party and Kazakhstan's Socialist Party, began to collapse from lack of public interest before they could even get off the ground.

The Minsk agreement of December 8, 1991 by joining together Russia, Belarus, and Ukraine in a Commonwealth of Independent States, destroyed any hopes the Central Asian republics had for preserving the Union and essentially left the republics political orphans. Central Asia's leaders, faced with no real alternative, joined the new Commonwealth on December 21, 1991, thus creating a basis of transition to complete independence.

Notes

1. Eelvin, Neil (2002), "Uzbekistan", *Eastern Europe, Russia and Central Asia*, London: Europa Publications. p. 488.
2. Ibid.
3. Krader, Lawrence (1963), *Peoples of Central Asia*, Bloomington, Indiana: Indiana University Press. p.153.
4. Bohr, Annettee (2002), "Turkmenistan History", *Eastern Europe, Russia and Central Asia*, London: Europa Publications. p. 425.
5. Rakowska-Harmstone, Teresa (1970), *Russia and Nationalism in Central Asia*, London: The Johns Hopkins Press. p. 10.
6. In the modern times the Upper flow of the Oxus (Amu-Dariya) is known as the Panj (Pyandzh) River, now a boundary between Tajikistan and Afghanistan.
7. Rakowska-Harmstone, Teresa, op.cit, p. 10.
8. Ibid. p. 11.

9. Ibid.
10. Payne, John (1990), "Tadzhiks", in Graham Smith (ed.), *The Nationalities Question in the Soviet Union*, London: Longman. p. 260.
11. Rakowska-Harmstone, Teresa, op.cit., p. 11.
12. Ibid. p. 12.
13. Ibid. p. 13.
14. Ibid.
15. The Yenisei region has been now named as the Tvga region which is situated in the Russian Federation.
16. Anderson, John (1999), *Kyrgyzstan: Central Asia's Island of Democracy?*,The Netherlands: Harwood Academic Publishers. p. 2.
17. Anderson, John (2002), "Kyrgyzstan History", *Eastern Europe, Russia and Central Asia*, London: Europa Publications. 2nd Edition.p. 229.
18. Akiner, Shirin (2002), "Kazakhstan History", *Eastern Europe, Russia and Central Asia*, London: Europa Publications. 2nd Edition. p. 1999.
19. Ibid.
20. Carley, Patricia M. (1995), "The Legacy of the Soviet Political System and the Prospects for Developing Civil Society in Central Asia", in Vladimir Tismaneanu (ed.), *Political Culture and Civil Society in Russia and the New States of Eurasia*, Armonk, New York: M.E. Sharpe Publication. p. 295.
21. Ibid.
22. Pierce, Richard (1960), "*Russian Central Asia: 1817-1917*",Barkeley and Los Angeles: University of California Press. p. 12.
23. Kaushik, Devendra (1976), *Socialism in Central Asia: A Study in the Transformation of Socio-Economic Relations in Soviet Central Asia*",New Delhi: Allied Publishers. p. 53.
24. Pierce, R.A., op.cit., p. 12-13.
25. Kaushik, Devendra, op.cit., p. 54.
26. Mandel, William (1944), *The Soviet Far East and Central Asia*, New York: Institute of Pacific Relations. p.100.
27. Ibid. pp.100-101.
28. Kaushik, Devendra, op.cit., p .53.
29. Patnaik, Ajay (1989), *Perestroika and Women Labour Forces in Soviet Central Asia*, New Delhi: New Literature. p. 10.
30. Akiner, Shirin (1997), "Between Tradition and Modernity: the Dilemma Facing Contemporary Central Asian Women", in Mary Buckley (ed.), *Post-Soviet Women: from the Baltic to Central Asia*, UK: Cambridge University Press. p. 265.
31. Ibid. p.262.
32. Wheeler, Geoffrey (1957), "Recent Development in Soviet Central Asia: Lecture, 1957", *The Geographical Journal*, vol. 123., no. 2., January. p. 139.
33. Kaushik, Devendra (1970), *Central Asia in Modern Times*, Moscow: Progress Publishers. p. 71.
34. Ibid.
35. Glenn, John (1999), *The Soviet Legacy in Central Asia*, London: Macmillan Press. p.65.
36. Sharma, R.R. (1976), "Intelligentsia and Politics of Underdevelopment and Development: A Case Study of Soviet Central Asia", *International Politics*, vol.15., no.2., pp.207-208.

37. Ibid. p. 209.
38. Sansawal, M.S. (1988), *Political Leadership in Soviet Central Asia: 1946-64*, New Delhi: Common Wealth. p. 41.
39. Imam, Zafar (1976), "Origin and Development of Socialism among the Muslims of Russia", *International Studies*, vol. 15., no.2., p. 197.
40. Mandel, William, op.cit., p.104.
41. Glenn, John, op.cit., p.67.
42. Ibid.
43. Narkiewicz, Olga A. (1972), "Political Participation and the Soviet State", in Geraint Parry (ed.), *Participation Politics*, Manchester: Manchester University Press. p.197.
44. Ibid.
45. Mandel, William M. (1992), "Soviet Central Asia", *Pacific Affairs*, vol. 15., no.4., December. p. 401.
46. Rywkin, Michael (1990), *Moscow's Muslim Challenge: Soviet Central Asia*, London: M.E. Sharpe. 1990. p.35.
47. Basmachis: The Basmachis were a local guerrilla group led by mullahs, tribal chiefs and landlords who resisted Soviet rule across the whole of central Asia and sustained their unequal struggle until the 1930s. By 1919 there were some forty Basmachi groups with some 20,000 fighters strung across the steppe from Ashkhabad to Ferghana and Dushanbe.
48. Mandel, William M., op. cit., p. 403.
49. Ibid. p.404.
50. Baradat, Leon P. (1986), *Soviet Political Society*, New Jersey: Prentice-Hall. p.108.
51. Article 3. The Constitution of the USSR, 1977, cited in Gordon B. Smith (1992), *Soviet Politics*, London: Macmillan Press. Second Edition. p.349.
52. Almound, Gabriel A. (1983), "Communism and Political Culture Theory", *Comparative Politics*, vol. 15., no. 2., January. p. 129.
53. Article 6. The Constitution of the USSR, 1977, cited in Gordon B. Smith, op.cit., p.342.
54. Article 51. The Constitution of the USSR, 1977, cited in Gordon B. Smith, op.cit., p.349.
55. Baradat, Leon P., op.cit., p.111.
56. Kaushik, Devendra, *Socialism in Central Asia: A Study in the Transformation of Socio-Economic Relations in Soviet Central Asia*, op.cit., p. 33.
57. (1976) *Great Soviet Encyclopedia*, 3rd Edition, vol. 12. New York and London: Macmillan INC. p.481.
58. Anderson, John (1997), *The International Politics of Central Asia*, New York: Manchester University Press. p.32.
59. Ibid.
60. Ibid.
61. Burg, Steven L. (1984), "Central Asian Political Participation and Soviet Political Development", in Yaacov Ro'i (ed.), *The USSR and the Muslim World*,London: George Allen and Unwin Publishers. p.41.
62. Ibid.
63. Anderson, John, op.cit., p. 34.
64. Ibid. p.36.

65. Ibid. p.37.
66. Burg, Steven L., op.cit, p.48.
67. (2001) *International Encyclopedia of the Social and Behavioural Sciences.* Oxford: Elsevier Science Ltd, vol. 22, p.14737.
68. Evans, Michael, op.cit., p.127.
69. Baradat, Leon P., op.cit., p.193.
70. Hazard, John N. (1980), *The Soviet System of Government* (Fifth Edition), Chicago and London: The University of Chicago Press. p.42
71. Baradat, Leon P., op.cit., p.195.
72. Hazard, John N., op.cit., p.44.
73. Baradat, Leon P., op.cit., p.211.
74. Ibid. p.212.
75. Sansawal, M.S., op.cit., pp.110-111.
76. Hough, Jerry F. (1976), "Political Participation in the Soviet Union", *Soviet Studies*, vol. XXVIII, no.1, January. p. 7.
77. Ibid. p. 9.
78. Burg, Steven L., op.cit., p.49.
79. Unger, Arych L. (1981), "Political Participation in the USSR: YCL and CPSU", *Soviet Studies*, vol.33., no.1, January. p.121.
80. Hough, Jerry F., op.cit., p.16.
81. Evans, Michael (1972), "Karl Marx and the Concept of Political Participation", in Geraint Parry (ed.), *Participation Politics*, Manchester: Manchester University Press. p.131.
82. Hazard, John N., op.cit., p.49.
83. Ibid. p.50.
84. Lodge, Milton (1968), "Soviet Elite Participatory Attitudes in the Post-Stalin Period", *The American Political Science Review*, vol.62., no.3., September. p.839.
85. Akiner, Shirin, op.cit.. p.268.
86. Kennedy – Pipe, Caroline (2004). Whose security? State Building and the Emancipation of Women in Central Asia. *International Relations.* vol. 18. no. 1. p. 92.
87. Ibid. p. 94.
88. Ibid.
89. Akiner, Shirin (1997), "Between Tradition and Modernity: the Dilemma Facing Contemporary Central Asian Women", in Mary Buckley (ed.), op.cit., p.269.
90. Ibid. p.272.
91. Kennedy–Pipe, Caroline, op.cit., p.101.
92. Mandel, William, *The Soviet Far East and Central Asia*, op.cit., p.116.
93. Akiner, Shirin (1997), "Between Tradition and Modernity: the Dilemma Facing Contemporary Central Asian Women", in Mary Buckley (ed.), op.cit., p.273.
94. Mandel, William, *The Soviet Far East and Central Asia*, op.cit., p. 100.
95. Luong, Pauline Jones (2002), *Institutional Change and Political Continuity in Post-Soviet Central Asia: Power, Perceptions, and Pacts*, UK: Cambridge University Press. Pp.5-6.

96. Article 48. The Constitution of the USSR: 1977, cited in Gordon B. Smith, op.cit., p.342.
97. Baradat, Leon P., op.cit., p.197.
98. Adams, Jan S. (1981), "Critical Letters to the Soviet Press: an Increasingly Important Public Forum", in Donald E. Schulz and Zan S. Adams (eds.), *Political Participation in Communist Systems*, New York: Pergamon Press. p.108.
99. Ibid. p.201.
100. Adams, Jan S., "Critical Letters to the Soviet Press: an Increasingly Important Public Forum", in Donald E. Schulz and Zan S. Adams (eds.), op.cit., p.110.
101. Gorbachev, Mikhail (1987), "*Perestroika: New Thinking for Our Country and the World*",London: Collings. p.22.
102. Ibid. p.24.
103. Ibid. p.34.
104. Ibid. p.35.
105. Lapidus, Gali W. (1992), "From Democratisation to Disintegration: The Impact of Perestroika on Nationality Question", in Gali W. Lapidus, Victorzalavsty, Phillip Goldman (eds.), *From Union to Commonwealth: Nationalism and Separatism in Soviet Republics*, New York: Cambridge University Press. p. 46.
106. (1986) Gorbachev's speech on "Further Democratization of Society and Promotion of the People's Socialist Self-Government", *XXVII CPSU Congress, Documents and Resolutions*, New Delhi: Allied Publishers Pvt. Ltd. p.76.
107. Ibid. p.77.
108. Babak, Vladimir (2004), "The Formation of Political Parties and Movements in Central Asia", in Yaacov Ro'I (ed.), *Democracy and Pluralism in Muslim Eurasia*, London & New York: Frank Class. p.144.
109. Ibid.
110. Ibid. p.145.
111. Ibid.
1120 Ibid. p. 146.
113. Lapidus, Gali W. "From Democratisation to Disintegration: The Impact of Perestroika on Nationality Question", in Gali W. Lapidus, Victorzalavsty, Phillip Goldman (eds.), op.cit., p.46.
114. Ibid.
115. Patnaik, Ajay (1996), "*Central Asia: Between Modernity and Tradition*", New Delhi: Konark Publishers. p.160.
116. Ibid.
117. Anderson, John, op.cit., p.57.
118. Ibid. p. 58.
119. Ibid. p. 59.
120. Ibid.
121. Patnaik, Ajay (2000), "Nation-State in a Multi-Ethnic Society: The Case of Central Asia", in Shams-Ud-Din (ed.), *Geopolitics and Energy Resources in Central Asia and Caspian Sea Region*",New Delhi: Lancer publisher. p.58.
122. Ibid.
123. Patnaik, Ajay (2005), "Ethnicity and Nationalism in Central Asia", in V.

Nagendra Rao & Mohammad Monir Alam (eds.), *Central Asia: Present Challenges and Future Prospects*, New Delhi: Knowledge World. p.65.

124. Ibid. p.67.
125. Patnaik, Ajay, "Ethnicity and Nationalism in Central Asia", in V. Nagendra Rao & Mohammad Monir Alam (eds.), op.cit., p. 66.
126. Olcott, Martha Brill (1992), "Central Asia's Post Empire Politics", *ORBIS,* vol.36., no.2., Spring. p.255.
127. Ibid.

3
Institutional Developments

Nation-building process of a contemporary nation state requires strong institutional designing which would accommodate the wills and aspirations of all sections of people. The effective and efficient stable political system of a nation state depends on its institutional developments. The design and formation of state institutions like legislature, executive and judiciary reflects the country's political system and governability. In the present political system in the contemporary world, institution building is the most important aspect to accommodate and give importance to all sections of people irrespective of discrimination. In the democratic form of government, institution building plays a major role for a stable society. At the same time, institution building is easier in a stable and mature society than in the newly independent states. In a democratic society, well-designed institutions would facilitate active citizen participation in the state affairs. Institutions are developed from the emerging political culture, system and governance process of the countries. Weak institutions could lead to destabilisation of the political system and anarchy and fail to protect the interest of all sections of society or citizens. Recently, Third World countries have experienced a lot of political crisis due to the weak political institutions and it leads to the domination of one organ of the political system over others. As a result, the ruling classes have systematically manipulated and dominated the political system according to their will and wishes in decision-making process and execution of executive orders. So, strong and balanced political institutions are required for growth, progress, prosperity and protection of the interests of all sections of society. This could be achieved by participation of all citizens in the political process of the nation state. After the Cold War period, political development especially in the Communist bloc provides a new imperative political knowledge regarding the transitional political developments from the Communist ideology to a democratic and liberal political system. The political culture, attitude, political behaviour and social acceptance of general community as well as political nomenclature of the Communist society also changed according to the new political scenario. They are trying to develop a conducive political atmosphere for institutional developments and political participation of all sections of society. Efficiently designed political institutions are the key yardstick and instrument for smooth functioning of the nation state in the contemporary political system. The newly independent Central Asian countries have been providing new theories to the democratic system and aspirations of its people for development of political culture and electoral participation.

The Central Asian republics attained their independence after the disintegration of Soviet Union in December 1991, though these republics were not willing to leave the Soviet Union. In the March 1991 referendum, 90 to 95 per cent of the electorate in the Central Asian republics had supported the preservation of the USSR, as against only 53.5 percent in the Russian republic favouring its continued existence.[1] In spite of the Central Asian willingness to remain in the Union the situation started changing following an abortive coup in Moscow in August 1991. As a result, on August 31, 1991, the Supreme Soviet of Uzbekistan and Kyrgyzstan declared the independence of their respective republics. On September 9, 1991, Tajikistan also declared independence through its Supreme Soviet. Only Turkmenistan proclaimed its independence last on October 26, 1991 following a referendum in which 94.1% of the electorate favoured such a course.[2]

Soon after attaining some sort of forced independence, the Central Asian republics faced numerous problems in their path. The most important problems were creating a national identity for the Central Asian peoples, pressure of large number of ethnic Russian minorities in Central Asian republics and problems emerging due to transitional nature of the economy from a command and state-regulated economic system to a market-oriented economy.

The Central Asian political elites tried their best to fulfill the needs and aspirations of the people and develop institutional mechanisms to iron out their problems. They also adopted different mobilisation strategies to take on the challenges posed by elements of social mobilisation. However, the experience differs from country to country depending upon the nature of problems posed by social forces. For example, in Tajikistan, structural disequilibrium between weak political institutionalisation and strong social mobilisation led to the breakdown of state authority. In Tajikistan, the regime faced intractable challenges from democrats, Islamic movements and various tribal and clan groups, each trying to take over political power.[3]

All the republics had secured their boundaries, territory, and legitimacy during the Soviet period itself. Ethno-national identities were most strongly visible among the intellectual elite, party members and the urban population. The rural population continued to identify with traditional *Mahalla* (community), village, residential, kinship, clan, and regional loyalties.[4]

After independence, all the five Central Asian republics (Kazakhstan, Kyrgyzstan, Tajikistan, Turkmenistan and Uzbekistan) have maintained their own territorial identity and statehood.

The Republic of Tajikistan is a mountainous, landlocked country located in the South East of Central Asia and shares its borders with Uzbekistan to the west, Kyrgyzstan to the north, Afghanistan to the south and China to the east. It spreads across 1426 thousand square kilometres having 8.160 million of population as on April 1, 2014.[5] Administratively, it is divided into one autonomous *Oblast*, two *Oblasts* (provinces), sixty two regions, seventeen cities and towns, fifty seven settlements and three hundred sixty nine *Djamoats dochot* (rural administration).[6]

The Republic of Kazakhstan is geographically situated in the heart of Eurasia and ranked as the ninth largest country in the world as well as the world's largest landlocked country sharing borders with China, Russia, Kyrgyzstan, Turkmenistan, Uzbekistan and a significant part of the Caspian Sea. It has 17.2 million population (as on January 1, 2014) and enters into the fifty most competitive countries of the world. The administrative and territorial structure of the republic includes fourteen areas, two cities of republican significance, one hundred and seventy five administrative areas, eighty seven cities, thirty four settlements and six thousand nine hundred and forty seven rural settlements.[7]

The Republic of Uzbekistan is situated in the centre of Eurasia on the Great Silk Route and is a doubly landlocked country in Central Asia. It shares its borders with Kazakhstan and the Aral Sea to the north, Tajikistan to the southeast, Kyrgyzstan to the northeast, Afghanistan to the south, and Turkmenistan to the southwest. It is spread over 448,900 square kilometres and has more than 30.4 million people as of January 1, 2014.[8] Administratively, it comprises twelve provinces, one autonomous republic and one independent city.

The Republic of Kyrgyzstan is a landlocked and mountainous country located in Central Asia and it borders with Kazakhstan to the north, Uzbekistan to the west, Tajikistan to the southwest and China to the east. Geographically, it covers 198,500 square kilometres and has more than 5.7 million population in 2014. It is divided into seven regions and twenty small settlements.

The Republic of Turkmenistan is a Central Asia country which stretches from the Caspian Sea on the west to Afghanistan in the east, also bordering Iran, Uzbekistan and Kazakhstan. It is divided into five provinces and one capital city district which cover 488,100 square kilometres of geographical area having a population of 5.11 million in 2014.

After the collapse of the Communist political system, these Central Asian countries had debated on whether the Parliament would operate on a full or part-time basis, as well as whether it would be unicameral or bicameral. In this debate central leaders were divided on both the aspects. At last they reached the conclusion and adopted their own constitution. The Kazakh Parliament ratified the country's first post-Soviet Constitution in January 1993. This Constitution contained 98 Articles and IX sections. On August 30, 1995, this Constitution was changed and through a national referendum with 89% of the electoral voting a new Constitution on September 6[9] was officially adopted. This Constitution was also amended on October 18, 1998; May 18, 2007 and February 2, 2011.

The Constitution of the Kyrgyz Republic was proclaimed on May 5, 1993 by the 12th Supreme Soviet of the Republic of Kyrgyzstan. This Constitution contained 97 Articles, divided into VIII chapters. This Constitution has also been amended many times, like on October 22, 1994; on February 10, 1996; on October 17, 1998; on February 2, 2003; in November 2006, October 2007 and June 2010 through referendums.

The Constitution of Tajikistan entered into force on November 6, 1994 though a nation-wide plebiscite. This Constitution contains 100 Articles and is divided into X chapters. This Constitution was also amended on September 26, 1999 and on June 22, 2003 through a national referendum.

The Constitution of Turkmenistan was adopted on May 18, 1992. This Constitution contains 116 Articles and VIII sections. This Constitution was also amended in 1995, 1999, 2003, 2006 and 2008.

The Constitution of Uzbekistan was adopted by the Supreme Council on December 8, 1992. This Constitution contains 128 Articles and is divided into six parts and 26 chapters. This Constitution has also been amended in 2003 and 2014.

All these Central Asian constitutions characterise their political system as secular, democratic, legal and social states whose highest values are given to the individuals, their lives, rights and freedoms. The fundamental principles of the activity of the republics are public concerns and political stability. They emphasise the separation of religion and politics. This provision has been incorporated in their constitution to refrain all the radical forces from the power orbit. All the Central Asian constitutions incorporated the principles of separation of power among the three branches of government to check the hegemonistic tendency on the part of any one apparatus of government. These constitutions, however, have not clearly mentioned the political system as unitary or federal or quasi-federal; but the practice implies that their structures are indeed unitary.

All the Central Asian constitutions claim their government to be democratic and based on law. The Constitution of Kazakhstan states that "the Republic of Kazakhstan is a democratic, secular, and unitarian state," and added that "the people of Kazakhstan are the sole bearer of the state power of the republic".[10] The 1993 Constitution of Kyrgyzstan also declares the country to be a secular and unitary state and places sovereignty with the people. The Uzbek Constitution, after declaring the state to be secular, democratic, and law-based, goes so far as to define the mission of the Uzbek people as "the creation of a humane democratic state based on the rule of law".

The Turkmen Constitution, in Article 1, states that Turkmenistan shall be a democratic, law-based and secular state. It designates the people of Turkmenistan as the sole bearer of sovereignty. The new Tajik Constitution was adopted only on November 6, 1994. Article 1 of the Constitution describes Tajikistan as "sovereign, democratic, law governed secular and unitary state".[11] Article 6 designates the people as the bearer of sovereignty and "the sole source of power of the state".

3.1 The Executive Branch

The governmental systems of all the Central Asian countries are republican and closer to a presidential form of government rather than parliamentary. The President is the head of the state in all five republics, and is also the symbol of the unity of people, state power and the guarantor of the Constitution and of individual and citizen rights. The President defines the fundamental directions of internal and external policy of the state and represents the republic within the country and in international forums.

The Constitution of Kazakhstan, in Article 40, defines the position of president. This article mentions: The President of the Republic of Kazakhstan shall be the head of state, its highest official determining the main directions of the domestic and foreign policy of the state and represents Kazakhstan within the country and in international relations. He shall be the symbol and guarantor of the unity of the people and the state power, inviolability of the Constitution, rights and freedoms of an individual and citizen. He also ensures by his arbitration concerted functioning of all branches of state power and responsibility of the institutions of power before the people.[12]

The Constitution of the Kyrgyz Republic mentions the position of President in the chapter three and Article 42. This Constitution elaborates: The President of the Kyrgyz Republic is the head of the state and is the highest official of the Kyrgyz Republic. He is the symbol of the unity of the people and state power, and is the guarantor of the Constitution of Kyrgyz Republic and of human rights and freedoms. He also defines the fundamental directions of internal and external policy of the state, represents the Kyrgyz Republic within the country and in international relations. He takes measures to guard the sovereignty and territorial integrity of the Kyrgyz Republic, and ensures the unity and continuity of state power and the coordinated functioning and interaction of state organs and their responsibility to the people.[13]

The 1994 Constitution of Tajikistan mentions the position of President in chapter four and Article 64. This Article states that "The President of the Republic of Tajikistan is the head of the state and of the executive power (Government). The President is the guarantor of the Constitution and laws, of the rights and freedoms of the persona and citizen, of national independence unity, and territorial integrity, of the continuity and longevity of the state, of the coordinated functioning and cooperation of governmental organs, and of compliance with the international treaties of Tajikistan".[14]

The Constitution of Turkmenistan describes the position of President in chapter three and Article 54. This Article mentions that the President of Turkmenistan is the head of state and of the executive power. He is the highest official of Turkmenistan, and acts as a guarantor of national independence, territorial integrity and adherence to the Constitution and international agreements.[15]

The Constitution of Uzbekistan mentions the position of President in chapter 19 and Article 89. This Article mentions that the President of the Republic of Uzbekistan is the head of state and executive authority in the Republic of Uzbekistan.

3.1.1 Electoral Process

All the constitutions of the republics clearly mention the electoral process and eligibility for the post of chief executives.

Kazakhstan

The Constitution of the Republic of Kazakhstan clearly mentions the eligibility and criteria of presidential election. Article 41 states: the President of the Republic shall be elected by universal, equal and direct suffrage under a secret ballot for a seven-year term in accordance with the constitutional law by the citizens of the Republic who have come of age. A citizen of the Republic shall be eligible for the office of the President of the Republic of Kazakhstan if he or she is by birth not younger than forty and has a perfect command of the state language and has lived in Kazakhstan for not less than fifteen years. Regular elections of the President of the Republic shall be held on the first Sunday of December and shall not coincide with the election of a new Parliament of the Republic. The candidate who receives more than 50 percent of the votes of the constituents that took part in the election shall be deemed elected. If none of the candidates receives the above number of votes, a second round of elections shall be held between the two candidates who obtained the largest number of votes. The candidate who receives the larger number of votes of the constituents who take part in the second round of elections shall be deemed elected.[16]

As per this constitutional provision, the first general presidential election was held in December 1991. In this election former Kazakhstan Communist Party First Secretary Nursultan Nazarbayev was the sole candidate and received 99 per cent of the vote.[17] On April 29, 1995, a nationwide referendum was held on the extension of President Nazarbayev's term of office until December 1, 2000. A total of 95.4 percent participated in this referendum and 91 percent of the electorate had voted in favour of this.[18] On October 8, 1998, the Parliament adopted a constitutional amendment for revising the date for the Presidential election to January 1999. The minimum age for holding the office of President was revised from 35 to 45 years and the maximum age of 65 was abolished. It also amended the terms of the President Office and extended it up to a 7-year term. Following this amendment, Nazarbayev was re-elected as President with 81.7 percent of the votes cast in which 86.3 percent of the registered electorates took part. The candidate of the Communist Party of Kazakhstan, Serikbolsyn Abdildin, came second polling 12.1 per cent of the votes cast.[19] The Organization for Security and Cooperation in Europe (OSCE) refused to monitor the election because the process was alleged to be unfair and also because it debarred certain candidates, including the former Prime Minister, Akezhan Kazhegeldin from the electoral process. However, on January 20, 1999, Nazarbayev was sworn in as President for a new term of office.

The Constitutional Council and the *Majilis* (the Lower House of Parliament) had called for the next Presidential election on December 4, 2005. This election was the second multi-party contested election since 1991. The election was contested by five candidates, namely, Mr. Yerassyl Abylkasymov (Communist People's Party of Kazakhstan), Mr. Alikhan Baimenov (Ak Zhol Party), Mr. Mels Yeleussizov (independent), Mr. Nursultan Nazarbayev (Otan Party), and Mr. Zharmakhan Tuyakbai ('For a Just Kazakhstan' Movement).[20] In this election, no woman candidate and no representative from the ethnic minority community had contested due to the mandatory requirement of the Kazakh language test. The *Sailau*, an e-voting system was used for first time in the Presidential election since independence. The official turnout was 76.78 per cent. Nazarbayev was again re-elected with 91.15 per cent votes for the post of President.[21] After that the Constitution was amended to allow no term limits to the President and reduced the presidential term from seven to five years in May 2007 and further amended on February 3, 2011 to allow the President to call an early Presidential election. Accordingly the election was held on April 3, 2011 and Nazarbayev was re-elected for a third term with approximately 95 percent of the votes against three nominal candidates.

Kyrgyzstan

The Constitution of Kyrgyzstan (amended on June 27, 2010) clearly mentions the election process of Executive Branch in the Articles 61 and 62. The President of the Kyrgyz Republic shall be elected for a term of six years and shall not hold office for two consecutive years. He may not be younger than 35 years of age and will not be older than 70 years. He has to have command over the official language and be a resident of the republic for not less than 15 years before the nomination of his candidature to the office of the President. The President of the Kyrgyz Republic shall be elected by citizens of the Kyrgyz Republic by a majority of actual votes cast and elections shall be held on the basis of universal, equal and direct suffrage by secret ballot. The number of candidates for the office of President of the Kyrgyz Republic shall not be limited. Any person who has registered and has obtained not less than 30,000 voter signatures may be a candidate for President of the Kyrgyz Republic. The election of the President shall be considered valid if more than fifty per cent of all voters in the republic have taken part in the election. In the first ballot, a candidate shall be considered elected to the office of President if he has obtained more than half of those votes cast in the election. If none of the candidates obtains more than half of the votes cast in the first ballot, only the two candidates who have obtained the largest number of votes shall appear on the second ballot. A candidate who obtains more than half of the votes cast in the second ballot shall be considered elected if not less than fifty per cent of all voters have taken part in the second ballot.[22]

After the adoption of constitutional provisions for election, the Presidential election was held on December 24, 1995. Asker Akayev was the popular candidate and other two opposition candidates, Apsamat Masaliyev and Medetkan Sherimkulov, were not so popular. In this election 81.1 per cent electorate participated and Akayev received 71.6 per cent votes.[23] He got elected for the second term. After the victory, Akaev expanded the presidential powers through a referendum. Thus Akaev, through frequent use of the institution of referendum, gradually converted the Kyrgyz political system from parliamentary democracy which the 1993 constitution had conceived to an executive Presidential system. Similarly, in the next presidential election, which was held on October 20, 2000, the incumbent President Akaev secured 74.4 percent of the votes. His main challenger Omurbek Tekebayev secured 13.85 percent of the votes. The OSCE criticised the Presidential elections and in a press release pointed out that "the Kyrgyz presidential elections fell short of the country's commitment to the OSCE".

In the Parliamentary election in February and March 2005 there were also reports of huge irregularities in the election process that contributed to public protests. As a result President Askar Akaev fled the state and an opposition leader Kurmanbek Bakiev was appointed as an acting President up to the next election. On July 10, 2005, a Presidential election was conducted by the Election Commission according to the resolution of Parliament on July 10. The dynamic of the Presidential race was shaped by an agreement on May 12 between acting President Kuemanbek Bakiev and Felix Kulov, a leading opposition leader released from prison following President Akaev's ouster. The agreement stipulated Felix Kulov's withdrawal from the electoral race and his immediate appointment as First Vice-Prime Minister. In this election one woman candidate namely Toktayyam Umetalieva contested for the post of President. It was for the first time that a woman candidate contested the post of President in Kyrgyzstan. Bakiev was declared the winner, with 88.71 per cent of the votes, on the basis of a reported turnout of 74.67 percent.[24] For the first time a southerner was elected as the head of Kyrgyzstan whereas since the Soviet period the northern clans had dominated the political scene that included the former President Askar Akaev and his administrative staff. The South is more traditional and a large number of Uzbek minority populations live in that region and have been politically marginalised for a long period of time.[25] This election created new history not only in Kyrgyzstan but also in the whole of Central Asia. For the first time since 1991 the incumbent was replaced as the head of the State. Over the period of time, President Bakiev was re-elected for a second term with 76 percent of the vote in July 2009. Due to corruption and rising prices of basic commodities, opposition activists and citizens protested against President Bakiev around the "White House" in Bishkek on April 7, 2010. As a result, this protest left 86 people dead and more than a thousand injured. Bakiev fled to his home in Jalalabad. Following these events, a provisional government was formed, headed by Ms. Roza Otunbaeva, a former foreign minister. By the referendum in 2010, Ms. Roza Otunbaeva was nominated as the interim President till 31 December 2011. Drastic amendments occurred to the Kyrgyzstan constitution on June 27, 2010 and accordingly the Parliament scheduled the Presidential election for October 30, 2011. In this Presidential election, 16 candidates contested. According to the CEC office, Mr. Atambaev received 62.52 percent, Mr. Madumarov 14.78 percent, and Mr. Tashiev 14.32 percent respectively and all other candidates garnered less than one per cent of votes cast.[26] As a result, Mr. Almazbek Atambaev was elected as a new President in this republic.

Tajikistan

Article 65 of the Tajikistan Constitution clarifies that the President is elected by the citizens of Tajikistan on the basis of universal, direct, and equal suffrage in a secret ballot for a five-year term. Any citizen aged between 35 and 65, who knows the state language and has lived in the territory of Tajikistan at least for the past 10 years, can be nominated to the post of President of the republic. Only a person whose nomination is signed by at least five per cent of the electorate shall be eligible for candidacy to the post of President. A person may not be elected to the office of President for more than two consecutive terms.[27]

According to Article 24 of the Constitutional Law on Elections of the President of the Republic of Tajikistan (Presidential Election Law or PEL), candidates for presidency can be nominated by political parties, the Federation of Independent Trade Unions, Union of Youth of Tajikistan, *oblast* and Dushanbe city *majlises* (councils), as well as representatives of *majlises* of towns and districts.[28] Article 66 of the Constitution establishes that more than half of the registered voters must take part in the election of the President for the election to be valid. A candidate must receive more than 50 per cent of votes cast in the election to win in the first round. If more than two candidates are running for presidency, and none of them receives the required number of votes, a second round shall be conducted within one month but not earlier than 15 days after the Election Day (Art. 35 PEL).[29]

The Presidential election is conducted by a three-tiered system of election commissions consisting of the Central Commission for Elections and Referenda (CCER), District Election Commissions (DECs) and Precinct Election Commissions (PECs). Additionally, polling stations are also established in foreign countries for casting their vote according to the presence of Tajik nationals. All citizens of Tajikistan who have attained 18 years of age have the right to vote, except those who have been declared incapacitated or are imprisoned by a court decision. The law describes that voters should be included in only one voter list. No central registration system has been maintained and it is administered locally. Citizens are included in the voter lists according to their place of permanent or temporary residence. Each PEC compiles a list of voters based on the data provided by local authorities. According to the CCER guidelines, the PECs may also involve representatives of the local community in compiling voter lists.[30]

In accordance with the constitutional provision of Tajikistan, the first election was held on November 6, 1994. Rakhmonov won the country's first direct Presidential election securing 58 percent votes cast against former Prime Minister Abdullojonov.[31] The second Presidential election took place on November 6, 1999. President Rakhmonov received 97 percent of the votes cast and his rival Davlat Usmonov got just 2 per cent. Ninety percent of the electorate participated in voting. The United Tajik Opposition (UTO) decided to return to the National Reconciliation Committee and participated in the Presidential election after the government released about ninety UTO fighters. The OSCE declined to send its observers alleging widespread malpractice. In June 2003, fifty-six changes were incorporated in the Constitution of Tajikistan through a referendum in which 96.39 per cent of the registered voters took part and 93.13 per cent of those who voted favoured the changes in the Constitution. The most significant change related to the dropping of restriction on the number of terms the President may serve and the removal or guarantees for free health care and education. This amendment has extended the President's term from five to seven years and allowed the incumbent to stand for two additional consecutive terms.[32] The Tajik President Rakhmonov can theoretically remain in office until 2020.[33] The third multicandidate Presidential election was held on November 6, 2006 and it was won by the incumbent President Emomali Rahmon of the People's Democratic Party of Tajikistan (PDPT) with 79.3 per cent of the vote.[34] The main contender to the incumbent President in this election was Olimjon Boboyev, who received about 7 percent of vote. After that the fourth multicandidate Presidential election was held on November 6, 2013. According to the CCER office, incumbent President Emomali Rahmon won the Presidential election with 84.32 percent of the vote. He contested against five candidates and the nearest contestant to him in this election was Ismoil Talbakov from the Communist Party who secured 4.93 percent of the vote. Other contestants like Tolibbek Bukhoriyev from the Agrarian Party received 4.49 percent, Olimjon Boboyev from the Party of Economic Reforms received 3.82 percent, Abduhalim Ghafforov from the Socialist Party received 1.48 percent and Saidjaffar Ismonov from the Democratic Party received 1.05 percent.[35] So, the present President has continued since independence.

Turkmenistan

The Presidential election process of Turkmenistan's new Constitution (2008) clearly mentions that the President must be a citizen of Turkmenistan, born in Turkmenistan, not younger than 45 years and not older than 70 years, who speaks the national language, has been living constantly in Turkmenistan and working in the state bodies, public associations, enterprise, institutions, organisations, for the past 15 years.[36] He/she is elected directly by the people of Turkmenistan for a term of five years and assumes office immediately after taking oath at a session of the People's Council. The Presidential election and the assumption of office occur in the manner established by law.[37]

In June 1992, the first election was conducted according to the constitutional provision. Saparmyrat A. Niyazov was elected unopposed with 99.5 per cent of the votes cast in a direct election. In November 1993, the Democratic Party of Turkmenistan proposed that Presidential election scheduled for 1997 be cancelled. The following month the *Majilis* (Parliament) voted for the extension of the term of Niyazov's office until 2002 on the ground that the Republic's political and economic stability depended on the realisation of Niyazov's 10 years of prosperity programme of reforms.

The extension of Niyazov's Presidency was endorsed by 99.99 per cent of the electorate in a referendum held on January 15, 1994. He was made President for life but he was reported to have announced that he would not continue beyond 5 years, i.e. 2007.[38]

In February 2001, Niyazov announced in Parliament that he would not like to continue beyond 2010 when the election for the next President would take place. This pronouncement of the Turkmen President was not seen as a renewal of his commitment to democratisation. On June 21, 2002, on the eve of the tenth anniversary of his election as President, he declared that he might step down in 2007 or 2008 and make way for a new leader.[39] On December 21, 2006, the President of Turkmenistan died due to heart failure. After the death of Niyazov, Turkmenistan went through a multicandidate Presidential election for the first time in history on February 11, 2007. Turkmenistan's acting President Gurbanguly Berdymukhammedov was approved as presidential candidate of the state's top legislative body along with five other contenders named Amanyaz Atajykov, Ishanguly Nuryev, Mukhammetnazar Gurbanov, Orazmyrad Garajaev and Ashyrniyaz Pomanov. After the end of the election, Gurbanguly Berdymukhammedov secured 89% of votes and was declared as the second President of independent Turkmenistan.[40] The Constitution was amended in 2008 and allowed the President to be elected for a term of five years without a limitation in the number of terms served. To be elected President, a candidate needs to win at least half of all votes cast. If no candidate succeeds, a second round is conducted within two weeks. Last but not the least, the fourth Presidential election was held on February 12, 2012 and Gurbanguly Berdymukhammedov was re-elected with 97% of the vote.

Uzbekistan

The Constitution of Uzbekistan in Article 90 mentions the eligibility and procedure of Presidential election. A citizen of the Republic of Uzbekistan not younger than thirty five years having full command of the state language and permanently residing in the territory of

Uzbekistan for at least 10 years, can be elected the President of the Republic of Uzbekistan. One and the same person may not be the President of the Republic of Uzbekistan for more than two consecutive terms. The President of the Republic of Uzbekistan shall be elected by citizens of the Republic of Uzbekistan on the basis of the universal, equal and direct suffrage by secret ballot for the term of seven years. The procedure for electing the President shall be defined by law of the Republic of Uzbekistan.[41] According to this electoral provision of the Constitution, the first Presidential election in independent Uzbekistan was held on December 29, 1991. Karimov got elected with 86 percent vote as President of Uzbekistan, defeating his only rival candidate Muhammad Solih (Erk Party).[42]

Another Presidential election was held on 9 January 2000 and President Karimov won an overwhelming victory. He secured 91.9 percent of the total votes cast. His only opponent, his personal friend and leader of the People's Democratic Party, Abdul Khafiz Jalalov polled only 4.2 per cent of votes and 95 percent of the total electorate participated in the poll. Both the OSCE and the US government criticised the election as undemocratic owing to the fact that opposition parties had been barred from nominating candidates. On January 27, 2002, a referendum was held to extend President Islam Karimov's term to 2007 by amending the constitution of Uzbekistan to allow for 7-year Presidential term.[43] Accordingly the third Presidential election took place on December 23, 2007 and the incumbent President Islam Karimov was further re-elected with 88 percent votes against another three candidates.

3.1.2 Executive Powers and Functions

The executive powers of all the Central Asian countries are vested in the hands of President. The political systems of these regions are presidential rather than parliamentary form of government in earlier independent political formations. Now it slowly moves to give certain powers to the parliament through constitutional amendments due to the pressure from the public, civil societies and international actors.

So, still the presidents enjoy more power than the legislatures. All the countries' constitutions themselves clearly mention the powers of the President in their own way.

Kazakhstan

The Kazakhstan Constitution elaborates the details of the powers of the President. These are the major powers: The President of the Republic of Kazakhstan annually addresses the people of Kazakhstan with a message on the state of the affairs and the main directions of the domestic and foreign policy of the Republic of Kazakhstan. He announces regular and extraordinary elections to the Parliament of the Republic, convenes the first session of Parliament and accepts the oath of its members to the people of Kazakhstan, calls extraordinary joint sessions of the Chambers of Parliament, signs laws submitted by the Senate of Parliament within fifteen working days, promulgates the law or returns the law on its separate articles for a second discussion and vote. He appoints the Prime Minister of the Republic from the majority party leader of the Parliament's consent, relieves him from office, determines the structure of the Government of the Republic with the advice of the Prime Minister, appoints to and relieves from office its members, as well as forms, abolishes and reorganises the central executive bodies of the Republic. He accepts the oath of the members of the government, presides at the meetings of the government on important issues, charges the government with bringing a bill into the *Majilis* of Parliament, annuls or suspends completely or partially the effect of the government's acts and those of the *akims* (regional heads) of the *oblasts*, major cities and the capital. He appoints the Chairperson of the National Bank of the Republic of Kazakhstan with the Parliamen''s consent, and relieves him from office. He appoints the Procurator General, diplomatic representatives to countries and the Chairperson and two members of the Accounts Committee for control over Execution of the Republican Budget for a five-year term. He adopts a resolution on conducting the all-national referendum.

In the event of a serious and immediate threat to the democratic institutions of the Republic, its independence and territorial integrity, political stability of the Republic, security of its citizens and the disruption of normal functioning of the Constitutional bodies of the state, the President shall have official consultation with Prime Minister and Chairpersons of the Parliamentary Chambers of the Republic and take measures, caused by a state of emergency in the entire territory or in particular areas of Kazakhstan. He immediately informs the Parliament of the use of the armed forces of the Republic. And he exercises other powers in accordance with the Constitution and the laws of the Republic.[44]

Kyrgyzstan

The new Constitution of Kyrgyzstan also mentions the powers of the President. The President has authority to call the elections to the *Jogorku Kenesh*, to make decision on calling early elections to the *Jogorku Kenesh* and local *keneshes* (parliaments) in accordance with procedure and in cases provided in the law to dismiss local *keneshes*. He signs and promulgates laws, returns laws with his objections to the *Jogorku Kenesh*, has the right to convene an extraordinary sitting of the *Jogorku Kenesh* and defines the issues for consideration thereof and has the right to address at the sittings of the *Jogorku Kenesh*. He also submits report to the *Jogorku Kenesh* on the candidates for election and dismissal as judges of the Supreme Court and local court judges as per the proposal of the Council. He appoints to the Prosecutor General with the consent of the *Jogorku Kenesh* and dismisses the Prosecutor General from office with the consent of not less than one third of the total number of the deputies of the *Jogorku Kenesh* or at the initiative of one third of the total number of the deputies of the *Jogorku Kenesh* approved by the two thirds of the deputies of the *Jogorku Kenesh*. He also appoints and dismisses the Deputy Prosecutor General with the consent of the Prosecutor General. He appoints and dismisses from office the members of the Government in charge of state agencies dealing with the issues of defense and national security as well as their deputies. He submits to the *Jogorku Kenesh* the candidates to be elected to the position of the Chairperson of the National Bank, deputy chairmen and members of the Board of the National Bank. He nominates to the *Jogorku Kenesh* the candidates to form one third of the members of the Central Commission on elections and referenda for election and dismissal and the candidates to form one third of the members of the Chamber of Accounts for election and dismissal. He appoints the Chairperson of the Chamber of Accounts from among the members of the Chamber of Accounts elected by the *Jogorku Kenesh* and dismisses the Chairperson in cases envisaged in the law.

The President represents the Kyrgyz Republic inside and outside the country and conducts negotiations and signs upon consent of the Prime Minister international treaties. He has the right to assign these powers to the Prime Minister, members of the Government as well as other officials. He signs instruments of ratification and instruments of accession and appoints upon consent of the Prime Minister, diplomatic representatives of the Kyrgyz Republic in foreign States and permanent representatives in international organisations and recalls them. He accepts the credentials and letters of recall of the heads of diplomatic missions of foreign States. The President decides upon the issues of naturalisation and denunciation of citizenship in the Kyrgyz Republic. The President is the Commander in Chief of the Armed Forces of the Kyrgyz Republic and defines, appoints and dismisses the highest commanders of the Armed Forces of the Kyrgyz Republic. The President chairs the Council of Defence which is established in accordance with the law and gives warning, on grounds specified by constitutional law, of the possibility of introducing a state of emergency, and where necessary to introduce a state of emergency in individual localities without prior declaration, providing prompt notification to the *Jogorku Kenesh*. He declares general or partial mobilisation, announces a state of war in the event of aggression to the Kyrgyz Republic and shall promptly submit this issue for consideration by the *Jogorku Kenesh*. He declares martial law in the interests of the defence of the country and the safety of its citizens and shall promptly submit this issue for consideration by the *Jogorku Kenesh*. The President exercises his/her powers by way of issuing decrees and orders which shall be mandatory for implementation in the entire territory of the Kyrgyz Republic.[45]

Tajikistan

Article 69 of the Tajikistan Constitution refers to the Presidential power as the Chief Executive power of the country. The main functions regarding the political system of the country are: The President has authority to represent Tajikistan inside the country and in international relations and establish or abolish ministries and state committees with the approval of the Supreme Assembly. He appoints and dismisses the Prime Minister and other members of the government and proposes them for approval to the Supreme Assembly. He forms the executive apparatus of the Presidency. He has the power to appoint and dismiss the chairmen of the Gornyy Badakhshan Autonomous *Oblast*, *oblasts*, city of Dushanbe, towns and *rayons*, and to propose them for approval to the relevant assemblies of people's deputies. He nominates the Chairman, Deputy Chairman, and judges of the Constitutional Court; the Chairman, Deputy Chairman, and judges of the Supreme Court; the Chairman, Deputy Chairman, and judges of the Supreme Economic Court and proposes them for appointment and recall to the Supreme Assembly. He appoints and dismisses the Procurator General and his deputies by the consent of the Supreme Assembly and the judges of the military courts, courts of Gornyy Badakhshan Autonomous *Oblast*, oblasts, city of Dushanbe, towns, and *rayons* at the proposal of the justice minister. He signs laws and annuls or suspends documents of state administration if they contradict the constitution and laws. He appoints with the approval of the Presidium of the Supreme Assembly the heads of diplomatic missions in foreign countries and representatives of the republic in international organisations, and declares a state of emergency throughout the republic or in separate parts of it and proposes it to the Supreme Assembly immediately for approval and to inform the United Nations Organization. He implements other powers prescribed in the constitution and laws.[46] Article 70 states that the President adopts orders and decrees within the framework of his authority, informs the Supreme Assembly about the country's situation, and submits necessary and important issues for discussion to the Supreme Assembly.

Turkmenistan

The Turkmenistan Constitution also mentions Presidential power regarding the political system of the country. These are: The President of Turkmenistan is the head of the state and has executive power; the highest official of Turkmenistan, acting as guarantor of the state independence and the status of neutrality of Turkmenistan, its territorial integrity, respect for the Constitution and fulfillment of international obligations. The President implements the Constitution and laws, supervises the execution of foreign policy, represents Turkmenistan in relations with other nations, appoints and dismisses ambassadors and other diplomatic representatives of Turkmenistan to foreign countries, with interstate and international organisations, accepts the credentials and letters of recall of diplomatic representatives of foreign countries. He/she is the Supreme Commander of the Armed Forces of Turkmenistan, orders general or partial mobilisation, use of armed forces and their military status, appoints the top command of the armed forces of Turkmenistan. He/she forms and presides over the National Security Council of Turkmenistan, the status of which is determined by law and approves the programme and basic directions of the political, economic and social development of the country.

He/she sends for consideration and approval of the *Mejlis* of Turkmenistan regarding the state budget and reports on performance of the budget and signs the laws, within no later than two weeks. He can use the right of suspensive veto for returning the law with his objections to the Parliament for a second hearing and vote, if he is not satisfied. If the Parliament, with at least two-thirds of the established number of deputies, confirms the decision earlier expected of him, the President of Turkmenistan signs the law. The President of Turkmenistan does not have the right of suspensive veto concerning the laws on amendments and additions to the Constitution. He/she forms the Central Commission for Elections and Referendums in Turkmenistan, makes changes in its composition and designates the date of the referendum, has the right to convene an early session of the *Mejlis*. He/she decides questions related to the grant of citizenship and removal from citizenship, grant of asylum and awards honours and other state awards of Turkmenistan and grants military and other special state titles and distinctions. With the consent of the *Mejlis*, he/she appoints and dismisses the Chairman of the Supreme Court, the Prosecutor General, the Minister of Internal Affairs, the Minister of Justice. He/she grants pardon and amnesty. In order to ensure the safety of citizens, he/she orders the state of emergency throughout the national territory or in certain areas of Turkmenistan. Use of the state of emergency is governed by the law of Turkmenistan. He/she issues decrees, decisions and orders, binding on the entire territory of Turkmenistan.[47]

Uzbekistan

The Uzbekistan Constitution mentions the power of the President regarding political affairs of the country. The provision of the Constitution mentions that the President of the Republic of Uzbekistan shall guarantee the observance of rights and freedoms of citizens, the Constitution and laws of the Republic of Uzbekistan and take necessary measures on the protection of sovereignty, security and territorial integrity of the Republic of Uzbekistan, implementation of decisions regarding its national-state structure. He presents to the Senate of the *Oliy Majlis* of the Republic of Uzbekistan nominees for appointment of diplomatic and other representatives of the Republic of Uzbekistan to foreign states. He also presents to the *Oliy Majlis* of the Republic of Uzbekistan annual reports on major matters of social and economic life, home and foreign policies of the country. He forms the office of executive authority and directs it, ensures interaction of the supreme bodies of authority and administration of the Republic, forms and abolishes ministries, state committees and other bodies of state administration with subsequent submission of decrees on these matters for approval by the chambers of the *Oliy Majlis* of the Republic of Uzbekistan. He represents to the Senate of the *Oliy Majlis* of the Republic of Uzbekistan a nominee for the election on the post of the Chairman of the Senate.

He represents for consideration and approval by the chambers of the *Oliy Majlis* of the Republic of Uzbekistan a nominee as the Prime Minister of the Republic of Uzbekistan and approves, upon the nomination of the Prime Minister of the Republic of Uzbekistan, members of the Cabinet of Ministers of the Republic of Uzbekistan and relieves the Prime Minister and the Cabinet of their posts. He appoints and relieves the Procurator General of the Republic of Uzbekistan and his deputies of their posts with their subsequent approval by the Senate of the *Oliy Majlis* of the Republic of Uzbekistan. He represents to the Senate of the *Oliy Majlis* of the Republic of Uzbekistan nominees on the posts of the Chairman and judges of the Constitutional Court, the Chairman and judges of the Supreme Court, the Chairman and judges of the Higher Economic Court, the Chairman of the Board of the Central Bank of the Republic of Uzbekistan, the Chairman of the State Committee of the Republic of Uzbekistan for Protection of Nature. He appoints and relieves judges of regional, inter-district, district and city, martial and economic courts of their posts and *Hokims* (Heads) of regions and the city of Tashkent of their posts with their subsequent approval by relevant *Kenghashes* of people's deputies. The President has the right to relieve, by his decision, *Hokims* of districts and cities of their posts, should they violate the Constitution, laws or perform acts discrediting the honour and dignity of a *Hokim*. He has the right to suspend and repeal acts passed by bodies of state administration, as well as *Hokims*. He signs and promulgates laws of the Republic of

Uzbekistan, has the right to return a law, with his objections, to the *Oliy Majlis* of the Republic of Uzbekistan for the second discussion and vote. In exceptional cases (real outside threat, mass disturbances, major catastrophes, natural calamities, epidemics) in the interests of citizens' security he introduces the state of emergency in the entire territory or in the particular localities of the Republic of Uzbekistan and within seventy two hours has to submit the adopted decision for approval by the chambers of the *Oliy Majlis* of the Republic of Uzbekistan. Conditions and the procedure for introducing the state of emergency shall be regulated by law and he/she also exercises other powers stipulated by the present Constitution and laws of the Republic of Uzbekistan.[48]

3.2 Legislature

The Parliaments of Central Asian states are the supreme representative body, exercising legislative functions. The Parliament of Kazakhstan consists of two chambers, the *Senate* (upper chamber) and the *Majlis* (lower chamber). The Senate comprises fifty five members, of whom 40 are elected at a joint sitting of the deputies of all representative bodies of the regions and the capital, while the remaining fifteen deputies are appointed by the President. The *Majilis* consists of 107 deputies elected in an order, established by the constitutional law. Elections of ninety eight deputies of *Majilis* are carried out on the basis of the universal, equal and direct right under secret ballot. Nine deputies of *Majilis* are elected by the Assembly of the people of Kazakhstan. The term of the powers of Senate deputies is six years and that of the *Majilis* is five years. One half of the elected deputies in the Senate are subject to election every three years. The elections of the deputies of the Senate are carried out on the basis of indirect electoral right under secret ballot.

The Kyrgyzstan Parliament called *Zhogorku Kenesh* comprises of two chambers—the Legislative Assembly (lower chamber) and the People's Assembly (upper chamber). The Legislative Assembly consists of 35 members and is a permanent chamber. The People's

Assembly comprises 70 members, sits twice yearly and represents regional interests. Members of both chambers are elected for a term of five years on the basis of universal, equal and direct suffrage by secret ballot. In 2003, a referendum passed by Parliament with majority votes created the new unicameral Parliament consisting of 75 deputies elected in single-mandate constituencies for a five-year term and further increased it to 120 deputies elected for a five-year term on the basis of proportional representation in 2010 through a constitutional amendment.

The present composition of Tajikistan Parliament has been the by-product of a Constitutional amendment in September 1999 which provided for the establishment of a bicameral legislative body. The parliament called as *Majlisi Oli* comprises of two Assembly (*majlises*)—*Majlis Namoyandagon* (Assembly of Representatives) and the *Majlis Milly* (National Assembly).[49] The lower assembly of representatives (*Majlisi Namayandagon*) has 63 deputies directly elected for five-year terms. Out of total 63 members, 22 members are elected under a proportional closed-list system within a single nationwide constituency with a 5 percent threshold for seat allocation. The remaining 41 members are elected in single mandate constituencies under a majoritarian system. In these contests, if no candidate receives more than 50 percent of votes cast in the first round, the two top candidates compete in a second round within two weeks. A 50 percent turnout of registered voters is required; otherwise, repeat elections must be held. The *Majlis Milly* consists of 34 seats and its members are indirectly elected. For this house, 25 members are selected by local deputies, 8 appointed by the President and 1 seat is kept reserved for the former President. All the members serve for a five-year term.

In Turkmenistan, supreme legislative power resides with the one hundred and twenty five deputies of the *Majlis*, a unicameral parliament which is directly elected from geographical constituencies with an approximately equal number of voters for a five-year term. The other supreme representative body of popular power is the

Khalk Maslakhaty. This is described as a supervisory organ with no legislative or executive function. The formation of *Khalk Maslakhaty* is a replication of the ancient Turkmen traditions, where all elders meet and decide the well-being of society.

The highest legislative body of Uzbekistan is the *Oliy Majlis* (the Supreme Assembly). It comprises 150 deputies, elected by territorial constituencies on a multiparty basis for a term of five years. The August 2002 Constitutional amendment adopted a bicameral legislature. The *Oliy Majlis* consists of two chambers named the Legislative Chamber (the lower chamber) and the Senate (the upper chamber). The term of powers of the Legislative chamber and the Senate of the *Oliy Majlis* is five years. Article 77 of the amended Constitution mentions that the Legislative Chamber of the *Oliy Majlis* will consist of one hundred twenty deputies elected by territorial constituencies on a multiparty basis. The Senate of the *Oliy Majlis* is the chamber of territorial representation and consists of members of the Senate (senators). Members of the Senate of the *Oliy Majlis* are elected in equal quantity— six persons—from the Republic of Karakalpakstan, regions and the city of Tashkent by secret ballot at relevant joint sessions of deputies of *Zhokarghy Kenes* of the Republic of Karakalpakstan, representative bodies of state authority of regions, districts, cities and towns from among these deputies. Sixteen members of the Senate of the *Oliy Majlis* are appointed by the President of the Republic of Uzbekistan from among the most authoritative citizens with large practical experience and special merits in the sphere of science, art, literature, manufacture and other spheres of state and public activity.

3.2.1 Electoral Process

The constitutional provisions regarding the election process of all the Central Asian legislatures are more or less same. The election processes are conducted by the Central Election Commission at the highest level and territorial and polling station election commissions at the middle and lower level. All the media and political parties are allowed to participate in these elections. The voter lists are prepared area wise and those who attain the age of 18 years and above will be included in the voter list. For contesting elections, candidates must be at least 25 years old, possess voting rights, higher education and citizens of respective countries residing for the past five years or more.

Kazakhstan

In Kazakhstan, the first lower house election was held in March 1994. In this election, Kazakh majority representatives were elected by the common people. Faced with a no-confidence vote in his Prime Minister Treshenko, Nazarbayev nominated A. Kazhegeldin as the new Prime Minister. In a style reminiscent of President Yeltsin of Russia, he packed off his Parliament in March 1995 after a stand-off with the Speaker. In 1995, the upper chamber election was held to fulfill 38 of the 40 regionally elected seats. The second election to the *Majlis* was held in October 1999. 65 candidates from nine political parties contested for the remaining 67 seats from single-member constituencies. All the 10 party-list seats were filled in the first round of elections (the pro-President Otan Party won 4 seats, and the Communist Party of Kazakhstan, the Agrarian Party of Kazakhstan and Civic Party of Kazakhstan each won 2 seats). Of the 67 directly contested seats, 20 were filled in the first round of elections and 'run-off' elections were held for 47 seats. Finally Otan party emerged as the largest party in the *Majlis* with 23 seats. The Civic Party won 13 seats. Three other parties registered their parties with their token presence. The independent candidates numbered 34. The OSCE which monitored the elections cited numerous breaches of the election law.

In the next election to the lower house of Kazakh Parliament (*Majlis*) held in October 2004, President Nazarbayev's party Otan (Fatherland) won seven out of the ten seats allocated on the basis of overall votes for a given party and 35 of the 67 single-seat constituencies giving it 42 out of 77 seats in the lower house. The rest of the seats with a single exception went to the party called Asar led by the President's daughter Dariga and to several other small parties of President loyalists. Only one seat in the 77 member Parliament went to an opposition party Ak Zohl.[50] Protesting against the alleged irregularities in elections the lone opposition member subsequently resigned from the membership of the lower house. The Parliamentary election in Kazakhstan was criticised by the OSCE observation mission for falling short of international standards. A spokesman of the US State Department also agreed with the criticism of serious shortcomings in voter lists, candidates' access to media and the tabulation of the results.[51]

Fig. 3 Kazakhstan Parliament Election Final Result January 2012

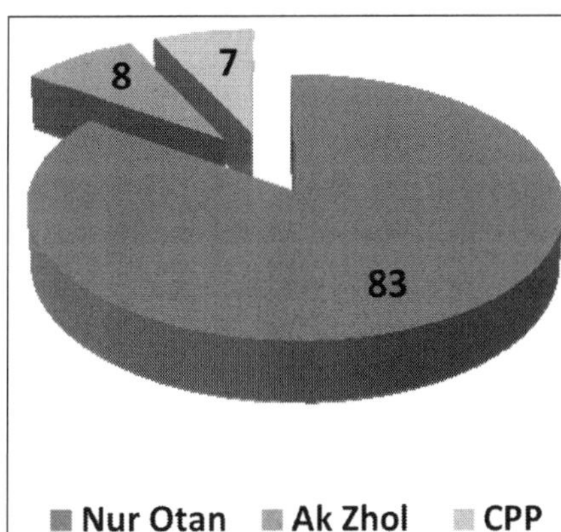

In June 2007, the Constitution of Kazakhstan was amended which included the election law, Law on Political Parties, the Law on Mass Media and the Law on Public Assemblies. After that *Majilis* election was held on August 18, 2007 and Nur Otan Party secured 88.42 percent votes and got all the 98 seats. Other six political parties which participated in this election shared 11.58 percent of votes.[52] After completion of five years, the next

Parliament election was held on January 15, 2012 and only three political parties Nur Otan, Ak Zhol and Communist People's Party crossed the seven percent threshold required to enter the *Majilis.* According to Central Election Commission, Nur Otan got 83 seats (80.99 percent vote share), Ak Zhol secured 8 seats (7.47 percent vote share) and Communist People's Party got to manage 7 seats (7.19 percent vote share) for representation in the lower house. Other four political parties were OSDP, Auyl, PPK and Adilet participated in this election secured below seven percent vote share and could not get any representation to the Assembly. Now Nur Otan is the dominant party in the *Majilis.*

Kyrgyzstan

The Kyrgyzstan Parliamentary election was also held on February 20, 2000 according to the new system. The number of seats in the legislative Assembly increased from 36 to 60, 15 of them being allocated to parties.[53] In this election the voter turnout was not high, with 57.8 percent of the electorate casting vote in the first round and 61.86 per cent in the second round. Direct elections were held for 45 seats in the Legislative Assembly and 45 in the People's Assembly and another 15 seats in the Legislative Assembly were allocated on the basis of proportional representation. Most of the candidates running in single-seat electoral districts failed to win 50 percent of the votes required to be elected. Only the former leader of the Kyrgyz Soviet Communists, Turdakum Usubaliyev, and Kyrgyz President Askar Akaev's brother got through the first round of the elections. Those who made it to the Parliament represented the El (People) party, the Communist Party, the Ata-mekum (Fatherland Party), and the Kairan El party. Observes were highly critical of the elections. In 2000, the Communist Party won 5 out of 15 seats, the Union of Democratic Force Election Bloc 4, Democratic Party of Women 2, the Political Party of the Afghan War Veterans 2, the Ata-Meken Socialist Party 1, and My Country Party 1.[54]

As a result of the February 2003 referendum the new Constitution proposed by President Akaev was approved by 75 percent of the votes polled. The referendum also approved the abolition of its bicameral parliament. The Constitution introduced the majority system of election to the Parliament. Under Art 54, the *Jogorku Kenesh* shall consist of 75 deputies who will be elected for a five-year term from single-member constituencies. The voting in the referendum was criticised by the Kyrgyz Committee for Human Rights which stated that "ballot boxes were carried from door to door to boost the turn out total". Elections for the new unicameral body or *Jorgorku Kenesh* were held on February 27, 2005, but the vast majority of positions remained undecided and was contested in a runoff election on March 13, 2005 and election irregularities caused widespread protests that resulted in the President being forced to flee the country. In this election, only 10 per cent of women participated and OSCE reported that in the first round 88 per cent Kyrgyz, 5 per cent Uzbeks and 4 percent Russians participated in this election.[55] The pro-presidential political party—Alga Kyrgyzstan—won a clear majority in that election.

The President tried to consolidate the executive power with his own associates and brought out a referendum in October 2007. According to this referendum, 75 deputies would be elected through a closed list of Proportional Representation system. Political parties would have to clear a threshold of 5% of registered voters i.e., based on all eligible voters as opposed to votes cast nationwide to enter the Parliament. Parties also would need to clear a second threshold of 0.5% of all registered voters in each of the country's seven regions, plus the cities Bishkek and Osh.[56] Following this referendum, the *Jogorku Kenesh* subsequently set the election date for July 23, 2009. In that election three political parties that were represented in the Parliament comprised the political parties of Ak Jol (71 seats), the Social Democratic Party of Kyrgyzstan (SDPK) (11) and the Party of Communists of Kyrgyzstan (8).[57]

In April 2010, President Kurmanbek Bakiev was ousted in a coup, which brought to power an interim government led by Roza Otunbayeva. She introduced the constitutional referendum in June 2010 for reforming the electoral system, the separation of powers, the judicial system, human rights and local self-government. This referendum was approved by 90.55 percent of the votes cast, with a turnout figure of 72.24 percent.[58]

Fig. 3.1 Kyrgyzstan Parliament Election Result 2010

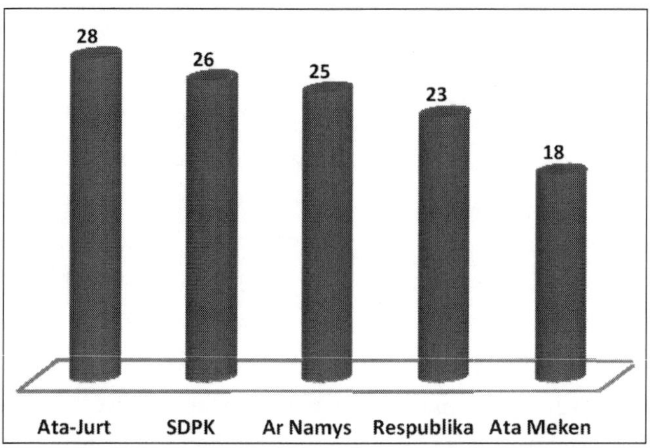

This referendum gave stronger powers to Parliament and resulted in a weakened presidency. It also extended the number of seats in Parliament from 90 to 120, and set the cap for the maximum number of seats in Parliament by any political party to 65. The new Constitution also would allow the Parliament to choose a Prime Minister and also to play a key role in forming the new government. In that direction, the new Parliament election was held on 10 October 10, 2010. According to the results declared by the Election Commission's office of Kyrgyzstan, five political parties had passed the two thresholds. The CEC allocated 28 parliamentary seats to Ata-Jurt, 26 to SDPK, 25 to Ar Namys, 23 to Respublika and 18 to Ata Meken. The voter turnout was announced at 55.31 which represents 28 female members

(23.33 per cent) and 14 members (11.66 per cent) belonging to a national minority. No political party had gotten a clear-cut majority in Parliament after the election process had gotten over. As a result, the coalition government came into force with five winning political parties in Parliament.[59]

Fig. 3.2 Parliament Election Mandates, 2005

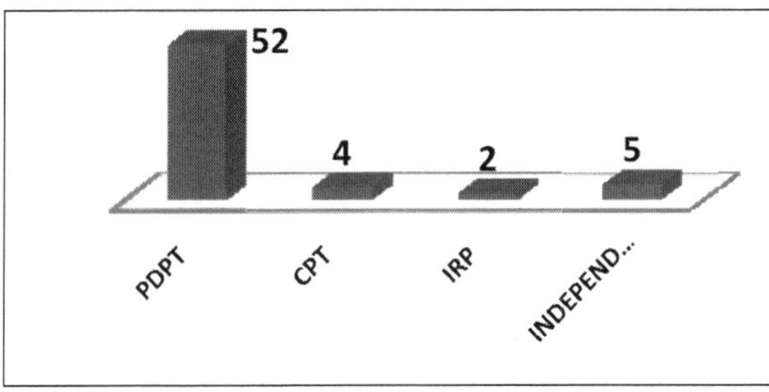

Sources: OSCE/ODIHR Election Observation Mission Final Report, 2005.

Tajikistan

After the end of the civil war, the first Parliamentary election was held for both the chambers of the Tajik Parliament in February and March 2000. The People's Democratic Party of Tajikistan (PDPT) secured 45 seats, the Communist Party of Tajikistan (CPT) received 13 seats and the Islamic Rebirth Party won 2 seats.[60]

The second election was held on February 27, and March 13, 2005 for the Assembly of Representatives and March 25, 2005 for the National Assembly. Total 195 candidates had contested and out of 195, 32 candidates were women. In this election, the percent of vote secured by different parties are: PDPT 74.9 percent, CPT 13.6 percent, Islamic Revival Party 8.9 percent, others 2.5 percent. In terms of number of seats: PDPT 52, CPT 4, Islamic Revival Party 2 and independents 5.[61] In the National Assembly election various political parties secured the following number of seats:PDPT 29, CPT 2 and independents 3.[62]

F: 3.3 Parliament Election Mandates, 2010

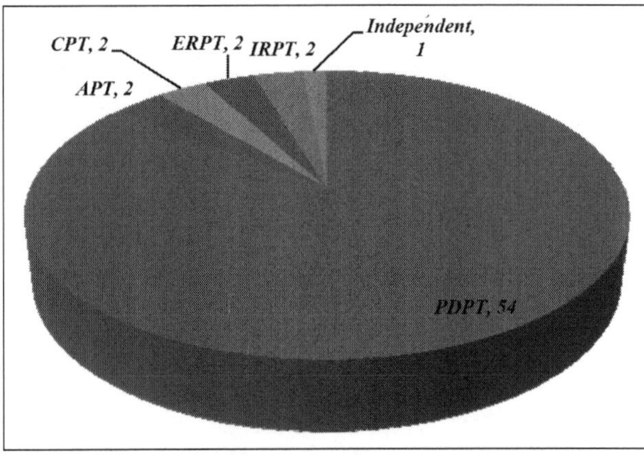

Sources: OSCE/ODIHR Election Observation Mission Final Report, 2010.

The third multiparty Parliamentary elections of lower chamber of Parliament (*Majlis Namayandagon*) were held on February and March 2010. According to the CCER, the dominant political party named PDPT has secured 54 seats and others like APT, CPT, ERPT, and IRPT had secured only two seats each along with one independent candidate. The People's Democratic Party of Tajikistan (PDPT) has been dominating the political system since independence.

Turkmenistan

The elections for the 50 regional representatives to the *Khalk Maslakhaty* of Turkmenistan were held in November 1992. On December 11, 1994, election to the 50-member *Majlis* were held with the participation of 99.8% of the electorate and 49 of the deputies were elected unopposed. The election of the *Khalk Maslakhaty* was held with the participation of 99.5% of the electorate on April 5, 1998.

The next election was held on a multiparty basis in the *Majlis* and also in the People's Council; the Democratic party of Turkmenistan was the only Party which put up candidates in the *Majlis* elections held in December 1999. According to official reports 99 percent of the electorate participated in these elections. After five years, another election of the *Majlis* took place on December 19, 2004 and January 9, 2005.[63] Only the elected representatives' names were announced without refereeing to the party list. The next Parliamentary elections were due to take place in 2009. However, on October 25, 2005, the *Khalk Maslakhaty*, or People's Council of Turkmenistan (PCT) adopted a Resolution on holding early elections to the *Mejlis*. The election was held on December 14, 2008 with a second round held in one constituency on December 28, 2008 and a revote in one constituency on February 8, 2009. No party-affiliated candidates were announced.

Fig. 3.4 Turkmenistan Parliament Election Result 2013

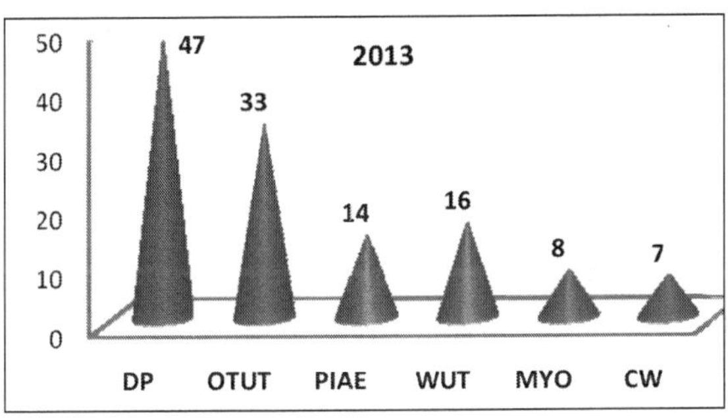

Last but not least, the *Majlis* of Turkmenistan election was held on December 15, 2013. For the first time, many political parties took part in this election to Turkmenistan's first ever multiparty unicameral Parliament, *Majlis*. According to the Central Election Commission (CEC), the total voter turnout was 91.3 percent out of all registered eligible voters. A total of 283 candidates nominated by two parties as well as citizens' groups, trade unions and a women-rights group were competing for five-year mandates in the 125-seat Parliament. However, all of the parties and groups were loyal to the then current leader Gurbanguly Berdymukhammedov.[64] The Democratic Party (DP) secured 47 seats, Organisation of Trade Unions of Turkmenistan (OTUT) secured 33 seats, Party of

Industrialists and Entrepreneurs (PIAE) secured 14 seats, Women's Union of Turkmenistan (WUT) secured 16 seats, Magtymguly Youth Organisation (MYO) secured 8 seats and Citizen Groups (CG) secured 7 seats in this election.

Fig. 3.5 Uzbekistan Parliamentary Election Result 2004-2005

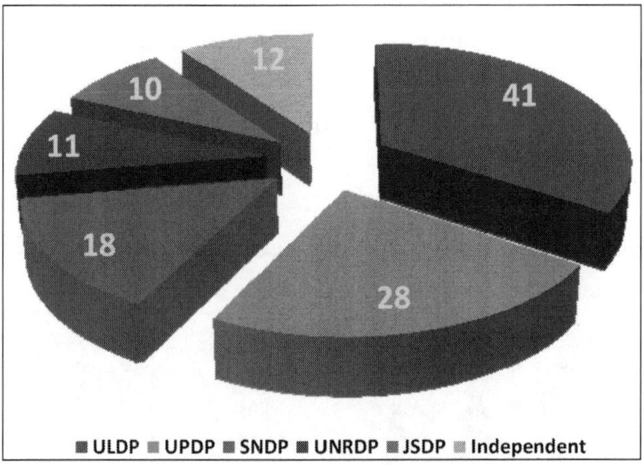

Sources: http://en.wikipedia.org/wiki/Uzbekistani_parliamentary_election,_2004%E2%80%932005

Uzbekistan

In September 1994, about 72 percent of the voters endorsed constitutional amendments proposed by President Karimov of Uzbekistan which included formation of a bicameral legislature, extension of the Presidential term from 5 to 7 years and the legalisation of religion-based political parties. 92 per cent of the voters participated in this referendum. Elections to the *Oily Majilis* were held in December 2000. The Peoples Democratic Party (PDP) secured the largest representation with 48 seats. Non-party local council's nominees however gained 110 seats. The Fidokorlar National Democratic Party was the second largest party with 34 seats. With Watan Tarrakkiyati Party, the Odolat Social Democratic party and Millee Tiklinish Democratic Party also achieved representation in the *Oily Majlis* winning, 20, 11, and 10 seats respectively. The OSCE sent only a limited number of observers alleging that Uzbekistan had reneged on earlier commitments to make the elections free and fair. Another referendum was held on January 27, 2002 and the referendum also approved the creation of a bicameral parliament.

The last Parliamentary election was held on December 26, 2004.[65] The Uzbekistan Liberal Democratic Party secured most of the seats. According to the Election Commission, Uzbekistan Liberal Democratic Party (ULDP), Uzbekistan Peoples' Democratic Party (UPDP), Self- Sacrifice National Democratic Party (SNDP), Uzbekistan National Revival Democratic Party (UNRDP), Justice Social-Democratic Party (JSDP) and independent candidates secured 41, 28,18,11,10 and 12 seats respectively.[66]

Fig: 3.6 Uzbekistan Parliament Election 2010

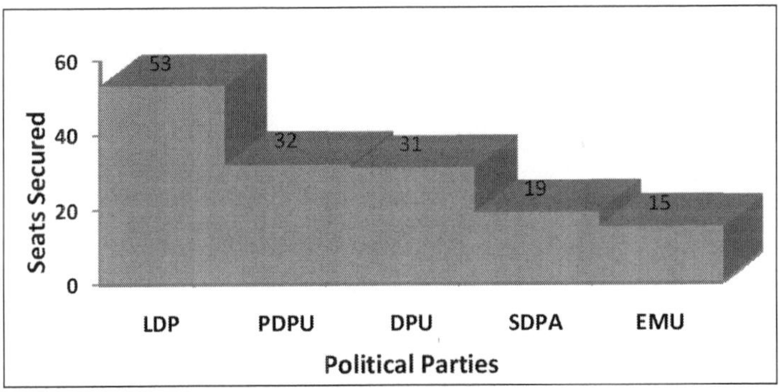

Sources: OSCE/ODIHR Election Observation Mission Final Report, April 2010.

After four years of functioning of the bi-cameral Parliament (*Oliy Majlis*), an amendment of the Constitution waspassed on December 25, 2008 regarding amendments to the law "On Elections of the *Oliy Majlis* of the Republic of Uzbekistan", which increased the number of deputies from 120 to 150. This amendment also introduced 15 reserved seats for representatives of the newly established Ecological Movement of Uzbekistan (EMU) and the remaining 135 deputies were to be directly elected in single-mandate constituencies on the basis of majority. Accordingly, the Parliament election was held on December 27, 2009 and January 10, 2010. In this election, Liberal Democratic Party secured 53 seats, People's Democratic Party of Uzbekistan (PDPU) secured 32 seats, Democratic Party of Uzbekistan Milliy Tiklanish won 31 seats, Social Democratic Party Adolat got 19 seats and Ecological Movement of Uzbekistan got 15 seats respectively.[67]

3.3 Political Practice

In spite of all the liberal provisions of the Central Asian countries' constitutions, the political system is different in practice from theory. It is well known in political discourse that there is a great deal of "democratic deficit". The political regimes are totally devoid of legitimacy, as well as long-term political strategic vision. The fragile character of the political system in these countries is largely due to "facade democracies",[68] which have been imposed from above. The 'facade democracies' have been instituted in these countries in accordance with the minimal principles of democracy which are called formal elections. The lack of elite–mass linkages and socio-political dialogue not only retards socioeconomic development, but also encourages traditionalist-conservative formations.[69]

3.3.1 Executive vs. Legislature

Initial adoption of the constitutions of the five republics stressed giving more or less equal power to both the organs. But later, the executive branch consolidated more power ignoring the legislative branch through constitutional referendum. In the Central Asian political system, the executive branch always dominates over legislative branch. The President controls all the activities of the state including that of the Parliament. When the laws or the other activities of the Parliament have contradicted the power of the President, in that case the President dissolves the Parliament and calls for fresh election. This regular exercise is very rampant in Kazakhstan and Kyrgyzstan but in the case of Tajikistan, Uzbekistan and Turkmenistan, the legislative bodies are in complete control by the President. The parliament being a body of state power and the voice of public interests, it bears responsibility to the nation for the quality of laws adopted. It is very difficult for the parliament's functioning under the conditions of an imperfect system of checks and balances, i.e. relating to the legislative, executive and judicial branches of power. Possessing vast authority, the head of the state supersedes and prevails over all the other branches, immobilising their initiatives.

In the case of Kazakhstan the role of Parliament under the first Constitution (1993) corresponded to the parliamentary–presidential form of government, while the second Constitution (1995) was adopted in the interest of one branch of government (executive) only.[70] Due to limits on the Parliament's organic powers, its role as the supreme representative and legislative body has been reduced to the level of a consultative institution intended to discuss and approve the President's and the government's legislative initiatives. Accordingly, the Parliament's influence on the formation of state policy is currently limited. The Constitution of 1995 declared Kazakhstan a presidential republic. According to the Constitution, the President became a direct participant of the law-making process. After the *Majlis* approved a draft law and the Senate adopted it, the law would acquire legal force only upon approval by the Head of the State, e.g., the President.[71]

As per Article 49 of the Constitution of 1995, the Parliament is the highest representative body of Kazakhstan, exercising the legislative functions.[72] However, a number of issues were removed from the legislative competence of Parliament and governed by the extra-legislative acts regulated by the Decrees of the President and the resolutions of the government.[73] Moreover, on the President's initiative, the Parliament is authorised to delegate legislative powers to the President for a period not exceeding one year. The Constitution also vested the President with the right to issue an edict having the force of a law if the Parliament did not meet the President's requirement to review, within a month's time, any draft law that the President declared urgent. In accordance with the Constitution of 1995 a two-chambered Parliament was formed. The underlying rationale was that a bicameral structure ensured a stable balance of force between the executive and legislative powers thereby improving the effectiveness of the law-making process. Two chambers should guarantee succession in the Parliament's activity. Criticism with regard to the implementation of a two-chambered system of Parliament is based on the fact that the Senate does not play an important role in the law-making process. Its purpose is to implement the will of the executive power. In Kazakhstan, which is a unitary state, there is no need to represent the regions and any deputy should get authority directly from the people. After the Constitution had been amended in 1998, a new Parliament was elected in 1999. It convened until November 2004. The elections were held on the basis of a mixed system that a majority system was used in the single-member constituencies, while a proportional system was used among the political parties. For the first time, political factions appeared in the Parliament.[74]

So, in Kazakhstan the President's powers in relation to the other branches of power have increased since 1995. He directly controls the successor to the Constitutional Court and the Constitutional Council. The six members of the Constitutional Council are nominated by the President, the Senate and the regional parliaments. The activities of the Constitutional Council are directly controlled by the President. The status of judges is not clearly defined. The Arbitration Court was abolished and the Prosecutor's office restructured, with part of its functions transferred to the newly established State Investigation Committee, which is subordinate to the President. The judiciary has lost any independence it enjoyed prior to 1995.[75] In the 2007 Constitutional Amendment, Parliament was empowered through some role in the appointment of important post of national importance and Prime Minister and Council of Ministers were more accountable to the Parliament and head of the state.

In Kyrgyzstan on May 5, 1993, the Supreme Soviet session of the Kyrgyz Republic adopted a new Constitution based on the democratic principle. The new Fundamental Law established a model close to the presidential–parliamentary form of government. The head of the state and the highest legislative body both had fairly wide powers.[76] The Parliament played an important role in forming the government and its structure, and also identified the main trends in the country's domestic and foreign policies. The Parliament and President had the right to submit the most important issue for a referendum. The Constitution created legal conditions in which the legislative and executive branches could function independently, thus making an agreement between them possible. The President could not rule independently of the *Jogorku Kenesh.*

However, in 1994, the President's power betrayed the first signs of strengthening at the expense of the Parliament. In December 1993, the country was shaken by cabinet crisis, and in September 1994, the legislature dissolved itself amid another crisis.[77] The President made skillful use of his address to the nation to fortify his position more. The dissolution of the Parliament was explained by the fact that the head of state and the legislative branch were at odds with each other. The national referendum of October 1994 set up a bicameral parliament elected in February 1995 in accordance with the majority system introduced to keep any potentially strong opposition party outside the parliament. This created a so-called 'pocket parliament'.[78] In December 1995, for the first time in its history, the nation went to the polls to elect a president from among several candidates. In that election process, the coalition supported the president for re-election and after the election process got over, the coalition demanded for another series of constitutional amendments in 1996. In this constitutional amendment, the republic acquired its final political image as an authoritarian state with elements of democracy.

The amended Constitution supplied the President with wide powers for forming the executive and judicial branches. In the absence of the checks and balances system, the hybrid regime could easily develop into a regime of personal power. In October 2000, about 10 parties united into an opposition People's Patriotic Movement bloc. The opposition was displeased with the President's wide powers, which it assessed as too wide and insisted that they should be redistributed in favour of the Parliament.[79] They also insisted on the presidential–parliamentary form of government and wanted the Constitution to be amended accordingly. To normalise the situation, in September 2002, a Constitutional Conference was convened to discuss a new version of the republic's Constitution. On the strength of the referendum of February 2, 2003, the Law on the new version of the Constitution of the Kyrgyz Republic was adopted on February 18, 2003. Maintaining the power balance, the *Jogorku Kenesh* received the following powers—the approval structure of the government recommended by the President, giving its consent to the appointment of the Prime Minister and the member of the government, control over the government, giving a vote of no-confidence in the government by a majority of no less than two-thirds of the votes of the deputy corps, giving its consent to appointment of judges of the local courts, etc (Art 58).[80]

In spite of that, the head of the state has more power to control the cabinet. Due to the 2005 unfair elections, the opposition groups demanded the resignation of President. Following a large demonstration and political crises, the President left the country. An interim government was set up under Kurmanbek Bakiev. The people at this time wanted to steer the country towards continued reforms rather than towards a new development model or a new social-political system. In January 2006, the opposition moved towards greater unity within a newly established people's coalition of Democratic Forces of 18 parties, movements and NGOs.[81] The new opposition insisted on more amendments to the Constitution regarding administrative and judicial reforms and more active anti-criminal measures. After the series of rallies in the capital city of Bishkek, finally a new Constitution was adopted on November 10, 2006.

This Constitution established a mixed form of government with wide powers to the Parliament; national security services earlier accountable to the President came under the Parliament; prominent heads were appointed by the Parliament but President retained power to dismiss them; the number of deputies increased to 90 and the party that wins fifty per cent of the seats acquires the right to form the government and nominate a candidate for premier to be approved by the President. If none of the party wins half of the seats, the head of the state has the right to invite one of the parliamentary parties to select a premier. The *Jogorku Kenesh* has the right to pass a vote of no-confidence in the cabinet if dissatisfied with its annual report. All the power structures retain their power until their term expires in 2010.[82] In that respect, former president Akaev said, "the new constitution has a reasonable balance of President and Parliamentary Authority, which meets the expectation of society".[83]

After the November 2006 Constitution, the President also signed another Constitution in January 2007. Many of the things remained the same and only few of the provisions of the Constitution got changed. According to the 2007 Constitution, the President in the end decided whether to dismiss the cabinet or not. This constitution introduced new provisions that the President may set goals and tasks before the cabinet. On his own discretion the President may interfere in the work of the cabinet, although the Prime Minister is responsible for the work of the cabinet. Representatives elected from the party list have the right to form a cabinet, which is better since voters elect MPs. Besides, the President is placed above Parliament in the hierarchy of power due to a provision whereby the President "commissions" MPs from a political party to nominate a prime minister. Therefore, relations between the President and Parliament are not of a relation of authority and subordination but relations of bodies that are independent of each other, having separate competencies and power in checking and influencing each other.[84]

On April 13, 2010, President Bakiev offered his resignation, due to huge protest by Opposition and common people. As first steps, the provisional government led by Roza Otunbayeva dissolved the Parliament, the Central Election Commission (CEC) as well as the Constitutional Court. It was announced as a so-called 'Return to Democracy' programme with the aim of a peaceful transition to democracy. In that direction, President Roza Otunbayeva brought out the referendum on June, 2010 aiming for parliamentary democracy. This referendum was historic among all the Central Asian countries for minimising executive powers and giving more power to Parliament. This referendum brought major changes in the executive and legislature branches to promote the democracy and proper representation.

This referendum has limited the President of the Kyrgyz Republic's power to serving a single six-year term. The President will invite names for the Prime Minister but under very restrictive conditions described under the powers of the Parliament. Members of the government would be chosen by the Prime Minister, who is not required to even consult the President in the parliamentary form of government. The President signs legislation but has no right of veto, just the right to send it back for reconsideration. That provision is certain to create a number of potential political chokepoints. On the other hand, in the event of the President's death or incapacity, the Speaker (*Toraga*) of the *Zhogorku Kenesh*, the national parliament, becomes President, with new elections required within three months. The Prime Minister is second in line of succession.

The Legislative Power section lays out the structure of the Parliament as well as its responsibilities, which include forming the government and electing its Speaker. The Parliament would consist of 120 deputies who serve a five-year term and are granted their seats on the basis of party lists. A Prime Minister and the Prime Minister's government are also subject to dismissal through a vote of no-confidence. A request for a no-confidence vote would require only one-third of all parliamentary deputies, and the vote itself would require only a simple majority. In this instance, it would revert to the President to decide whether to dismiss the government. If there are two votes of no-confidence within a three-month period, the government must be dismissed. The Prime Minister may also call for a vote of confidence in the government, no more frequently than once a year; if it fails, the President must call for new Parliamentary elections. Under this new provision, the role and responsibility of the government could be moving towards a parliamentary form of government.

The President of Tajikistan has ample power to control the whole region single-handedly. The President appoints and dismisses the heads of the regional, city and district administrations. According to the Constitution the President is the head of the administrations and at the same time head of the local representative bodies. Thus, the whole system of the state power including executive, representative and judicial branches is controlled by the President for the country. There is only one independent body—the Parliament—which is not controlled by the President.[85] But in some cases the President is influencing some of the parliamentary decisions.

The political transition in Uzbekistan can be characterised as a centralising tendency favouring the President and at the same time this is happening in a rapid and deliberate way. The President is establishing strong presidential rule and controlling the regional powers, media, political parties and grassroots organisations.[86] In that context the president of Uzbekistan Islam Karimov argued, "There is no unified democratic model, which equally fits for all states and takes into account all their peculiarities and conditions. Any democracy must be based on historical, national and religious features of each country. The constituent of the democratisation process has become the development of parliamentarianism in the republic. From the very beginning we were aware of the fact that for the fundamental development of democracy we need an effectively functioning parliament, which could meet modern world standards. At first, a new single-house parliament the *Oliy Majlis* was formed. After that a new multiparty parliament consisting of 250 deputies elected in territorial single-mandate election districts was elected at the beginning of 1995. Subsequently, relaying on the experience of the parliament performance and proceeding from the new requirements and opportunities, and taking into account the experience of foreign countries, the parliament reform was carried out at the beginning of 2005 and a two house parliament, the *Oliy Majlis*, was formed."[87]

At the first joint session of the Legislative Chamber and the Senate of *Oliy Majlis* on January 28, 2005, the President said that the country should pay attention to strengthening the role of the legislative power and achieving a balance among legislative, executive and judicial powers to reform and modernise the life of the country. Part of the Presidential powers should be transferred to the upper house of the Parliament, Senate, and to the government. Besides, professional lower house of the Parliament should be formed and its powers and rights should be expanded. The role and responsibilities of the Prime Minister and the government should be strengthened. He also added that concrete measures on achieving independence and freedom of judicial power must be undertaken.[88]

In the constitutional amendment of April 10, 2014, the Constitution has given more role and responsibility to the Parliament in the political system. Under this system, the President has the right to appeal to the *Oliy Majlis* of the Republic of Uzbekistan on major matters of domestic and foreign policy of the country. The Cabinet of Ministers are responsible for conducting effective economic, social, financial, monetary policy, development and implementation of programmes for the development of science, culture, education, healthcare and other sectors of the economy and the social sphere. It can implement measures to protect the economic, social and other rights and legitimate interests of citizens. It coordinates and directs the work of state and economic management bodies, and ensures control over their activities in accordance with the law. It provides the implementation of laws of the Republic of Uzbekistan, decisions of the *Oliy Majlis*, decrees, resolutions and ordinances of the President of the Republic of Uzbekistan.

The Cabinet of Ministers within the constitutional norms in accordance with the current legislation issues resolutions and ordinances binding on all bodies, enterprises, institutions, organisations, officials and citizens in the entire territory of the Republic of Uzbekistan. The Cabinet of Ministers, in its work, is responsible before the *Oliy Majlis* of the Republic of Uzbekistan and the President of the Republic of Uzbekistan. The Cabinet of Ministers tenders its resignation to the newly-elected *Oliy Majlis*, but continues to operate until the formation of the new Cabinet of Ministers in accordance with the decision of the President. The Prime Minister of the Republic of Uzbekistan organises and directs the activity of the Cabinet of Ministers being responsible for efficiency of his work. She/he presides at the sitting of the Cabinet of Ministers and signs its decisions. The Prime Minister who heads the Cabinet can be appointed by a political party who obtains the most deputy seats in the elections to the Legislative Chamber of the *Oliy Majlis*, or by several political parties that obtain equally highest number of seats. Members of the Cabinet of Ministers are appointed by the President of the Republic of Uzbekistan upon nomination by the Prime Minister. A no-confidence vote to the Prime Minister can be moved any times and if it does not receive vote of at least two-thirds of the total number of the deputies of the Legislative Chamber and the Senate of the *Oliy Majlis*, the President of the Republic of Uzbekistan can decide on the dismissal of the Prime Minister from office. As a result, the entire Cabinet of Ministers could resign together with the Prime Minister. The new nominee for the Prime Minister for consideration and approval of the chambers of the *Oliy Majlis* of Uzbekistan can be proposed by the President after consultation with all the political parties represented in the Legislative Chamber of the *Oliy Majlis*. In the case of double rejection by the *Oliy Majlis* of the nominee for the post of Prime Minister, the President of the Republic of Uzbekistan can appoint an acting Prime Minister and dissolve the *Oliy Majlis* of the Republic of Uzbekistan.[89] So this amendment can give the stepping stone for moving towards a parliamentary form of government.

In Turkmenistan, all the powers are controlled by the executive branch. On the contrary, in these countries ethnic cleavages and cultural divergences are quite deep, and both civil society and the private sector are still weak. Seventy years of Communist rule has left a legacy of mistrust between the government and the governed, as well as a political culture characterised by authoritarianisms, intolerance, mistrust, and clientism. On September 26, 2008 the *Khalk Maslahaty* (the People's Council) and a body of popular representation met for its special XXI session to approve the policies of "national revival" and accepting the new draft of the Turkmen Constitution. This Amendment abolished the People's Council's existence and divided the power between the President and the Parliament of Turkmenistan. Now Parliament enjoys certain rights of the Council such as amending and adopting the Constitution, conducting referendums, announcing Presidential and Parliamentary elections, ratifying and denouncing international treaties, and addressing issues of border delimitation and territorial division within Turkmenistan. The new Constitution gives the presidential right to lead the State Security Council and to select its members. The authority also appoints the regional and city mayors. All the constitutional amendments have been trying to give some power to the Parliament. In spite of that, there is still no clear-cut separation of powers between the executive, legislative and judicial branches of government.

3.3.2 Personality Cult and Authoritarian Tendencies

The political ideology that has replaced Communism in Central Asia can best be described as "secular authoritarianism" with a dose of free-market philosophy. Central Asian leaders have concluded that, given present conditions in their countries, a period of authoritarian rule is a necessary stage in the transition from Communist totalitarianism to liberal democracy. Kazakh president Nurusultan Nazarbaev illustrated this trend when he said that the path from totalitarianism to democracy lies through enlightened authoritarianism.

These growing authoritarian tendencies have been accompanied by the cult of personality. The extent of the cult of personality differs from country to country. In this respect, Turkmenistan seems to have gone farthest, with late President Niyazov's personality dominating the country's politics. The late President Niyazov had also used Turkmenistan's tribal and paternalistic tradition to consolidate and legitimise his position. He had effectively used such titles as Turkmenbashi, meaning the leader of the Turkmen.[90] Since 1994, when Turkmenbashi was made President as a result of a referendum, there have been no Presidential elections. In 1999, he was announced President for life and in 2003, he was appointed Chairman of the country's highest legislature—*Khalk Maslakhaty*—on the same condition.[91]

The leaders of Turkmenistan, Uzbekistan, and Kazakhstan have taken steps towards authoritarianism and personal rule to extend their Presidential terms beyond 1996-1997 through the holding of referendums rather than Presidential elections. The first country to do so was Turkmenistan, which held a referendum on January 5, 1994, to extend the term of Niyazov's Presidency until the year 2002. Uzbekistan held a referendum on March 26, 1995, to extend the President's terms of office until the year 2000. The Uzbek government claimed that 99.3 percent of the voters participated in the referendum and by a majority of 99.6 percent approved the extension of the President's term of office. All the Central Asian countries' heads of the state hold President's office from independence by amending frequent constitutions and laws except Kyrgyzstan and Turkmenistan.

The Central Asian states have moved from a single-party authoritarian system to a personalised authoritarianism of their Executive Presidents—Niyazov, Karimov, Nazarbayev, and Rakhmonov. All these republics have not succeeded in forging an effective party system of their own though efforts in this direction were made. All power is concentrated in the hands of the President and he alone exercises it, quite often arbitrarily, and at times in violation of the Constitution which is changed to suit the drive towards concentrating power in the hands of the Executive President. Checks and balances, independent judiciary, free press and media and democratic rights of the citizens are conspicuous by their absence.

Karimov changed the name of the Communist Party of Uzbekistan to People's Democratic Party (PDP) which legally inherited the property of the Communist Party of Soviet Union in Uzbekistan. The party had a membership of 3,51,000 as against 3,000 members of the Erk party. In 1993 a new Constitution was promulgated which gave the President power to exclude a Member of Parliament on grounds of participation in unconstitutional acts directed at destabilising the socio-political situation. Censorship of press was strengthened and the Erk paper was closed down. The paper of Birlik appeared irregularly from Moscow. Karimov encouraged businessmen and bankers to form a new opposition party Watan Tarrakkiyati (Progress of the Homeland) in May 1997 to replace the only legal opposition party Erk. This pocket opposition party is led by a poet named Azim.

From the above discussion of the unfolding political scenario in the Central Asian republics since their independence, it is evident that their transition from single-party authoritarian rule to a multiparty democracy has often been attributed to the objective need for giving priority to stability. The intense concentration of power by the existing ruling elite makes it impossible for new political leadership or ideas to emerge in a peaceful manner. Practically, in the entire tradition of constitutional practice in the Central Asian region, only in Kyrgyzstan, the Parliament functions, somehow, according to the constitutional mandate whereas in other republics Parliaments have been rendered powerless. Generally, the people do not trust the Parliament which can bring some change to the system or the economy. People have faith upon the Presidential system due to the traditional respect for power. The other reason for the growth of authoritarianism in Central Asia could be that the peoples of Central Asian region are from the steppes and the nomadic tribes.[92]

Another reason leading to authoritarian system is the lack of efficient political parties, a middle class and an independent mass media which are usually considered to be the vital agents in liberalising and democratising the society. The elite group that prevails over and dominates the Central Asian social hierarchy does not allow any other group to enter into the arena of politics. The present political leaders are always facilitating their kin and kith to enter into politics by providing education from Western countries. There is also the struggle between the elite and the counter-elite for power than the common people posing any kind of competition to the power-sharing relationship. And the bottomline in all these indicates the situation that these elite groups have never tried to act in the larger interest of the nation but they see the future of their own.[93] By thwarting the development of institutions like free press, competing political parties and an independent judiciary, the present leaders of the Central Asian republics have eliminated the possibilities of political change being effected without a convulsion. The unpredictability of succession only breeds instability. The unimpressive performance of opposition candidates in the Presidential election cannot be solely explained in terms of election malpractices, rigging of polls, intimidation of voters or discriminatory electoral regulations. The Presidential elections have underscored the absence of viable opposition parties or movements in the region. So, the Central Asian political system is not democratic in the true sense but it looks like.[94]

Presidents of the Central Asian region are monopoliSing every sphere. In the case of Turkmenistan, on the second anniversary of independence, all papers carried headlines such as: 'Turkemnbashi is our might', 'Turkmenbashi is our hope' 'Turkmenbashi is the sacred symbol of the independent, flourishing Turkmenistan', 'Realisation of Turkmenbashi's plans is our sacred duty'.[95] The Parliament proclaimed Niyazov's birthday, February 19, a national holiday. The city of Krasnovodsk has become Turkmenbashi. In June 1997 the Presidium of the Turkmen Parliament renamed the Bay of Krasnovodsk in the Caspian Sea the Bay of Turkmenbashi. In total about 100 major things in the republic are named after the President.[96]

All opposition parties were made illegal on the basis of restrictive laws on elections. A new representative body of power was formed—Supreme Council, in which there was not even one member from the opposition parties and movements. The President extended his powers without an election by means of a national referendum, which would have been impossible to do in an unconsolidated regime. The Islamic Renaissance Party (IRP) with republican organisations in Tajikistan and Uzbekistan represents radical Islam with all its ambiguities in Central Asia. The party never attracted enough support in Turkmenistan to organise a branch in that republic. The Tajik and Uzbek parties enjoyed a surge of interest on the eve of the Soviet collapse, but are banned from politics.

The leadership in Tajikistan and Uzbekistan has retained its distrust of popular sovereignty. In spite of constitutional guarantees, the leadership in these states has curbed freedom of expression and association. States exercises rigid control on the mass media. No debate over government policies is allowed. Political opposition is suppressed. No independent party is registered. A possible exception might develop in Tajikistan, where the state allowed the registration of a splinter group from the opposition Democratic Party in July 1995. The pre-Soviet and Soviet experiences have left a legacy of authoritarian culture.

3.3.3 Kinds of Change: Political Reforms in the Offing

In the wake of the March 2005 events, that is, 'Tulip revolution' in Kyrgyzstan, Akaev fled from the capital of Kyrgyzstan in the face of popular protests, and it added another chapter in the post-Soviet democratic upsurge in Central Asia. The rulers of Central Asia especially have concentrated power in the hands of extended family networks and seek to prolong their hold on power by bringing family or regional clan networks into the political process.[97] After Akaev fled the country, a Constitutional Conference of the Kyrgyz Republic was convened on the initiative of Ch. Baekova, Chairperson of the Republic's Constitutional Court, and a decision of *Zhogorku Kenesh* (the Parliament).[98] The one hundred and fourteen people who attended the conference represented the head of state, the cabinet, the deputies, and the civilian sector. Omurbek Tekebaey, Speaker of the newly elected *Zhogorku Kenesh*, a very popular opposition member and leader of the Socialist Ata Meken Party, was elected the Conference Chairman.

The provision of the Constitution has been changed. In the new provision the next President should be deprived of the right to organise referendums at his will and to amend or change the Constitution. The Premier, on the other hand, should be given more power when it comes to appointing ministers. It was decided to restore the Parliament's former (10 out of 75 deputies) numerical strength and to elect two-third of its deputies on the basis of proportional representation as a step towards more developed party democracy. By May 15, 2005, the amended Constitution was ready for publication. Supported by the civilian sector, it appeared in the local media.

The hastily organised election was fraught with another political crisis caused by the bitter rivalry between the North and the South. This would have deprived the republic of its revolutionary dynamics and democratic conquests. The revolutionary leaders spared no effort to pacify the democratic-minded public, while the two recognised leaders who formed a "political tendem"—Kurmanbek Bakiev, who represented the South, and Felix Kulov, who represented the North—entered into an agreement and promised to carry out the constitutional reform. On January 5, 2006, under pressure from the democratically minded public, President Bakiev signed a decree on preparations for the referendum of the Kyrgyz Republic, under which national voting on the constitutional order was to be carried out in the fourth quarter of 2006. It was pointed out that to the nation and the power structures should be explained the differences among the three possible forms of governance—parliamentary, presidential, and mixed (semi-presidential).

On the other aspect, it was emphasised that the role of the President is only to mediate among various groups in their respective region. In that contest, the President of Kyrgyzstan is to mediate between the northern and southern regions. In this country, the series of street demonstrations and frequent amendments to the Constitution could lead to the destabilisation of the country.[99] The 'revolution' in Kyrgyzstan was only a clash between the southern and the northern leadership. These societies are not reorienting their traditional values and clan/regional loyalties. In the Central Asian countries, clan, family and solidarity groups are fighting between themselves for survival. They want justice and food, rather than the political system.[100] Ajay Patnaik argues that in the Central Asian case, the democracy is promoted from above not from the below.[101]

Presently most of the Soviet-period elites are heading the Central Asian states. No question is being asked nor can be asked to the rulers by the citizens. Even after the death of the Turkmenistan President, there is no expectation of change in the society in the near future. In the electoral process, power and wealth go together to contest or participate in the election process. This is the main reason for destabilisation in the region. Traditional respect for power determines the vote and this is the reason for the high turn-out of voters. Administration plays a major role to influence the voters rather than political parties. In the electoral process, administration always manipulates and controls the voting pattern.[102] So, democracy and political participation is very limited and it also varies from country to country. Turkmenistan is one side of the coin and other republics are another side of the same coin. For a stable and advanced political system, this region requires a vertical and hierarchical political system. The main reason of political defects in this region are lack of experience of multiparty system, political tradition that did not promote parliamentary system, no experience of power sharing and lack of middle class.[103]

The biggest challenge to the political system of Central Asia is in the form of the nature of rule of the groups in power. The cornerstones of such rule are networks of patronage underpinning governance, the monopoly of the ruling groups over the main assets, the dominant role of the security sector and a strong leader as a centerpiece of a political regime.[104] Networks are based on the principle of personal loyalty. In Tajikistan and Kyrgyzstan kinship and regionalism are key factors in networks. In Uzbekistan, although power is highly centralised with a strong Presidency on the top, the pyramid on which the power rests is not hollow, but it consists of a number of pillars. The tension between geographical groups or clans, namely Tashkent, Samarkand and the Ferghana Valley, define Uzbekistan's politics.[105]

In Kazakhstan, the current influence groups are formed along the principle of personal loyalty and affiliation and interact with each other on the basis of hard, pragmatic interests. The groups can be structured in a hierarchy, with President Nazarbayev's own group at the top of the pyramid and all groups maintaining links to the President. Political battles happen not for the electorate, but for influence with the head of the state.[106] Recently, after immense pressure from various angles, President of Kazakhstan Nursultan Nazarbayev introduced a number of constitutional amendments. The new changes are aimed at increasing the Parliament authority in forming the government.[107]

To sum up, Central Asian political systems are more authoritarian than liberal. The executive concentrates more power in its hand instead of investing more power in the hands of the legislative organs. The family, clan and mafia relations from top to bottom help to concentrate more powers in the hands of the group in power. In the electoral process also members of Central Election Commission and other subordinate commissions are controlled by the President, which does not symbolise a free and fair election method as practiced by mature democracies. Very few political opponents are nominated as members of the electoral committee. No opposition political parties are allowed in Uzbekistan and Turkmenistan. Media and civil society are controlled by the President. This state of the affairs is called super presidentialism in Central Asia. After the 'Tulip Revolution' in Kyrgyzstan and Andijan movement in Uzbekistan and external powers' influences, the political system of this region has changed to some extent. Kyrgyzstan, Uzbekistan, Turkmenistan and Kazakhstan are moving towards a mixed presidential and parliamentary form of government in the sense that they are giving more power to the parliament. The Ukraine crisis and merger of Crimea with Russia teach the lesson to the Central Asian countries to liberalise the political system and promote parliamentary democracy with ensurance of proper representation to all ethnic minorities. Still, the political system of Central Asian countries needs more political reforms and a greater role of legislature.

Notes

1. Kaushik, Devendra (2004), "Central Asia since Ozodi: An Appraisal", in K. Warikoo and Mahavir Singh (eds.), *Central Asia since Independence*, New Delhi: Shipra Publications. p. 1.
2. Ibid.
3. Menon, Rajan and Hendrik Spruyt (1998), "Possibilities for Conflict and Conflict Resolution in Post-Soviet Central Asia", In Barnett R. Rubin and Jack Snyder (eds.), *Post-Soviet Political Order: Conflict and State Building*, London: Routledge. p.114.
4. Central Asian Human Development Report 2005, Bratislava, Slovak Republic: Published by *the UNDP Regional Bureau for Europe and the Commonwealth of Independent States*. p.167.
5. *Tajikistan in Figures, 2013*, TAJSTAT, Agency on Statistics under President of the Republic of Tajikistan, www.stat.tj assessed on 9th September 2013. p.12.
6. Ibid. p. 9.
7. *Kazakhstan in Figures 2011*, Published by The Agency on Statistics of the Republic of Kazakhstan.
8. *Information on the Republic of Uzbekistan*, Published by The State Committee of the Republic of Uzbekistan on Statistics.
9. "*Kazakhstan*" 2005, The Europe World Year Book, 46th edition, vol-II, London and New York: Routledge. p. 2479.
10. Hunter, Shireen T. (1996), *Central Asia since Independence*, Washington D.C: Praeger. p.41.
11. Ibid.
12. Article 40, *The Constitution of the Republic of Kazakhstan*, Almaty, 1995.
13. Article 42, *The Constitution of the Republic of Kyrgyzstan*, Bishkek, 1993.
14. Aritcle 64, *The Constitution of the Republic of Tajikistan*, Dushanbe, 1994.

15. Aritcle 54, *The Constitution of the Republic of Turkmenistan*, Ashgabat, 1994.
16. Article 41, *The Constitution of the Republic of Kazakhstan*, Almaty, 1995.
17. Babak, Vladimir, Demian Vaisman and Irina Vladimirskaya (2004), "Republic of Kazakhstan",in Vladimir Babak, Demian Vaisman and Aryeh Wasserman (eds.), *Political Organization in Central Asia and Azerbaijan*, London: Frank Cass Publishers. p. 100.
18. "Kazakhstan" (2001), *Eastern Europe, Russia, and Central Asia*, 2nd Edition, London: Europa Publications Limited. p.197.
19. Kaushik, Devendra, "Central Asia since Ozodi", in K. Warikoo and Mahavir Singh, op.cit., p.10.
20. Report on Republic of Kazakhstan Presidential Election, 4th December 2005, Prepared by *OSCE/ODIHR Election Observer Mission*, Warsaw, 21 February 2006. p.12.
21. Ibid. p.22.
22. Article 43-45, *The Constitution of the Republic of Kyrgyzstan*, Bishkek, 1993.
23. Abazov, Rafis, "Kyrgyzstan's Struggle for Democracy and Stability", in K. Warikoo and Mahavir Singh (eds.), op.cit., p.45.
24. Report on Republic of Kyrgyzstan Presidential Election, 10th July 2005, Prepared by *OSCE/ODIHR Election Observer Mission*, Warsaw, 7 November 2005. p.23.
25. Sjoberg, Fredrik M. (2005), "Post-Revolutionary Syndrome in Kyrgyzstan: the Struggle for Power Continues", *Central Asia-Caucasus Analyst*, Wednesday, July 13. p.1.
26. Report on Republic of Kyrgyzstan Presidential Election, 30th October 2011, Prepared by OSCE/ODIHR Election Observer Mission, Warsaw, 10th January 2012. p.18.
27. Article 65, *The Constitution of the Republic of Tajikistan*, Dushanbe, 1994.
28. Report on Republic of Tajikistan Presidential Election, 6th November 2006, Prepared by *OSCE/ODIHR Election Observer Mission*, Warsaw, 18 April 2007. p.5.
29. Ibid.
30. Report on Republic of Tajikistan Presidential Election, 6th November 2013, Prepared by *OSCE/ODIHR Election Observer Mission*, Warsaw, 5th February, 2014. pp.9-10.
31. Tajikistan. (2002). *Eastern Europe, Russia and Central Asia*. 2nd edition. London: Europa Publications. p.398.
32. *Report on Republic of Tajikistan Presidential Election*, November 2013, Prepared by OSCE/ODIHR Election Observer Mission, Warsaw 31, July 2013. p.5.
33. Kaushik, Devendra *(2004)*, "Central Asia Since Ozodi", in K. Warikoo and Mahavir Singh, *Central Asia: Since Independence*, Shipra: Delhi. p. 18.
34. *Report on Republic of Tajikistan Presidential Election*, 6th November 2013, Prepared by OSCE/ODIHR Election Observer Mission, Warsaw, 5th February 2014. , p.4.
35. Yuldoshev, Avaz (2013), "CCER Announces the Final Results of the 2013 Presidential Election in Tajikistan", *ASIA-Plus*, 14th November. http://www.news.tj/en/news/ccer-announces-final-results-2013-presidential-election-tajikistan.

36. Article 51, *The Constitution of the Republic of Turkmenistan*, Ashgabat, 2008.
37. Ibid. Article 52.
38. Kaushik, Devendra, "Central Asia Since Ozodi", in K. Warikoo and Mahavir Singh., op.cit., p.15.
39. "Another Resignation Tease by Niyazov", *Radio Free Europe/Radio Liberty (RFE/RL)*, Central Asia News Line, 27 June, vol.2., no. 22, 2002. p.1.
40. "Turkmenistan: the First Election in 16 years", *Vremya Novostei*, 12th February 2007.
41. Article 90, *The Constitution of the Republic of Uzbekistan*, Tashkent, 1992.
42. Vaisman, Demian, "Republic of Uzbekistan", in Vladimir Babak, op.cit., p.359.
43. "Uzbek Lawmakers Rubberstamp Referendum Result", *Radio Free Europe/ Radio Liberty (RFE/RL)*, Central Asia News Line, 11 April, vol.2, no. 14, 2002. p.1.
44. Article 44, *The Constitution of the Republic of Kazakhstan*, Almaty, 1995.
45. Article 64 & 65, *The Constitution of the Republic of Kyrgyzstan*, Bishkek, 2010.
46. Article 69, *The Constitution of the Republic of Tajikistan*, Dushanbe, 1994.
47. Article 50-58, *The Constitution of the Republic of Turkmenistan*, Ashgabat, 2008.
48. Article 92, *The Constitution of the Republic of Uzbekistan*, Tashkent, 1992.
49. Article 48, *The Constitution of the Republic of Tajikistan*, Dushanbe, 1994.
50. Buluktaev, Yuri (2005), "2004 Elections in Kazakhstan: Strategy and Tactics of the Political Parties", *Central Asia and Caucasus*, no.1, vol.32, p.20.
51. Ibid.
52. Report on Republic of Kazakhstan Parliament Elections, 18 August 2007, Prepared by *OSCE/ODIHR Election Observer Mission*, Warsaw, 30 October 2007.
53. Elebaeva, Aynura (2007), "Political Transformations in Kyrgyzstan (1991-2006)", *Central Asia and the Caucasus*, vol.44, no.2, p.70.
54. Ibid.
55. Report on Republic of Kyrgyzstan Parliament Elections, 27 February and 13 March 2005, Prepared by *OSCE/ODIHR Election Observer Mission*, Warsaw, 20 May 2005. p.20.
56. Gavin, Weise (2010), "Understanding the Proposed Kyrgyz Parliament", An IFES Briefing Paper, May 15.
57. Ibid.
58. *Final Results 2010 by CEC*. Assessed from website: http://www. shailoo.gov.kg/ru/news/svodnaya-tablica-cik-kyrgyzskoj-respubliki-po-itogamvsenarodnogo-golosovaniya-na-referendume-27-iyunya-2010-goda-svodnaya-tablica-cikkyrgyzskoj-respubliki-po-itogam-vsenarodnogo-golosovaniya-na-r/#more-3819.
59. Report on Republic of Kyrgyzstan Parliament Elections, 10 October 2010, Prepared by *OSCE/ODIHR Election Observer Mission*, Warsaw, 20 December 2010. p.23.
60. Kaushik, Devendra (2001), "A Decade of Independent Tajikistan: Some Reflections", *Contemporary Central Asia*, vol.5, no.2, 2001. p.12.
61. Report on Republic of Tajikistan Parliament Elections, 28 February 2010,

Prepared by *OSCE/ODIHR Election Observer Mission*, Warsaw, 6 July 2010. p.6.

62. Report on Republic of Tajikistan Parliament Elections, 27 February and 13 March 2005, Prepared by *OSCE/ODIHR Election Observer Mission*, Warsaw, 31 May 2005. p.21.
63. Kurtov, Azhdar (2006), "Elections in the Turkmenistan Power System", *Central Asia and Caucasus*",vol.38, no.2, p.105.
64. "Turkmenistan Votes in First Ever Multi-Party Legislative Polls", *Ria Novosti*. dated 15/12.2013 http://en.ria.ru/politics/20131215/185587034/Turkmenistan-Votes-in-First-Ever-Multi-Party-Legislative-Polls.html.
65. Report on Republic of Uzbekistan Parliament Elections, 27 December 2004, Prepared by *OSCE/ODIHR Election Observer Mission*, Warsaw, 7 March 2005. p.7.
66. *Uzbekistan Parliamentary Election, 2004-2005.* Assessed from http://en.wikipedia.org/wiki/Uzbekistani_parliamentary_election,_2004%E2%80%932005.
67. Uzbekistan Parliamentary Election, 27 December 2009, Prepared by OSCE/ODIHR Election Observer Mission,Warsaw, 7 April 2010. p.23.
68. Sharma, R. R. (2005), "Central Asia's Quest for Democratic Identity",in V. Nagendra Rao and Mohammad Monir Alam (eds.), *Central Asia: Present Challenges and Future Prospects*, New Delhi: Knowledge World. p.27.
69. Ibid.
70. Aitkhozin, Kabdulsamikh and Yuri Bulukteav (2004), "The Role of Parliament within the System of State Power", *Policy Studies*, vol.5, December. Published by Public Policy Research Center, Kazakhstan. p.22.
71. Ibid. p. 8.
72. Ibid. p.10.
73. Ibid. p.7.
74. Ibid.p 10.
75. Cummings, Sally N. (2000), *Kazakhstan Center-Periphery Relations*, London: Royal Institute of International Affairs. p.8.
76. Aynura Elebaeva, op.cit., p.69.
77. Ibid.
78. Ibid.
79. Ibid. p.70.
80. Ibid.
81. Ibid. 72.
82. Ibid.p.76.
83. *The Current Digest of Post Soviet Press*,vol.58, no.45, 2006. p.7.
84. Gulnara Iskakova, "*Consitutional Reform and Power of the Highest Government Bodies in Kyrgyzstan: A New Balance*, available at http://www.ipp.kg/en/analysis/386/.
85. Aliev, Hassan (1997), "Forming of Political System of Tajikistan: Political and Juridical aspects", *Democratic Institutions*, NATO Fellowship Programme. p.9
86. Luong, Pauline Jones (2002), "*Institutional Change and Political Continuity in Post-Soviet Central Asia*", Cambridge: Cambridge University Press. p.121.
87. Ismailov, Abdulla (2007),"The Basic Priorities of Democratization and

Renovation of the Society at Modern Stage in the Republic of Uzbekistan", Paper presented in IDSA-ISRS Bilateral seminar on *Emerging Geopolitical Dynamics in Central Asia: India-Uzbekistan Relations.* New Delhi. April 11-12.

88. "President Declares Long-Term Priorities of Uzbekistan", 28th January 2005. Available at http://www.press-service.uz/eng/gsection.scm?groupid=4658&contented=6096.
89. "President of Uzbekistan Signs the Law that Makes Amendments to the Constitution", 17th April 2014. UZ Report assessed from http://news.uzreport.uz/news_2_e_118755.html.
90. Akbarzadeh, Shahram (1997), "The Political Shape of Central Asia", *Central Asian Survey*, vol.16, no.4, p.521.
91. Truevtsev, Konstantin (2007), "Central Asia: Political Legitimization Models", *Central Asia and Caucasus*, vol.44, no.2, p.29.
92. Interview with *Aleksei V. Malashenko*, Scholar-in-Residence, Carnegie Moscow Centre, Russia, on 17th April, 2007.
93. Interview with *Grozin Andrey Valentinovich*, Head of Central Asia and Kazakhstan Department, Institute of CIS Studies, Moscow, Russia, on 6th April 2007.
94. Interview with *Irine Zvyagelskaya*, Institute of Oriental Studies, Academy of Sciences, Moscow, Russia, on 2nd April, 2007.
95. Dudarev, K. P. (2001), "A Post-Communist Authoritarian Regime",in Alexei Vassiliev (ed.), *Central Asia: Political And Economic Challenges in the Post-Soviet Era*,London: Saqi Books. p.136.
96. Ibid.
97. Patnaik, Ajay (2003),"The Spirit of Bandung: Security and Stability in Central Asia",*Contemporary Central Asia*", vol. vii, no.3, p.9.
98. Kurmanov, Zaynidin (2006), "Kyrgyzstan after the Revolution: Political Development and Choice of the Form of Government", *Central Asia and Caucasus*, no.2, vol.38, 2006. p.52.
99. Interview with *Aleksei V. Malashenko*, Scholar-in-Residence, Carnegie Moscow Centre, Russia on 17th April, 2007.
100. Interview with *Irine Zvyagelskaya*, Deputy Head of International and Political studies, Institute of Oriental Studies, Academy of Sciences, Moscow, Russia, on 2nd April, 2007.
101. Keynote address delivered by *Ajay Patnaik* at the Academy of Third World Studies, Jamia Millia Islamia, New Delhi , on 14th March, 2007.
102. Interview with *Irine Zvyagelskaya*, Deputy Head of International and Political studies, Institute of Oriental Studies, Academy of Sciences, Moscow, Russia, on 2nd April, 2007.
103. Interview with *Vyacheslav YA Belokreuitsky*, Chairman, Near and Middle East Department, Institute of Oriental Studies, Russian Academic of Sciences, Moscow, Russia on 6th April 2007.
104. Anna Matveena, "EU stakes in Central Asia", *Chaillot Paper*, no.91, July 2006, p.14, published by Institute for Security Studies, European Union, Paris.
105. Ibid., p.16.
106. Ibid.

107. "*A New Stage in the Democratization of Kazakhstan: the Expedited Development of a Free Democratic Society*", Address of N.A. Nazarbayev, President of the Republic of Kazakhstan, to the Joint Session of the Chamber of the Parliament of the Republic of Kazakhstan, Astana, 16th May 2007, available at http:/ www.kazind.com/speeches/president/kaz_presinjoint-session.htm.

4
Non-State Actors

Non-state actors have been playing a very prominent role, contributing proactively in the progress of the nation building process and helping in building a legitimate state apparatus in the modern nation state. These actors may be involved from various social, economic and political settings of the country and positively contribute for the developments of democratic process and political participation. The nation state has created a positive political environment for greater involvement of non-state actors in the process of political representation, policy making, execution and implementation. The success of a nation state depends on how to create enabling environments for participation of non-state actors in the political process mainly in the newly independent states.

4.1 Political Parties

In a democratic political process, political parties play a major role in facilitating and socialising its citizens about the political system. Political parties act as political agents for smooth functioning of a political system. The main functions of political parties are representation, elite formulation, party recruitment, socialisation, mobilisation and political force and they help immensely in running governmental system in a proper way. They establish the relationship between government and citizens. Citizens actively participate in the political system of the country through political parties. In every country, whether authoritarian or liberal, political groups are always trying to mobilise citizens for capturing political power and strengthening their party base. So, a political party is the main medium for facilitating democratisation of a nation.

After the disintegration of the Soviet Union, Central Asian constitutions provided for multi-party political system in a liberal way. But, the emergence of political parties and groups in the Central Asian region is the outcome of the reform policies started by Mikhail Gorbachev in the 1980s. During that time political groups were formed to approach the issue of environment, language and ethnicity rather than political interests. From late 1990, many of these groups were transformed into political parties, and their focus shifted towards gaining independence and engagement in political activities. The number of political parties has sharply increased only after independence for political purposes. The majority of these parties and interest groups do not have very large membership. They, therefore, have adopted very attractive slogans in order to collect funds and to enrol new members. The avowed aim of these informal and formal alternative groups is to establish a multi-party political system.[1] But, the formation and dissolution of political parties in Central Asia remains a very fluid process. In fact, political parties have not yet established deep roots within the society. The shifts in policies and regulations from time to time have caused for the dissolution and formation of many political parties. All the Central Asian countries except Turkmenistan are multi-party based political systems.

Kazakhstan

In Kazakhstan many political parties are functioning in the political process. Political pluralism and a multi-party system have become features of Kazakhstan society and any citizen of Kazakhstan is free to associate himself or herself with any public or political grouping.[2] In that respect Article 23 of the Kazakhstan Constitution mentions that Citizens of the Republic of Kazakhstan shall be given the right to freedom of forming associations. The activities of the public associations shall be regulated by law.[3] There are some main political parties which have played a major role in both the Presidential,

Parliamentary and Local government elections and in social, economic and political developments of the country.

Communist Party of Kazakhstan (CPK): This party was officially registered on February 28, 1994 and reregistered in 1997. The members are mainly from scientific intelligentsia, civil services, working class and pension holders. The main principles of this party are directed towards freedom and social justice based on the principles of scientific socialism and priority of common human ideals. In the political arena the party struggles for the restoration of power of the Soviets, and the establishment of a parliamentary republic. In socioeconomic arena it aims at the restoration of socialist-type ownership in the form of private and state-owned property and their combination, intolerance of exploitation of people, return to planned management of national property, monopoly of state in foreign trade, suspension of privatisation and restoration of social guarantees like right to labour, rest, lodgings, free healthcare and education. This party recognises parliamentary methods of struggle for power and at the same time, it uncompromisingly opposes the present official political course. Thus, the main methods of mobilisation by the party are ideological, political and organisational work with population. [4]

Republican Political Party "OTAN": This party was formed in December 1998 supporting the candidature of N. Nazarbaev at the Presidential election of 1999. The party received an official registration on February 12, 1999. This party was united with several parties who had announced their dissolutions. Among these parties were the Party of National Unity of Kazakhstan, Democratic Party, Liberal Movement of Kazakhstan and "For Kazakhstan–2030" Movement. It has branches in all regions of the country. It shows loyalty to official policy. Many well-known public figures, scientists, and businessmen are in this party. This is the major party which won the highest seats (43) in the September 2004 Parliamentary elections.[5]

Republican People's Party of Kazakhstan (RPPK): This party was formed at the Constituent Assembly that took place in Almaty on

December 17, 1998 and was officially registered by the Ministry of Justice on March 1, 1999. The goals of the party consist of creating a democratic state with socially oriented market economy. Its principal goal is to improve the quality of life of the population by conducting political and economic changes. As its main challenge, RPPK views the reform of political system meaning liquidation of monopoly for power and providing for all-state accountability and control of society. RPPK stays in opposition to official politics of authoritarianism. It is evident that RPPK has all the necessary financing for undertaking its activity. There are several newspapers to act as mouthpieces for the party including *XXI Century*, *451 Fahrenheit*, and the Kazakh newspaper *Sol Dat*. Due to governmental obstruction and the group's own organisational shortcomings this party remained dormant for almost two years.[6]

Democratic Party "Azamat": This party was formed on March 27, 1999 on the basis of people's movement "Azama" and registered by the Ministry of Justice. It includes civil servants, representatives of scientific and artistic intelligentsia, owners of small business, non-political and non-governmental organisations. For the propaganda of its ideas and information of its activity, "Azamat" uses newspapers like, *XXI Century*, *Caravan*, and commercial TV channel and others. In the political arena, it promotes the formation of a multi-party government that people would trust, and favours increase of parliamentary powers connected with control over the activity of the government. In the economic and social sphere, it demands checks on uncontrolled handing over of main objects of national economy to suspicious international companies, to secure with legislation the principle of open ownership of property including all of the taxed real property, demonopolisation of economy and banking system, decrease in the number of taxes and simplification of tax collection process, stressing of the priority of development of domestic market, support of national producers, development of small and medium business and taking of effective measures in defence of pensioners, disabled, families with low income and population in zones of ecology crisis. At the beginning this party was among the parties that stood for uncompromising opposition to the President and the government especially concerning its goals. The initiative for the formation of a bloc of opposition "People's Front of Kazakhstan" belongs to the leaders of Azamat.

Asar (All Together): This political party in Kazakhstan was led by the President's daughter Dariga Nazarbayeva. It was registered on October 25, which was Kazakhstan's Republic day.[7] In the 2004 Parliamentary elections, the party won 11.4 % of the popular vote and 4 out of 77 seats at the last legislative elections. Following calls from its leader Dariga Nazarbayeva for a united ruling party, and allegations that her father was becoming increasingly concerned by the group's independence, Asar merged with Otan. This party has now merged with Otan party.

Bright Path (Ak Zhol): This party was registered on April 3, 2002 and reregistered on December 12, 2002 with the initiative of several members of the political council of the public association "The Democratic Choice of Kazakhstan". The main aim of this party is to maintain independence, democracy, freedom and justice in Kazakhstan.[8] In the legislative election of 2004 the party won 12.0 % of the popular votes and 1 out of 77 seats. A dissident faction was formed in 2005 and was named the Naghyz Ak Zhol (True Bright Path). At the last Presidential election held on December 4, 2005, the party's candidate Alikhan Baimenov won 1.61 % of the popular vote.

The Democratic Choice of Kazakhstan: This party was registered on February 21, 2004. This is an opposition party that works towards the democratisation of the socio-political sphere. It wants to limit the President's powers and extend those of the Parliament.[9] In 2004, by aligning with the Communist Party of Kazakhstan it won 3.4 percentage of the popular vote and no seats at the last legislative election.

Kazakhstan facilitates the playing of a greater role of political parties in the political process. At present 10 registered political parties are functioning in the country. 98 *Majilis* deputies are directly elected every five years to the lower house of Parliament through a proportional system with party lists in one nationwide constituency. So the political parties' role in Kazakhstan politics is very vital for smooth functioning of the political process.

Kazakhstan's law on political parties prohibits parties based on ethnic origin, religion, or gender. Parties need to obtain at least seven per cent of the total number of votes to enter the *Majilis.* As per a 2009 amendment to the Election Law, if only one party passes the threshold, the party receiving the second highest number of votes will also be given at least two seats in the *Majilis.* This amendment also facilitates, liberalises and expands the space for political debate. This significantly reduces the number of requirements for registering a political party, decreases required membership size for a party to be registered, simplifies the registration process and the funding of political parties to strengthen their role in public life, regulates the legal and technical process of establishing a political party and provides public financing of political parties.

In Kazakhstan, the Nur Otan Party has been playing a dominant role in Parliament over the years. In 2007 Parliamentary elections, the National Democratic Party Nur Otan obtained 88 per cent of the votes and took all seats in the *Majilis.* For the first time in history, Kazakhstan Parliament has got multiparty representation in the January 2012 Parliament election. In this election, Nur Otan obtained 80.99 per cent of the votes and received 83 mandates, Ak-Jol received 7.47 per cent and 8 mandates, and CPPK received 7.19 per cent and 7 mandates. Of the remaining parties that were declared not to have passed the seven per cent threshold, the OSDP received 1.68 per cent of votes, Auyl 1.19 per cent, the PPK 0.83 per cent, and Adilet 0.66 per cent. Although, the pro-government political parties were winning the election but a precedent of multi-party representation to the Parliament from single-party dominance has been established.

In spite of that many restrictions have been imposed on political parties. Ten political parties are currently registered with the Ministry of Justice (MoJ). The MoJ has refused registration to several other political parties for a number of years. The registration of the Alga party has been refused since 2005 due to 'technical' problems with application documents. Two other parties, Khalyk Rukh and Ata Meken, have been previously denied registration for similar problems with their members' lists. The merger of the All-National Social Democratic Party (OSDP) and the Democratic Party Azat was rejected by the MoJ due to technical issues with the dissolution of the latter. As a result, the parties could not participate in the elections jointly, as OSDP-Azat, and members of Azat had to formally join the OSDP in order to compete in these elections. The Communist Party of Kazakhstan (CPK) was suspended by a court in October 2011 and thus unable to stand in these elections[10]. Apart from that, mergers of political parties are very rampant in Kazakhstan before the start of election process. Four parties representing supporters of the current Government merged by the end of 2006, and as a result "Nur-Otan"—a new pro-Presidential pro-reform party able to effectively represent interests of its numerous supporters—emerged on the political stage of Kazakhstan. Also in 2006, a Leftist Nationwide Social Democratic Party was registered joining the ranks of several other opposition parties. The beginning of 2007 saw a robust process of mergers and consolidation of political parties, including opposition ones, particularly in the run-up to the August 18, 2007 Parliamentary elections.[11]

Kyrgyzstan

In Kyrgyzstan political atmosphere is more favourable and liberal than other Central Asian countries, so that a large number of political organisations and political parties are functioning smoothly. Article 8 of the Kyrgyzstan Constitution mentions political parties, trade unions and other public organisations that may be organised in the Kyrgyz Republic on the bases of free will and unity of interests. The state shall guarantee the rights and lawful activities of the public associations. The Constitution also mentions that political parties may participate in state affairs to nominate their candidates for the election to the *Jogorku Kenesh*, state posts and to bodies of administration and to form factions in representative bodies.[12] The most important political groups are:

Ata-Jurt (Fatherland): This political party was founded on December 9, by former Foreign Minister and Ambassador to the United States, Roza Otunbaeva. She joined with three opposition parliamentarians to found the party in preparation for the February 2005 Parliamentary elections. However, she was personally barred from standing for office due to a new enacted law in which candidates had to reside in the country for the last five years.

Ata-Menken (Fatherland) Socialist Party: This Socialist Party was founded and led by Omurbek Tekebayev. The party was registered on December 16, 1992 following a split between Tekebayev and the conservative Erkin Kyrgyzstan party. This party calls for a democratic state, economic reforms and evolutionary social development and favours the bringing about of a reasonable compromise between various social sectors and government bodies. The party supported Tekebayev in the 2000 Presidential elections, where he came second with 14% popular votes. On May 20, 2004 the party joined in electoral alliance with other parties in preparing for the February 2005 Parliamentary elections.[13]

Ar-Namys (Dignity) Party: This party was founded on July 9, 1999 by Felix Kulov. The party quickly became the nation's leading opposition party but was barred from the 2000 Parliamentary elections. However, since the party was barred, its members formed a bloc with the Democratic Movement of Kyrgyzstan. With Kulov serving time for criminal charges, the party's members worked over the next years to both clear his name and establish a broad opposition coalition. In 2001, the party formed the People's Congress of Kyrgyzstan, an electoral alliance with three other opposition parties.[14] Kulov was chosen as Chairman. However, in 2004 the party joined other opposition groups for fair elections to the Parliament in 2005.

The Alga Kyrgyzstan (Forward Kyrgyzstan) Party: This party was founded on September 7, 2003. The current chairman of the party is Bolot Begaliev but one of its notable founders was Bermet Akayeva, eldest daughter of former President Askar Akaev. However, Bermet did not run as a candidate of the party. In the February 2005 Parliamentary election, the party won 19 seats. The party was formed by the merger of five separate parties. On December 8, 2003 the Birimdik Party agreed to merge with the party.[15]

The Communist Party of Kyrgyzstan: This party was founded in 1999, following a split in the Party of Communists of Kyrgyzstan. Significantly, it did not participate in the 2000 Parliamentary elections. The party is affiliated to the Communist Party of the Soviet Union of Oleg Shenin.

The constitutional framework of Kyrgyzstan has provided enough space for political parties. Only political parties are entitled to nominate candidates for the Parliament. Presently all the political parties are governed by the 1999 Law on Political Parties. In the last Parliamentary election which was held in October 2010, 29 political parties participated and only five political parties were able to send their representatives. These are Ata-Jurt, SDPK, Ar-Namys, RESPUBLIKA and Ata-Meken.

Tajikistan

Like other countries in Central Asia, political parties in Tajikistan are limited and only the government and pro-government parties are playing major role than other political parties. The exception in this country is that even religious-based political parties are allowed to participate in the political system. The main political parties are:

The People's Democratic Party: This political party in Tajikistan is the ruling party, and is led by Emomali Rakhmonov, the current President of Tajikistan. In legislative elections held in 2005 and 2010, this party secured 52 and 54 seats out of 63 seats.[16]

The Communist Party: This party has been functioning from the former Soviet Union. In the previous legislative elections held in

2000, 2005 and 2010, this party won 13, 4 and 2 seats respectively out of 63 seats.

The Islamic Renaissance Party: This party's primary objective is to promote the ideology of Islam, while it talks of equal rights for all nationalities and it upholds humanistic goals at the same time. It has also alliances with the secular opposition parties in support of popular sovereignty, civil society and economic reform. This political party in Tajikistan has secured two out of 63 seats in each election in the previous legislative elections held in 2000, 2005 and 2010. [17]

Party of Economic Reforms (PER): The Party of Economic Reforms was established by Olimjon Boboyev in 2005 ahead of the Parliamentary election. The main objectives of this party are to create the idea of a multiparty-system and to distract the neutral and moderately opposing voters from the real opposition. It advocates for a genuine reform of the structure of the Tajik economy.[18] This party has managed to secure 2 seats in the 2010 Parliament election.

Agrarian Party (AP): The Agrarian Party was established by Amir Karakulov in 2005, ahead of the Parliamentary elections. This party mainly focuses on the issue of agricultural production. The party advocates for a halt in export of raw materials from Tajikistan, and for the country to switch to the production and export of finished products.[19]

In the electoral process of executive and legislature, the People's Democratic Party has dominated from the inception of the independent political system. This party is getting more popular day-by-day that shows in the figure below. The Communist Party is losing popularity in comparison with previous elections. The Islamic Renaissance Party has managed to keep equal representation in all elections. Recently, political environment has become more conducive for playing a greater role in the political process in comparison with the previous period particularly after 2005. This country has been trying to promote the multi-party system in the political process. However, ruling and pro-ruling political parties are dominating the political system.

Fig. 4: Parliament Election Mandates of 2000, 2005 and 2010 by political parties

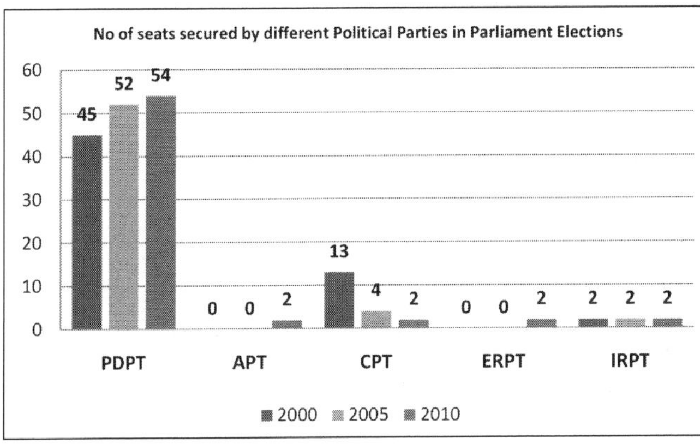

Turkmenistan

Like other countries, Article 28 of the Turkmenistan Constitution mentions that citizens have the right to form political parties and other social associations, which operate within the framework of the Constitution and laws. The formation and activity of political parties and other social associations having as their goal violent change of the constitutional order, allowing violence in their activities, agitating against the constitutional rights and freedoms of citizens, advocating war, racial, national, social, or religious animosity, encroaching on the health or morality of the people, or forming militaristic associations or political parties based on national or religious traits are forbidden.[20] Practically, the political parties' role was very limited and there was not enough space for political parties up to 2009 in the unicameral Parliament. The law was formulated in 2012 on political parties and provided an opportunity to establish new political parties. In the last 2013 Parliamentary election many political parties and interest groups participated and were represented in the unicameral Parliament. The present government is led by the Democratic Party of Turkmenistan (DPT), which has dominated national politics for the last two decades.

The Democratic Party of Turkmenistan is the ruling political party in Turkmenistan. Only one political party is legally allowed to hold effective power up to 2013. It was led by all the outgoing and ongoing presidents of Turkmenistan. Before 1991 the party was called the Communist Party of the Turkmen SSR. [21]

The Party of Industrialists and Entrepreneurs: This party was established in August 2012 as the first legal opposition party in this country. The party leader Ovezmammed Mammedov was elected to the Assembly of Turkmenistan in a by-election held for five vacant seats on June 10, 2013. The party is widely seen as a tool of the ruling DPT to prevent criticism over Turkmenistan being a single-party state rather than an actual opposition party.[22]

Turkmen Union of Democratic Forces: This political party was created in Vienna, Austria on November 23, 2003. Former Foreign Minister Awdy Kulyýew, former ambassador to Turkey Nurmuhammet Hanamow, former central bank chief Hudaýberdi Orazow and former Deputy Agriculture Minister Saparmyrat Yklymow are the founding members.[23]

Uzbekistan

Uzbekistan Constitution mentions that political parties shall have registered in accordance with the procedure prescribed by law and got the status of associations in the Republic of Uzbekistan.[24] Political parties shall express the political will of various sections and groups of the population and through their democratically elected representatives shall participate in the formation of state authority. Political parties shall submit public reports on their financial sources to the *Oliy Majilis* or their plenipotentiary body in a prescribed manner.[25] Many political parties have been banned in the course of time. The constitutional amendment of 2014 has given more space to strengthen the role of political parties in the political process. At present five political parties are existing in the Uzbek mainstream politics. The main existing political parties are:

The Uzbekistan People's Democratic Party: This party emphasises the principle of law and order in order to keep the nation out of extreme nationalism or Islamic fundamentalism. This political party in Uzbekistan won 28 out of 120 seats at the last election in 2005[26] and 32 seats in 2010.

The Uzbekistan Liberal Democratic Party: This political party in Uzbekistan in the legislative elections in 2005 won 41 out of 120 seats[27] and 53 seats in 2010.

The Self-Sacrifice National Democratic Party: The party's leader is Aslam Tursunov. In the legislative election of 2005, it won 18 out of 120 seats [28] and 31 seats in 2010.

The Uzbekistan National Revival Democratic Party: This political party in Uzbekistan has won 11 out of 120 seats in 2005.[29]

The Justice Social Democratic Party: At the legislative elections of 2005, the party won 10 out of 120 seats and 19 seats in 2010.

The position of Central Asian political parties are divided into three parts e.g. ruling party, pro-government party and opposition party. The ruling and pro-government parties enjoy more powers than opposition political parties. The rules of registration of political parties are frequently changed from election to election. In Central Asia, all the presidents of the republics are organising their own political parties. Niyazov had created the idea of a Presidential party from the beginning and during the first decade of independence all the ruling leadership had well understood the need of a solid party. Nazarbayev and Akaev made an attempt to achieve this objective by involving their daughters to organise pro-government parties. Karimov began his Presidency by delegitimising religious and nationalist parties on the Right and social-democratic parties on the Left, and formed five legal parties of the centre all being pro-government. But, Rakhmonov set up his own pro-governmental group, the Peoples' Democratic Party.

A new development, that is, the gradual acceptance of political parties by authoritarian rulers across Central Asia emerged. However, the parties' early reluctance was because of the potential and capability of parties to influence the fundamental changes in balances among regional networks, clans, cliques and families from which the presidents derived their personal powers. From the presidents' perspective, parties, like parliaments, were fine so long as they constrained these forces, but would pose a threat as soon as they aspired to change fundamentally the relations among them. President Bakiev has already sought radical redress for the North's long-term dominance of Kyrgyz politics, and the consequences may prove destabilising. In the long run parties may bring about a fairer balance of power in each country, but the authoritarian rulers rightly judge that in the process this could undercut their own power base. Uncontrolled parties, even more than the principle of "one person one vote," could unleash uncontrollable forces within these new yet deeply conservative states. This realisation has led to the non-registration or banning of parties in every country in the region. This runs the danger of moving powerful forces outside the system, where they can pose a yet greater danger. A more effective method, practiced in all states except Uzbekistan, allow candidates to run as individuals, unaffiliated with any party. This retards the growth of parties, but at the potential price of elevating the status of rivals to the President.[30]

Detailed laws on everything from party finances to the maintenance of membership lists by region can also be used effectively to curtail party activity. In Tajikistan the election law requires parties to publish their platforms in full. When a party competing in the 2005 Parliamentary elections failed to do so, it was banned. A simpler and more effective method by which governments can keep parties in check is through cooptation. This can mean giving key party figures or their supporters remunerative administrative posts or handing them outright payments. This cursory account of the techniques by which authoritarian rulers can control the work of political parties might suggest that it is a one-sided battle, with all of the most effective weapons in the hands of the state. If this were so, one would have to conclude that political parties, like presidential votes, offer few prospects for evolution towards more open systems. Yet the picture is more complex and, in the end, more positive. In Tajikistan, Rakhmonov's People's Democratic Party received all possible support from the President prior to the 2005 Parliamentary elections, yet it was placed a weak third in the balloting.[31]

Presidential parties in Kazakhstan and the Kyrgyz Republic fared no better. In Kazakhstan's November 2004 Parliamentary vote, Dariga Nazarbayeva's Azhar Party received substantial subsidies, not to mention unlimited access to the national television station run by Ms. Nazarbayeva herself. Yet Kazakhs gave more votes to the heretofore marginal Ak Zhol Party. The differential might have been yet greater, had not many local officials illegally promoted Azhar. Similarly, Bermet Akaeva's Presidential party failed to shine even in the grossly corrupt first Parliamentary election of March 2005. Even though she had disingenuously tried to distance herself from her father, Akaeva herself lost the election in her Bishkek constituency. Nor has Karimov succeeded in his efforts to champion one of Uzbekistan's five pro-government parties over others. No sooner had he accepted the nomination of this group than the Liberal Democratic Party (LDP) began to advance rapidly. Appealing to young entrepreneurs, the LDP presented itself as the outspoken champion of economic reform. Following the voters' shifting loyalties, Karimov changed his idea, and by the December 2005 Parliamentary elections was actively signalling his support for the LDP.[32] The consistent picture in all Central Asian countries is for the legal parties to develop slowly and steadily. They have used all legal tools at their disposal to challenge dubious restrictions imposed by the government. The supposedly authoritarian rulers either failed to manipulate the parties as wished, and failed in the effort to elicit from voters the preferred outcome, or were forced to follow rather than lead the electoral process.

In every country, political parties would seem to be at a particular disadvantage. For example, in Uzbekistan, the five legal parties were all creations of the state, and are by definition pro-government. Yet there is a steady evolution of the gradual limited democratic process which has been inevitable. As these political parties tried to translate a programmatic and social focus into practical actions, all five parties benefited from contacts with like-minded parties abroad.

Due to internal and external pressures, all the Central Asian countries have amended the constitutions and given more space to the political parties in the present political arena.

4.2 Oppositions

The roles of the opposition in Central Asian countries are very minimal. They enjoy some rights in Kyrgyzstan than in other states. In Kazakhstan, the law and regulation of political parties was passed on April 15, 2003 and amended further. Kazakhstan's Justice Ministry announced the results of the process of reregistering political parties. In the last legislative elections in 2012, only 10 political parties participated but in 2006, 13 political parties participated. So the restriction of registering political parties still exists. Reregistration was established as a requirement for parties to function legally in the country. The government touted the exercise as a requirement for parties to function legally in the country and as a way to strengthen Kazakh democracy. But most independent observers saw it as a ploy by President Nursultan Nazarbaev to decimate opposition to his regime. [33]

Most of the exiled political leaders in Turkmenistan are operating primarily out of Moscow, and are known as much for fighting amongst themselves than offering a serious alternative to the authoritarian regime. They took, however, a potentially major step towards professionalising and consolidating their efforts. A communiqué issued by representatives of four opposition groups in 2003 announced that they were joining forces as the Union of Democratic Forces of Turkmenistan with the goal of replacing the existing regime with a democratic government based on a parliamentary system. Among those gathered in Prague were former Turkmen Foreign Minister Avdy Kuliev, Aleksander Dodonov and former Ambassador to Turkey Nurmuhammed Hamanov, co-founder of the People's Democractic Movement of Turkmenistan.[34] Now Turkmenistan is trying to facilitate and accommodate the opposition through constitutional amendments.

In Kyrgyzstan, the movement 'Reforms for the People' was formed for the removal of the then President Askar Akaev. But the movement was also criticised by some leading opposition figures who might have been expected to sympathise with its aims. The movement was founded by representatives of 22 opposition political parties, public organisations and NGOs, including the Communist, Erkindik, and Asaba parties, the "Kyurgyuzstan" bloc of deputies in the Legislative Assembly, the Kyrgyz Committee on Human Rights and others. General Ismail Isakov, a lawmaker who serves as chairman of the Parliamentary Security Committee, was selected to head the movement.[35] So, the role of the opposition is visible in Kyrgyz politics.

In Uzbekistan, Sandzhar Umarov, the son of a prominent Soviet physicist, headed the Uzbek opposition movement known as the Sunshine Coalition. In the wake of the public disturbances that were suppressed in Andhijan, the democratic coalition demanded the removal of a "corrupt government". Umarov was arrested in Tashkent on charges of financial wrongdoing meant for being an open dialogue with the opposition. Umarov asked Russian Prime Minister Sergei Lavrov to promote the democratisation of Uzbekistan and help the Sunshine Coalition obtain registration.

After Sandzhar Umarov's arrest, the leaders of the European Union placed harsh criticism at the Uzbek authorities. Both houses of the US Congress interceded for Umarov in a special resolution. American human rights activists called it a historic moment and christened Umarov as the Uzbek Mandela. They recalled that the Tashkent court sentenced the opposition leader to a lengthy prison term. In addition, the convicted man would have to pay a fine of $8.3 million and the assets of the companies he owned would be confiscated.[36]

The Kazakh opposition, which took a real beating during the 2004 Parliamentary elections, hoped to turn the next Presidential elections, set for December 2006, into a Ukrainian-style route. Most members of the opposition had already settled on a single candidate, Zharmakhan Tuyakhai, former Parliament speaker and deputy chairman of the pro-Presidential Otan party, who broke with Nazarbayev in 2003. It is hard to gauge how much popular support the opposition enjoys, and Nazarbayev might try and diminish the appeal of the opposition by setting himself up as an agent of political reform. Nazarbayev maintains that he is committed to real, albeit gradual, political reform, to be accompanied by concrete steps to improve the social and economic conditions of the Kazakh people.[37]

The Tajik opposition also believed that it had a better chance of defeating President Emomali Rakhmonov in 2006 than of getting the recent parliamentary results overturned. Tajikistan held Parliamentary elections on the same day of the first round of elections held in Kyrgyzstan, and these also fell far short of international norms. The four opposition parties—the Democratic, Communist, Islamic and Social Democratic parties—had strongly protested the election results and had pressed for a new election. But they have not been able to translate these protests into large popular demonstrations against the Rakhmonov government, largely because the population of Tajikistan is still partially traumatised by the lengthy civil war that began in the early 1990s.[38]

The Uzbek government made some largely symbolic steps to introduce a few promised political changes. However, the absence of formal political institutions that can moderate elite competition means that the period of political transition will be a time of potential instability in Uzbekistan. Excluded political groups seeking to expand their influence are likely to appeal to regional and sub-national groups as they seek ways to expand their potential power basis. For much the same reason, the role of religious opposition groups particularly the least radical ones may expand as well.[39] In spite of government control, opposition political parties are still active in Central Asia.

Due to financial crises and government regulations these are facing lots of problems. But their potential cannot be minimised.

The role of the opposition is very visible at the time of election and electoral process. No significant contribution has been noticed over the period of times in policy making and implementation level like other democracies. Most of the political nomenclature are continuing their office and don't have experience to share the power between the elite. In Kyrgyzstan, opposition has substantial role in politics and other Central Asian countries are trying to promote the opposition through liberalisation of the political system.

4.3 Civil Societies

Civil society institutions are playing a critical role in a democratisation process. These institutions are viewed as a set of horizontal social links, of autonomous institution vis-à-vis the state and of associations created by free and responsible citizens to protect their interests.[40] These institutions also generate social capital for the development of the nation-state. Civil society institutions are working in every field and where government agencies fail to reach the common people, civil society institutions are reaching. A UNDP report based on NGO sector capacity assessment broke down all organisations into the following five categories in 1999. These are: protection of rights of specific groups, common interest groups, charity organisations, associations protecting rights of ethnic minorities, and development associations.[41] In Central Asia, Civil society institutions are booming in the field of economy, environment, gender issues and politics. Civil society in this region is called the third sector. The state controls the public expression of opinion but it cannot control the private sphere. As the Soviet state weakened and subsequently collapsed, the people had a chance to take a closer look at what their society looked like.[42]

After independence, all the Central Asian countries have given space for the growth of civil society institutions. In accordance with the Constitution of Uzbekistan, Article 9 mentions that major matters of public and state life shall be submitted for a nationwide discussion and put to direct vote of the people (a referendum). Article 32 also mentions that citizens have the right to participate in the administration of public and state affairs directly and through their representatives. Such participation shall be through self-government, the holding of referendums and the democratic formation of government bodies.[43] In the same direction, Kazakhstan Constitution (Article 5) also mentions that in the Republic of Kazakhstan, ideological and political pluralism shall be recognised. The merger of non-government and government institutions or the establishment within government bodies of political party organisations shall not be allowed. Non-government associations shall be equal before the law. Interference by government in the affairs of non-government associations and interference by non-government associations in the affairs of government, the vesting of non-government associations with the responsibilities of government bodies and government funding of non-government associations shall not be allowed.[44] But the Turkmenistan constitution does not elaborate much about the non-governmental organisations. Article 28 mentions that citizens have the right to form social associations and Article 29 mentions that every citizen has the right to participate in the management of the affairs of the society.[45] Article 8 of the Kyrgyzstan Constitution also mentions that public associations may be organised on the basis of free will and unity or interests. The state shall guarantee the rights of lawful public associations.[46] Article 28 of the Tajikistan Constitution guarantees that citizens have the right to form associations and each citizen has the right to participate in the formation of social associations.[47]

Due to such space in the legal system, many civil society institutions have come up and concentrate on many issues. In the initial stage, many civil society organisations are concentrating on environmental issues in this region. For instance, the first environment-based NGO, Ecological Movement of the Kyrgyz Republic, was officially registered in 1993. By November 1997, over 70 ecological NGOs were registered at the first forum of ecological

NGOs of this republic.[48] After the institutional growth of this sector, many civil society groups are working as consultant agencies dealing with various issues and collaborate with various international agencies for economic sustenance. Many businessmen started funding this sector for social influence and business purposes.

Apart from that, civil society is also active in various other areas. By 2002, Kazakhstan had already established groups of non-profit organisations dealing with environmental issues which were about 15 per cent, human rights protection (8 per cent), gender-equality issues (14 per cent), medical (13 per cent), social-support issues (7 per cent), supporting public initiatives (6 per cent), the disabled (7 per cent), children and young people (14 per cent), and culture, arts, science and education (13 per cent) of all NGOs.[49] According to Kazakhstan's Ministry of Justice, in mid-2001, the country had about 2,500 registered voluntary citizens' associations. However, that number apparently did not include all groups or organisations that comprise the non-government non-profit sector.[50] In Uzbekistan there are only about 200 NGOs. However, this number does not include more than 10,000 *Mohallas*, a traditional form of self-organisation at community level.[51]

In Turkmenistan, civil society activity is very limited compared to other Central Asian states where NGOs are flourishing. In total there were about 150 NGOs by the middle of 2001.[52] The groups that do exist are discouraged by the government from conducting awareness campaigns, sending members abroad for seminars, or inviting foreign guests. There have been some successes in establishing NGOs that work on the environment and on women's issues, although many are in some way dependent on government structures. One example of a successful independent NGO is the environmental group *Catena*. It is tolerated because it provides funds for ecological projects and expertise from abroad but it also reportedly comes under pressure from the authorities. This sector, however, does offer some possibilities for engagement by the international community, particularly as public services come under increased pressure. Health, small and medium-sized enterprises, education and the environment are all areas that may hold promise for developing more NGO structures, although government suspicion and bureaucratic obstacles will remain serious problems. The NGO sector not only provides useful services, but also offers a chance for qualified Turkmen who do not wish to work in government structures to remain engaged in the country's development.

The Tajikistan National Unity and Revival Movement (TNURM) created in July 1997 united efforts of different social strata and forces to establish an environment of peace, mutual trust, and consent. The experience of resolving civil problems within the political movement deserves close analysis, only because TNURM is headed by the President and this movement has effective channels for strengthening social partnership.

Due to various social unrest and disturbances in these newly independent countries, authorities control various activities of civil societies. For instance, Kyrgyzstan adopted the law regulating NGO activities from October 15, 1999. Under this law, the functions and tasks of NGOs consist in pursuing the goals of NGOs set out in their articles of association. The law does not provide for NGO participation in formulating and executing the policy process. Relations with government are set out in Article 5.3 of the law reading "Interference by government bodies or officials in the operations of non-profit organisations and, equally, interference by non-government organisations in the operations of government bodies and officials shall not be allowed except as provided for in the law." This norm could be interpreted discretionarily, including in a way restricting NGO involvement in taking and executing policy decisions. [53]

After the Andijan movement in Uzbekistan in March 2006, the Uzbekistan government tightened the screw on civil society functioning. As a result, most of the foreign NGOs are closing their offices. On March 6, 2006, the human rights organisation, Freedom House, ended its operations. The offices of the International Research and Exchanges Board and the Internews Network have been closed. Meanwhile, Uzbek organisations found guilty of accepting money from the US and other external agencies, have been shut down by the dozens, even if their activities had nothing to do with politics or human rights. The Uzbek Ministry of Foreign Affairs revoked the accreditation of journalists working for Radio Liberty, and Britain's BBC news service decided on its own to close its office in Tashkent and recall its correspondents, saying that they were being harassed.[54]

The Western strategy for introducing greater openness into the governance of Central Asian states has led to confrontation. During 2005-06 this resulted into steep conflict between the governments and civil society organisations in the Kyrgyz Republic and Uzbekistan. Earlier, Turkmenistan had severely restricted such organisations. By late 2005 Kazakhstan began to move in the same direction. Many NGOs are choosing to leave the region, if they are not meanwhile expelled. Also, many international groups have lost the hope of a peaceful transition and are looking ahead to a regime change as a precondition to progress. But, Kyrgyzstan's experience since March 2005 gives cause for concern as to the viability of this option. NGOs may not be a very effective tool for achieving an open and participatory system. However, there is increasing evidence that some aspects of the electoral process and associated activities are effective.[55]

In Central Asia, certain representatives of civil society continue to be perceived as dissidents and political opponents. They also face interference with their activities. This particularly affects human rights defenders and organisations which are known for their strong criticism of governmental failures to improve human right records. Moreover, the fact that there are sometimes individuals with purely political agendas hiding behind NGO labels, contributes to reinforcing some governments' reluctant attitude to NGOs. This has sometimes led to a vicious circle. When the governments seek to control illegal political activities, the entire NGO community suffers from restrictions. In turn, real NGOs are often forced to operate underground that retards the impact of their activities and encourages even more criticism of the governments.

In Central Asia, NGOs have come across strict regulations which involve lengthy registration period and high fees. Sometimes, arbitrary rejection of certain kinds of NGOs raises suspicions that obstacles to allowing a variety of NGOs to the surface are politically motivated and that legislation is introduced only as a measure to prevent unwanted groups being active in society.

In the political sphere, some civil society groups are very active in the policy planning, formulation and implementation levels. These groups are co-coordinating various ethnic organisations and smooth functioning of political parties. Use of the right on legislative initiative is an important form of participation in the law-drafting activity of civil societies. In all the republics, there is very limited scope for civil society institutions. State institutions have such right, as a rule, through the President, the Parliament and its committees and members and the government. Only the Kyrgyz Republic has a norm, which gives the right on the legislative initiative to 30,000 voters. This norm is only a formal right, which is impossible to implement due to lack of the norm defining an order, forms and methods of implementation of the right of the legislation initiative for 30,000 voters. There are no regulations for collection of signatures, calculation procedure and control of these signatures etc.

In the Central Asian region, civil society organisations are adopting strategies for fighting on many social and political issues in a coordinating manner. Kyrgyz NGOs also show this tendency for uniting on the basis of working agendas. The "Coalition" is the most successful case of NGO consolidation. There are also women and youth organisations working together. Numerous women NGOs have been very successful in bringing out issues of gender imbalance at the family, community, and state levels by engaging females with various backgrounds. Although most of the politically active NGOs are located in the capital Bishkek, there are nevertheless strong networks of activities outside the cities. There are a number of youth organisations and newspapers that seek active involvement in political life. The March 24, 2005 events of Kyrgyzstan showed that youth networks such as "Birge and Kelkel" have strong public support. A widely published youth newspaper *Limon* is famous for developing caricatures of known government figures that reflects on recent developments. Kyrgyz people did stand up for their liberty. Following the fraudulent Parliamentary elections of 2005 in which the leading opposition members were either barred from running or faced the full use of government resources to defeat them, the people of Kyrgyzstan protested against these results and demanded genuinely free elections. The people had long been frustrated by the one-man rule and the corruption that had developed around the former President, and were no longer willing to accept that their representatives be handpicked by the government.[56]

For promoting democratic atmosphere, many external actors are also providing funding to civil society institutions in the Central Asian regions. In Kyrgyzstan, assistance provided by the United States directly to Kyrgyz civic groups and indirectly through NGOs such as National Democratic Institute, International Republican Institute, Freedom House, Internews and International Foundation for Electoral Systems was instrumental in helping creating the space for political dialogue, raising civic awareness and providing support for civil society. [57]

National innovations are even more apparent using the example of the transitional organisational structures that exist in all of the Central Asian countries for interaction between the vertical power and civil society. The National Institute of Democracy and Human Rights (NIDHR), situated in Turkmenistan, can be seen as a kind of bridge between the state and the "third sector". In Central Asia, a number of consultative bodies are working under government for coordinating between government agencies and civil society institutions. In Kazakhstan, a number of consultative bodies operate under the government. According to the guidelines for the establishment, operation and liquidation of consultative bodies under the government of the Republic of Kazakhstan and for working groups established on instruction from the government, such bodies can be set up as commissions and working groups. In other words, such bodies are largely designed to coordinate inter-ministerial action. Commissions or working groups include officials of ministries, departments and organisations responsible, under the country's legislation, for the issues within the purview of the commission or working group. Several consultative bodies including NGO representatives are operating under the government. These are the Commission for the Promotion of Small Business, Youth Council and Council for Interaction with Religious Associations.[58]

In Uzbekistan, many civil society institutions are participating on the policy planning and formulation levels. Under the Law on "*Oliy Majlis* of the Republic of Uzbekistan", representatives of non-government organisations, print and electronic media may be invited to the sittings of commissions and committees. Furthermore, *Oliy Majlis* committees and commissions invite representatives of NGOs, experts and academics to participate in their deliberations; they refer for peer review both bills drafted by the committee or commission or submitted to them as part of a legislative initiative; they also request the expert opinion of nongovernment organisations, academics and experts, on matters within their purview; they request documents, written conclusions, reports and other materials from NGOs. In an *Oliy Majlis* regulation on the Rules of Procedure of *Oliy Majlis* of the Republic of Uzbekistan it is stated that plenary of *Oliy Majlis* can be attended by representatives of non-government associations, workers' collectives, research centres, print media, radio and television as well as other persons invited by the Council (*Kengash*) of *Oliy Majlis.* [59]

For better social stability and development in Kazakhstan, the Assembly of the Peoples of Kazakhstan (APK) was established in 1995 by a Presidential decree in accordance with Article 78 of the Constitution to strengthen social stability and inter-ethnic accord. The Assembly is underpinned by APK rules that the head of state approved on March 1, 1995 in Decree No 2066. The APK operates by interacting with government and non-government bodies, including religious organisations, and regional self-governing authorities as well as international organisations and organisations of other states whose activities are not contrary to the goals and objectives of the APK. Decisions taken by the Assembly take the form of recommendations. APK members are appointed by the President from among representatives of centres of ethnic culture, veterans' councils and other persons taking into account their authority in the eyes of the general public, their voluntary and political activities and a track record of practical work. All candidates are reviewed by a meeting of the Assembly Board and referred for approval to the Chairman of the APK—the President—who has the discretionary right to turn down proposed nominees and replace them with other persons. The Assembly has its organisational units in all regions of the country.[60]

In Kyrgyzstan, on April 19, 2001, a meeting of representatives of almost a hundred NGOs with the Head of the President's Administration was held at the Government Building on the initiative of the Legal Issues Foundation supported by the NGO Association and the Administration of the President of the Kyrgyzstan. The meeting was devoted to interaction between NGOs and the Republic's authorities. The topics discussed at the meeting included interaction between NGOs and government on taxation, the need to explain to government officials the social role, objectives and specific features of NGO operations and the need to introduce in Kyrgyz legislation the institution of a public contract for NGOs in areas such as education programmes, the environment medicine etc. The participants concluded that it was necessary to establish a permanent Council for NGO Affairs working under the President. Participants proposed candidates for members to the Council. The Council was formed including 21 leaders of different NGOs. Domestic media extensively covered the meeting.[61]

In Kazakhstan there is a Standing Assembly for drawing up proposals for further democratisation and development of the civil society. Judging from the decisions made—the Memorandum on Adherence to Democratisation and Development of a Civil Society—there are several important resolutions on questions of judicial and legal reform. The Standing Assembly is demonstrating the same efficiency as the civil forum and has successfully involved oppositional political organisations in its activity. According to the Kazakh President, "We have created functioning institutes of the civil society, including over five thousand NGOs".[62] The conception of the Development of a Civil Society in the Republic of Kazakhstan for 2006-2010 was approved and adopted in 2006. The main idea behind this legislation is equal partnership between the government and civil society institutions. This document enforced the government's initiative to establish constructive and productive relations with NGOs in order to build an open, democratic and prosperous society of a free people.[63]

While addressing the joint session of the Kazakh Parliament, President of Kazakhstan Nursultan Nazarbayev commented that processes of political liberalisation are impossible without advanced civil society. On the other hand, the development of civil initiative is impossible without the strengthening of the NGO networks and trade unions. The laws "On the State Social Mandate" and "On Social Partnership in the Republic of Kazakhstan" were passed to ensure the involvement of Kazakhstan's NGOs in solution to the crucial social problems. They are aimed at establishing a new model of relationship in the sphere of social policies, establishing a stable and efficient system of relationships between the state and the public sector.[64] Apart from that many independent foreign NGOs have been opening their branches in the Central Asian region like the International Crisis Group, the Institute for War and Peace Reporting, Soros Foundation, James Foundation, Human Right Watch and Organisation for Security and Co-operation in Europe (OSCE) and they are playing a leading role in coordinating with other regional civil societies and create affiliated NGOs in various regions. Thus, the role civil societies are playing is very crucial for the democratisation process and for smooth functioning of the political party system. They are co-coordinating various social forces and could help stabilise the social system.

4.4 Media

The constitutions of all the Central Asian countries provide for free media and freedom of speech. Media is called the fourth pillar of democracy. It acts as the mouthpiece of society and various organisations. In Central Asia most of the ruling political elites, political parties, social organisations and ethnic minority groups maintain both electronic and print media. Many media agencies are pro-government and ruling party publications. Even many private-owned media outlets are extremely pro-government because their owners are members of the ruling party. However, many opposition parties also have their own publications mainly in Kazakhstan, Tajikistan and Kyrgyzstan. Many foreign media organisations are working in this region. In Turkmenistan, the media is totally controlled by the government. In every country of Central Asia, there are separate media legislations to control the media. After the Andijan incident of Uzbekistan, the government exercises total control over the media agencies because the authorities understood that the independent press is the main enemy.[65] The BBC's Uzbek service closed its Tashkent bureau for six months in October 2005. The same month, Internews, a media focused non-governmental organisation, lost its final appeal and shuttered its offices in Uzbekistan.[66]

Media of all types in Central Asia are very venerable due to censorship, access to information, libel and defamation, taxes and excessive government control. A Paris-based media research organisation, 'Reporters without Borders' conducted press freedom ranking of 166 countries in 2014. In this report, Tajikistan secured 115th place, Turkmenistan 178th place, Kazakhstan 161th place and Kyrgyzstan 97th place within Central Asia.

In Tajikistan, the civil war, though over, continues to cast a shadow over the media. Independent media often rely on foreign grants for financial support. Government-owned newspapers include *Jumhuriyatr* in Tajik, *Sadoi Mardum* (in Tajik), *Khalq Ovozi* (in Uzbek) and *Narodnaya Gazeta* (in Russian). *Asia Plus*, *Ruzi Nav* and *Nerui Asia Plus* maintain webpages, which feature materials in Russian and English from the affiliated Asia Plus news agency. The major political parties also publish newspapers such as the Islamic Renaissance party's *Najot* and the Communist Party's *Nidoi Ranjibar*.[67]

Due to the strong hold of authoritarianism, fear of instability and government control over information flow, the authorities are hesitant to disseminate sensitive information to the public in Central Asia. For getting official information, journalists are harassed immensely. The authorities, however, deny that there is a lack of press freedom. Darigha Nazarbaeva—the daughter of Kazakh President Nursultan Nazarbaev and a media magnate in her own right—said that one need walk only five minutes in Almaty to find a publication that elaborates "what a bad president we have and how I've monopolized the entire press."[68]

Uzbekistan's cabinet passed a resolution on February 24, 2006, regarding "basic rules regulating the professional activities of foreign media correspondents in Uzbekistan." This 2006 resolution mentioned in point 21 that "Accredited foreign correspondents are forbidden to call for the violent change of the existing constitutional system, the violation of Uzbekistan's territorial sovereignty by promoting war and violence, cruelty, ethnic, racial and religious animosity. They are also forbidden to interfere in the internal affairs of Uzbekistan, to insult the honour and dignity of Uzbek citizens, to interfere in their personal lives, or to perform other actions, responsibility for which is mandated by Uzbek law."[69] This 2006 resolution explicitly states that foreign correspondents cannot "interfere in the internal affairs of Uzbekistan", leaving undefined what such unwanted "interference" might constitute. The new text also regulates interactions between foreign correspondents and Uzbek citizens, stating that foreign correspondents are forbidden "to insult the honour and dignity of Uzbek citizens, to interfere in their personal lives."

In Turkmenistan, media is fully controlled by the government and very recently internet media services opened in this country. The access to information about what is happening in their own country is severely limited, but this is mediated to a degree by their access to foreign satellite and online media. There are six nationwide state television channels plus one serving the capital, as well as four state radio broadcasters. Residential areas host multiple satellite dishes providing access to an array of more than 300 news and entertainment channels from outside the country. There are 27 newspapers and 25 magazines in circulation. State newspapers *Türkmenistan* and *Neitralnyi Türkmenistan* are considered the main papers. *Rysgal* is described as the only private newspaper in the country, a weekly owned by the Union of Industrialists and Entrepreneurs. The state communications company *Türkmentelecom* has provided internet services. At the end of 2012 the Parliament passed a new Law on Mass Media, replacing the 1991 Law on Press and Other Mass Media. This new law places greater emphasis on preventing violations of media freedom than on providing safeguards to protect it.[70]

Kazakhstan's President said "In our country, we have established freedom of speech, there is no censorship and independent mass media is thriving. You may recall the attempt during the previous session of Parliament to limit freedom of the media. I had to veto the bill and thereby once more assert our firm commitment to freedom of speech".[71] He also stressed that political modernisation implies the enhanced positions of mass media, the enabling of independence of mass media's editorial practices and the protection of journalists' right. At the same time, mass media should understand their role in the process of democratisation, their responsibility to society and should act exclusively within the legal framework. This is exactly the approach of the state in establishing and passing the laws, dealing with information policy. Recently, the private mass media companies dominate the information environment in Kazakhstan, and this is the result of democratic aspiration of Kazakhstan. While improving the guarantees for freedom of the press, it is always essential to bear in mind the following: words today can have a creative role, they can mobilise people for solving urgent problems and can strengthen the stability in the country. But words can also destabilise the society. That is why the freedom of speech in any democratic state does not mean absence of control, and does not abolish the responsibility of the mass media before the society", underlined Nazarbaev.[72] The 2009 Amendment has provided to remove administrative barriers and re-registration requirements for mass media and extends the rights of journalists. The Senate passed a new law "On Television and Radio Broadcasting" on December 28, 2011 regarding control over broadcasting by the government.

In all the Central Asian countries, the authorities are able to manipulate the courts to make sure that the harsh laws are applied as the rulers deem appropriate. Journalists are regularly in courtrooms in Kazakhstan, Tajikistan and Kyrgyzstan.[73] The government controls printing press and has a near monopoly over media activities in this region. Many opposition media are being harassed by governments and the courts. Due to the shortage of finance and legal hurdles, private and opposition media are facing immense problems for their smooth functioning. In spite of that, many media organisations are making consistent efforts to highlight the misdeeds and failures of the governments. Media highlights many issues of political parties that have helped to sustain the democratic atmosphere.

4.5 Ethnic Minorities

The Central Asian countries are multi-ethnic states and ethnic minority groups are very significant in number in every state since the Soviet period.

In Kazakhstan, according to 2009 census data, population comprises of the Kazakh people 63.1 per cent, Russian 23.7 per cent, Ukrainian 2.1 per cent, German 1.1 per cent, Tatar 1.3 per cent, Uzbek 2.9 per cent and Uighur 1.4 per cent.[74] Over 100 other ethnic groups make up the remaining 4.5 per cent of the population. According to the 2014 census of Kyrgyzstan, population comprises of the Kyrgyz people (72.6 percent), Uzbek (14.4 percent), Russian (6.4 percent), Dungans (1.1 percent) and others constitute 5.5 percent. In Turkmenistan, population comprises the Turkmen people (85 percent), Uzbek (5 percent), Russian (4 percent), and others (6 percent) according to 2003 figure. Turkmen is the official language of Turkmenistan, though Russian is still widely spoken in cities as a language of inter-ethnic communication. In Uzbekistan, Uzbeks comprise a clear majority of 80 per cent of the total population. Other ethnic groups include Russian (5.5 per cent), Tajik (5 per cent), Kazakhs (3 per cent), Karakalpak (2.5 per cent), and Tatar (1.5 per cent) Kazakh.[75]

In Tajikistan, the main ethnic group is of Tajiks, accounting for 84.2 per cent of the population. Other groups include Uzbeks (12.2 per cent), Kyrgyz (0.8 per cent) and Russians (0.5 per cent). Smaller ethnic groups make up the remaining 2.3 per cent of the population.[76] Although Uzbeks are significant in number, there was no overt discrimination against Uzbeks or other minority groups, nor were any formal barriers placed in the way of their full participation in the electoral process. At the same time, however, members of the Uzbek minority did not appear to be actively engaged in the elections as candidates. Political parties did not have messages designed to appeal to Uzbek voters.[77] The recent Presidential election reflects that voter education materials and broadcasts were produced in the Tajik language. The lack of voter information materials in national minority languages did not cause serious discontent in these communities. In areas with significant minority populations, ballots were printed in minority languages. There are two representatives of national minorities among the CCER members. Ethnic composition of PECs and DECs generally corresponds to the ethnic composition of the total population in respective districts. However, in some areas with a large ethnic Uzbek population, members of this national minority were under-represented in the election administration.

In these elections, the number of candidates from minority groups was marginal and minority issues were not raised during the campaign. Only one person belonging to the Uzbek minority was elected from a single-mandate constituency so far. No candidates from a minority entered Parliament on party lists. Political parties distributed some campaign materials in minority languages, such as Russian, Uzbek, and Kyrgyz; this was observed by the OSCE/ODIHR EOM in the Sughd region and in Dushanbe. In some areas with significant minority populations, ballots were printed in minority languages. In most minority-populated DEC areas observed, up to 50 per cent of members were from minority groups.[78]

Due to this huge number of ethnic minorities in Central Asia, all the political parties are trying to seek their involvement, influence and participation in the political affairs. Their role in Turkmenistan, however, is very limited. In Turkmenistan, however, the gap between Turkmen and non-Turkmen continues to widen. Niyazov, the former President of Turkmenistan, stated in 2000 that the 21st century is the Golden Century of the Turkmens, which clearly marks the establishment of an ethnic divide between citizens living in the same country. Politically, Russians are denied any participation in the country's administration and state structures. There are no ethnic Russian ministers, deputies, or other high-ranking officials. The only advantage ethnic Russians still possess is the chance to gain dual citizenship. In 2000, Turkmenistan and Russia signed an agreement allowing dual Turkmen and Russian citizenship for ethnic Russians permanently living in Turkmenistan.[79] Even in Uzbekistan, the Russian minority's role is very minimal in the political sphere. But the political parties are still trying to seek their support in politics.

In the political process, minorities are playing significant roles in some countries. Tajikistan has several national minorities, of which Uzbeks are by far the largest, numbering as many as 25 per cent of the population. There was no overt discrimination against Uzbeks or other minority groups, nor were any formal barriers placed in the way of their full participation in the electoral process. At the same time, however, members of the Uzbek minority did not appear to be actively engaged in the elections as candidates. Political parties did not have messages designed to appeal to Uzbek voters.[80]

National minority issues appeared to be a factor in the election process in certain regions of Kyrgyzstan. In the 2005 Parliamentary elections, out of the 389 candidates that contested the first round of election, 88 percent were Kyrgyz, 5 per cent were Uzbeks, and 4 per cent were Russians. In comparison with the overall demographic figures, national minorities were significantly underrepresented as candidates. Nevertheless, the final composition of the Parliament ensured a certain level of representation to national minority groups. In this Parliamentary election 2005, according to official information, the Parliament includes 60 Kyrgyz, 7 Uzbeks, 3 Russians and 3 other deputies.[81] Of the 120 members of Parliament, 14 belonged to a national minority in the last election. The law requires that at least 15 percent of candidates on party lists be members of ethnic minorities.

Due to the significant presence in the Parliament of minorities, especially of Uzbeks, the latter demanded Uzbek to be made an official language in Kyrgyzstan. On June 7, 2006, President Bakiev stated that the Uzbek language will not be recognised as an official language. The President called upon the Members of Parliament to stop destabilising the situation. However, Parliamentarians, Kadyrian Batyrov and Abdumutalip Hakimov, noted in their speeches that the Uzbek people are native residents of the southern part of Kyrgyzstan and the Uzbek language has a right to gain official status. The Governor of Jalalabad oblast, Iskender Aidaraliev, who also participated in the meeting said "Nobody is violating the right of Uzbeks who make up 24 percent of the total population of oblast". The day before the rally, in the support of Uzbek language the Governor noted in a televised address that "there are 35 Uzbek language schools in the oblast, Uzbek television and newspapers operate on the same level as the Kyrgyz ones."[82]

Uzbeks are the second biggest ethnic group in the territory of Kyrgyzstan, totalling a million people. Thus, a lingering sense of irritation and resentment of minorities has been a feature of Kyrgyz politics and society under Akayev, but the government has publicly discouraged the expression of such feelings. In Kyrgyzstan, the representation of minorities in Parliament, ministerial appointments and senior civil service jobs has sharply diminished. The President dismissed the only ethnic Uzbek governor of Osh province, Anvar Artykov, elected by popular vote. Rather than a sign of any inclination of President Bakiyev towards nationalism, this may be explained as the weakness of his government, which has not been able to make an explicit commitment to create an atmosphere of inter-ethnic peace and harmony. Thus, expressions of ethnic prejudice and nationalist feelings are not discouraged and have increasingly entered into the public domain.[83]

The case of Kazakhstan though indicates that in the recent developments in state-building policy there is not going to be based on a mass linguistic transformation favouring the Kazakh language. While the 1993 Constitution accorded Russian the status of "language of inter-ethnic communication," the 1995 Constitution conferred "official" status upon it as well. In November 1996, the Lower House of the Kazakhstan Parliament passed a draft revision of the language law fixing a time period in which non-Kazakhs and Kazakhs would learn Kazakh, but the law was only adopted by both Houses of Parliament in July 1997. The deadline for learning the Kazakh language by all citizens was January 1, 2006. However, alongwith the Constitutional provision, the new language law clearly says that "Russian is used on a par with the Kazakh language in state organisations and organs of local self-government."[84]

Both the 1993 Constitution and the 1995 Constitution declared that 'Kazakhstan was created on the basis of Kazakh self-determination', but equal rights for all citizens, regardless of race, nationality, language or religion have been guaranteed. The new Constitution provides automatic citizenship with no language or residence requirement whoever desires it. Article 5 of the new draft prohibits the establishment of any social organisation that looks for forcible change in the constitutional order, undermines state security, violates territorial integrity, or promotes 'social, racial, national, religious, class, or tribal discord'. The new Constitution imposes an absolute ban on any propaganda or campaign pointed towards the above objectives.

Despite such provisions, Russian minority has disproportionately lesser participation in the political process due to manipulation by the authorities. In the March 1994 elections in Kazakhstan, it was found that out of 756 candidates, 77 per cent were ethnic Kazakhs and only 18 per cent were Russians. A quarter of the Parliamentary seats were reserved for candidates from the state list, a slate of 64 nominees personally drawn up by Nazarbaev, from which 42 deputies were to be elected. The President manipulated the new legislative body's ethnic composition in many cases, forcing the election of at least one Kazakh from a Russian-dominated oblast and vice versa, and putting up for election representatives of other ethnic groups that would be unlikely to otherwise gain representation. Nevertheless, election results showed that Kazakhs succeeded in 59 per cent (105) of the Parliamentary seats, while Russians managed to take 48 seats, or 27 per cent.[85] Thus, in Kazakhstan, ethnic minorities still represent a significant number in the legislative organs due to the influence of minority groups in political, social and economic sphere.

The creation of a model nation-state with a multi-ethnic society like Kazakhstan is the best form of state. The large minority with high skills and education is an asset for the new state. The attempt to prevail over ethnic minorities by the dominating majority threatens the social stability of the emerging state. The nationalising effort might be helpful in creating a sense of national solidarity among the Kazakhs but the issue of ethnicity has to be addressed.[86] According to Ajay Patnaik, "the society in Central Asia is not affected by majority–minority divide based on national identity alone. There are religious–secular, radical–moderate divisions, not to speak of regional and clan group rivalries. These divisions provide space to national minorities and keep open the prospects of their bargaining for a better status."[87]

4.6 Women

In Central Asian countries, there is no discrimination between man and women in public and political life. However, traditional attitudes sometimes hindered women from holding high office or playing active roles in political life. Women are involved in electoral process in all the Central Asian countries. There were no legal restrictions on the participation of women in politics. In Kyrgyzstan, the election code requires that the names of male and female candidates be intermixed on party lists and that no more than 70 percent of candidates on a party list can be of the same gender. Women held the positions of finance minister, healthcare minister, prosecutor general, president of the National Bank as well as one of the vice prime ministerial posts under the Parliamentary coalition formed in September 2012. A woman held the position of vice speaker of Parliament, and altogether 25 women representing five political parties occupied seats in the 120-member Parliament. As of 2011, women occupied 19 percent of the 675 senior government positions.[88] In Kazakhstan there were three female ministers, 26 members of the *Majilis* (lower house of Parliament) and two senators were women.[89] No significant representation has been found in Kazakhstan.

In Tajikistan, there are two female ministers but no ministers from minority groups. A deputy prime minister; the minister of labour, migration, and employment; and several deputy ministers are women in this current house. In the 63-member lower chamber of Parliament, there are 10 female members and one minority group member. In the 33-member upper chamber of Parliament, there are five women and one member of a minority group. The government and political parties are putting efforts to promote their involvement, such as the 1999 Presidential decree that mandated every ministry or government institution to have a female deputy.[90]

In Turkmenistan, there were 21 women in the 125-member Parliament, including the speaker of Parliament in the year 2013. Women also served in other prominent government positions, including as Deputy Chairperson of Parliament, Vice Premier of the Cabinet of Ministers for culture, television broadcasting, the press, Minister of Education, Minister of Culture, Director of the State Archives, and Director of the National Institute for Democracy and Human Rights.[91]

In Uzbekistan, there were 33 women in the 150-member lower chamber of Parliament, including speaker Dilorom Toshmuhammedova, and 15 women in the 100-member Senate, along with two women in the 28-member cabinet. During the 2009 Parliamentary elections, more than 30 percent of candidates were women, following a recommendation from the UN Committee on the Elimination of Discrimination against Women.[92]

To sum up, in the Central Asian political culture, which has emerged after independence, the participation of political parties is very limited in Turkmenistan, Uzbekistan and Tajikistan. But in the Kyrgyz case, the political atmosphere is liberal, which facilitates mushrooming growth of political movements and political parties. Presently there are more than forty political parties. But in practical terms, there are two groups, one is southern and another is northern, and they are bargaining with each other. In Kazakhstan, many political parties are functioning, but the government and pro-government political parties are getting more advantages than other political parties in terms of finance and legal matters. Groupism and regroupism are the general phenomena in Kazakhstan, affecting opposition political parties against ruling forces. Many political parties are formed at the time of election, but the frequent changes in the rules and regulations of the governments regarding the formation of political parties create hindrances in getting registration as political parties in Central Asia.

The participation of oppositions in Central Asian political process is very limited in Uzbekistan, Turkmenistan and Tajikistan due to the strong control of the government. In Kyrgyzstan, many opposition groups are participating in the political process in terms of demonstrations, gheraos and other means for demanding constitutional amendment, combating corruption and other causes. The civil society institutions are playing a very limited role in Turkmenistan, Tajikistan and Uzbekistan in the sphere of politics. In Uzbekistan, many independent think tank organisations emerged independently, but they have turned into pro-government organisations. In Kazakhstan and Kyrgyzstan, many civil society organisations are taking part in the political process. In the case of minorities, Kazakhstan is more willing to accommodate the minorities in the Parliament, civil service and other affairs of the state machinery. Mainly Russian and other minority groups are taking part in the election process, policy planning and at the implementation levels. In Kyrgyzstan, Uzbek minorities are playing a stronger role than other groups. But in Turkmenistan, Uzbekistan and Tajikistan, the role of minorities is very limited. Every country has constitutionally guaranteed independent mass media. But in Central Asia, most of the media are playing a limited role than local media or national media. First time in the history after the death of former Turkmen President, electronic media showed various entertainment programmes nationwide, symbolising the strong control of the state over media agencies. Many opposition news papers exit in Kazakhstan and Tajikistan. In short, the role of political parties, mass media, civil society, women and minorities cannot be minimised for facilitating democratisation process in Central Asia. Despite so many constraints and difficulties, these non-state actors are continuously working for the expansion of liberal impulses in the political process and for the creation of a stronger democratic culture in Central Asia.

Notes

1. Badan, Phool, (2001), "Emerging Political System in Central Asia in the Post-Soviet Period", *India Quarterly*, vol. LVII., no.3., July-Sept. p.104.
2. *Address of the President to the people of Kazakhstan* on 18th of February 2005, Documents cited in Contemporary Central Asia, vol. IX, no.2&3, August-December. 2005. p. 92.

3. Article 23. *The Constitution of the Republic of Kazakhstan*, Almaty. 1995.
4. Kurganskaia, Valentina, (2005), "The Party System in Kazakhstan and the Ethnic Issue", *Central Asia and Caucasus*, vol.32, no.2., p.77.
5. Olcott, Martha Brill (2005), *Central Asia's Second Chance*, Washington D.C.: Carnegie Endowment for International Peace. p.272.
6. Ibid.
7. "Kazakh President's Daughter Elected to Head New Political Parties", *Radio Free Europe/Radio Liberty* (*RFE/RL*), Central Asia News Line, vol.3, no. 37, 31st October 2003. p.1.
8. Kurganskaia, Valentina, op.cit., p.73.
9. Ibid. p.76.
10. *Report on Republic of Kazakhstan Parliament Elections*, 15 January 2012, prepared by OSCE/ODIHR Election Observer Mission, Warsaw, 3rd April 2012. p 4.
11. *Kazakhstan Democracy*. Assessed from http://www.kazakhembus.com/page/kazakhstan-democracy
12. Article 8. *The Constitution of the Republic of Kyrgyzstan*, Bishkek. 1993.
13. *Report on Republic of Kyrgyzstan Parliament Elections*, 27 February and 13 March 2005, Prepared by OSCE/ODIHR Election Observer Mission, Warsaw 20 May 2005. p.12.
14. Olcott, Martha Brill, op.cit., p.274.
15. Ibid.
16. Hunter, Shireen T. (1996), *Central Asia since Independence*, Washington D.C: Praeger. p.45.
17. *Report on Republic of Tajikistan Parliament Elections*, 27 February and 13 March 2005, Prepared by OSCE/ODIHR Election Observer Mission, Warsaw, 31 May 2005. p.19.
18. *Tajikistan* (2013), European Forum for Democracy and Solidarity. Assessed from http://www.europeanforum.net/country/tajikistan.
19. Ibid.
20. Article 28. *The Constitution of the Republic of Turkmenistan*, Ashgabat. 1994.
21. Borishpolets, Ksenia (2006), Elections in Central Asian States: Political Rivalry in a Transitional Society, *Central Asia and the Caucasus*, vol.37, no.1, p.31.
22. Turkmenistan Gets Its Second Political Party, *Radio Free Europe*, 11 June 2013.
23. Blagov, Sergei (2003), *Turkmenistan: A Study in Democracy Denial*".December 6. Assessed from http://www.atimes.com/atimes/Central_Asia/EL06Ag02.html.
24. Article 56. *The Constitution of the Republic of Uzbekistan*. Tashkent. 1992.
25. Article 60. ibid.
26. *Report on Republic of Uzbekistan Parliament Elections*, 26th December 2004, Prepared by OSCE/ODIHR Election Observer Mission, Warsaw, 7 May 2005. p.5.
27. Ibid. 8.
28. Ibid.
29. Ibid.
30. Kurganskaia, Valentina (2005), "The Party System in Kazakhstan and Ethnic Issues", *Central Asia and the Caucasus*, no. 2, vol.32, p. 67.

31. Starr, S. Frederick, "Clans, Authoritarian Rulers, and Parliaments in Central Asia", *Silk Road Paper*, Uppsala University, Sweden, p.21. Available at www. www.silkroadstudies.org/new/docs/silkroad papers/0605 starr_clans.pdf.
32. Ibid.p. 22.
33. Curtains for Kazakh Opposition Parties, *Radio Free Europe/ Radio Liberty (RFE/RL)*, Central Asia News Line, vol.3, no.15, 18th April 2003. p. 1.
34. Turkmen Opposition Units, *Radio Free Europe/ Radio Liberty (RFE/RL)*, Central Asia News Line, vol. 3, no. 33, 3 Oct. 2003.
35. Kyrgyz Authorities Space New Opportunities Group, *RFE/RL News Line*, vol 2, no. 32, 22nd August 2002. p. 1
36. "An Uzbek Mandela", *The Current Digest of Post Soviet Press*, April 10, vol.58, no. 10, 2006. p. 14.
37. Kaushik, Devendra (2004), "Central Asia since Ozodi: An Appraisal", in K. Warikoo and Mahavir Singh (eds.), *Central Asia since Independence*, New Delhi: Shipra Publications. p.5.
38. Olcott, Martha Bill (2005), "The Next Act in Central Asia's Transition Drama", *Moscow Times*, April 12.
39. Ibid.
40. *United Nations Development Programme Report* on "Policy Process Reform: Institutionalization of Consultations between Government Institutions and Non-Government Organizations in the CIS Countries, Conditions, Forms, Practice", Bratislava, August, 2002. p.10.
41. Shishkaraeva, Elmira (2006), "Review of the History of Establishment and Development of the NGO Sector in the Kyrgyz Republic", *Soros-Kyrgyzstan Foundation*, Bishkek. p. 74.
42. Carley, Patricia M. (1995), "The Legacy of the Soviet political System and the Prospects for Developing Civil Society in Central Asia", in Vladimir Tismaneanu (ed.), *Political Culture and Civil Society in Russia and the New States of Eurasia*", Armonk, New York: M.E. Sharpe Publication. p. 297.
43. *The Constitution of the Republic of Uzbekistan*, Tashkent, 1992.
44. *The Constitution of the Republic of Kazakhstan*, Almaty, 1995.
45. *The Constitution of the Republic of Turkmenistan*, Ashgabat, 1994.
46. *The Constitution of the Republic of Kyrgyzstan*, Bishkek, 1993.
47. *The Constitution of the Republic of Tajikistan*, Dushanbe, 1994
48. Shishkaraeva, Elmira, op.cit., p. 42.
49. *United Nations Development Programme Report* on "Policy Process Reform: Institutionalization of Consultations between Government Institutions and Non-Government Organizations in the CIS Countries, Conditions, Forms, Practice", Bratislava, August, 2002,op.cit., p.40
50. Ibid.
51. Ibid. p.39.
52. "Cracks in the Marble: Turkmenistan's Failing Dictatorship", *International Crisis Group Asia Report*, No. 44, 17 January 2003, p. 28. Available at www. crisisweb.org.
53. *United Nations Development Programme Report* on "Policy Process Reform: Institutionalization of Consultations between Government Institutions and Non-Government Organizations in the CIS Countries, Conditions, Forms, Practice", Bratislava, August, 2002, op.cit., p. 57.

54. "The Uzbekistan Opposition Harassed", *The Current Digest of Post Soviet Press*, April 14, vol.58, no. 10, 2006. p.3.
55. Starr, S. Frederick, op.cit., p.14.
56. Patnaik, Ajay (2003), "The Spirit of Bandung: Security and Stability in Central Asia", *Contemporary Central Asia*, vol.VII, no.3, December. p.10.
57. Statement by Edil Baisalov, President of the Coalition for Democracy and Civil Society (Kyrgyzstan), *Before the House Committee on International Relations*, US House of Representatives, May 5. 2005.
58. *United Nations Development Programme Report* on "Policy Process Reform: Institutionalization of Consultations between Government Institutions and Non-Government Organizations in the CIS Countries, Conditions, Forms, Practice", Bratislava, August, 2002, op.cit., p.58.
59. Ibid. 59.
60. Ibid. p.60.
61. Ibid. p.61.
62. *Address of the President to the People of Kazakhstan* on 18th of February 2005, cited in *Contemporary Central Asia*, op.cit.
63. Diachenko, Sergey (2007), "The Government and NGOs in Kazakhstan: Strategy, Forms, and Mechanisms of Cooperation", *Central Asia and Caucasus Analysis*, vol.43, no.1, p.53.
64. N. A. Nazarbayev address on "*A New Stage in the Democratization of Kazakhstan: the Expedited Development of a Free Democratic Society*, op.cit.
65. "Uzbekistan: New Media Resolution Tightens the Screws", *RFE/RL News Line*, Vol.15, March 13, 2006.
66. Ibid.
67. OSCE media report on Tajikistan, 2002. Available at www. osce .org.
68. Kimmage, Daniel, "*Muzzled Media*", available at http://www.rferl.org/featuresarticle/2006/6/1A688624-452A-4DDC-835E-FABF08DEB0F7.html.
69. Ibid.
70. OSCE media report on Turkmenistan 2013. Available at www. osce .org.
71. *Address of the President to the People of Kazakhstan* on 18th of February 2005, cited in *Contemporary Central Asia*, op.cit.
72. N. A. Nazarbayev address on "*A New Stage in the Democratization of Kazakhstan: the Expedited Development of a Free Democratic Society*", op.cit.
73. Pannier, Bruce (2006), "Central Asia: Bureaucratic Obstacles Hinder Journalists", *RFE/RL News Line*, April 28. Available at http://www.rferl.org/featuresarticle/2006/04/a43c5c6c-59c7-40e1-9144-0345d9861b81.html
74. Ethnic Composition of Kazakhstan (census data), 2009 available at http://en.wikipedia.org/wiki/kazakhstan.
75. Uzbekistan demography, available at http://en.wikipedia.org/wiki/Uzbekistan.
76. The state population census of 2010. Available at: http://www.stat.tj/en/img/526b8592e834fcaaccec26a22965ea2b_1355502192.pdf.
77. *Report on Republic of Tajikistan Parliament Elections*, 27 February and 13 March 2005, Prepared by OSCE/ODIHR Election Observer Mission, Warsaw, 31 May 2005. p. 17.
78. *Report on Republic of Tajikistan Parliament Elections*, 28 February 2010,

Prepared by OSCE/ODIHR Election Observer Mission Final Report, Warsaw, 6 July 2010.

79. "Cracks in the Marble: Turkmenistan's Failing Dictatorship" *ICG Asia Report* No. 44, 17 January 2003, Osh/Brussels. Available at www.crisisweb.org.
80. *Report on Republic of Tajikistan Parliament Elections*, 27 February and 13 March 2005, Prepared by OSCE/ODIHR Election Observer Mission, Warsaw, 31 May 2005. p. 17.
81. *Report on Republic of Kyrgyzstan Parliament Elections*, 27 February and 13 March 2005, Prepared by OSCE/ODIHR Election Observer Mission, Warsaw, 20 May 2005. p.20.
82. Osmonov, Joldosh (2006), "Uzbek Community in Kyrgyzstan Want Uzbek as Official Language", *Central Asia–Caucasus Analyst*, Wednesday, June 14.
83. Matveena, Anna (2006), "EU Stakes in Central Asia", *Chaillot Paper*, no. 91, July. p.30.
84. Patnaik, Ajay (2005), "Ethnicity and Nationalism in Central Asia", in V. Nagendra Rao and Mohammad Monir Alam (eds.), *Central Asia: Present Challenges and Future Prospects.* New Delhi: Knowledge World. p.74.
85. Patnaik, Ajay (2004), "State Building in Kazakhstan", in K. Warikoo and Mahavir Singh (eds.), *Central Asia Since Independence*, New Delhi: Shipra Publications. p.68.
86. Ibid.
87. Patnaik, Ajay (2003), *Nations, Minorities and States in Central Asia*, New Delhi: Anamika Publishers. p.121.
88. Kyrgyz Republic 2013 Human Rights Report. p.20. Assessed from www.state.gov/documents/organization.
89. Kazakhstan 2013 Human Rights Report. p.22. Assessed from www.state.gov/documents/organization
90. Tajikistan 2013 Human Rights Report. p. 18. Assessed from www.state.gov/documents/organization.
91. Turkmenistan 2013 Human Rights Report. p.18. Assessed from www.state.gov/documents/organization.
92. Uzbekistan 2013 Human Rights Report. p.24. Assessed from www.state.gov/documents/organization.

5
Conclusion

The Central Asian political culture is shaped by its history, culture, tradition and social formations. From the earliest to the present day of its civilisational growth, Central Asian political systems have been characterised by a paternalistic authoritarian political system. This political system has the minimal participation of citizens. Prior to the conquest of Russia, the Central Asian people were basically from the steppe region and nomadic in nature. Administrative system was vertical and hierarchical rather than horizontal. The origins of *Khanates* or autonomous kingdoms were developed mainly through the combination of nomadic and settled societies. The nomadic society was united from top to bottom by kinship. This society in form was a series of concentric circles. The nomadic village was composed of a series of extended families. This village in turn was combined with related villages to form a large unit, the clan, all the members of which had descended from a single ancestor many generations back. The clan was combined with other clans to form a confederation, all related by ties of descent in common from a single founder, traced from father to son. This clan confederation was the basis of a political unit, the state or principality.

In most of the regions the political structure was less oppressive because the people were not seen as slaves to the land and the rulers did not enjoy arbitrary and absolute rule. The *Khans* (leaders) were elected at a meeting of various local rulers, nobles and clan elders. In addition to this aristocracy of *Khans*, on a more local level the elders met to choose a leader to represent them in negotiating disputes among families and regulating migration. A *Khan* had to prove his military power to remain as a ruler. The government was tyrannical and oppressive giving cruel punishment to its opponents. The clergy enjoyed a high status and respect in a society where illiteracy and superstitions were widespread. The people of the region had no right to participate in political process even if they were aware of various activities of the governments. At that time Central Asia consisted of three *Khanates*—Kokand, Bukhara and Khiva.

During the colonial period, the Tsar appointed the Governor-General and he enjoyed wide powers both for military and civil administration of the territory. He had also great power in matters relating to Bukhara and Khiva. He appointed from among the representatives of Russian nobility, military officers and the administrative officers. In the administrative hierarchy, the military governor stood at the apex of the administration and all the powers were concentrated in his office. Military officers were heads of *Uyezd* (region) and city administration. Besides the above two levels, the Tsarist government also made use of the so called popularly elected lower village administration. The post of *Volost* (lowest administrative unit consisting of a few villages) administration and village official were filled through election. Their appointments were confirmed by the military governor of the *Oblast* (province). These elected officials worked under the control of the *Uyezd* (region) administration. But in actual practice, the process of election was merely a farce. Those who had good contacts with the Russian administration and were loyal got elected to this post. The Russians monopolised both the election and selection processes. Thus, the political systems of the Central Asian countries were very authoritarian in character and the people participated (very minimally) in the political process under the control of the Governor-General during the colonial period.

After the success of the Bolshevik revolution and demarcation of the Central Asian territories, these countries came under the Soviet rule. Under the Soviet political system, Central Asian countries were governed by a single political party, i.e., the Communist Party with the Marxist-Leninist principles. All the issues were decided by the Soviet Communist Party in the name of 'democratic centralism'. Democratic centralism means the election of all bodies of state authority from the lowest to the highest, their accountability to the people, and the obligation of lower bodies to observe the decisions of higher ones. Democratic centralism combines central leadership with local initiative and creative activity, and with the responsibility of each state body and official for the work entrusted to them. The Soviet authorities abolished the court of *Qazi* and introduced the centralised civil judicial system all over the region.

The constitution of the USSR established a federal system. The constitution recognised the autonomous republics as sovereign Soviet Socialist states and it guaranteed the right to secede freely from the USSR. Their territorial integrity was assured and each was left to its own territory. In reality, none of these provisions and rights was to be taken seriously. In effect, the Soviet government was federal in form and unitary in spirit. In the federal system, the Soviet Union was supreme and controlled all units or republics. All the republics had their own constitutions, though finally controlled by the Centre. In the Central Asian case, the first or second secretary was always a Russian, who was in charge of military or security areas. This secretary was more powerful than the others. On the other hand, the other officials were appointed from the native people.

Central Asian participation in modern sectors was limited by cultural and historical conditions. These included: first, a tradition of looking to other Turkic peoples primarily *Tatars* for cultural leadership. Secondly, a Muslim cultural heritage which inclined Central Asian intellectuals towards humanistic careers rather than scientific and technical ones, and which severely restricted the participation of women in public and social life. Thirdly, an instinctive chauvinism of the Europeans—primarily Russians—who dominated the political system and especially of those Europeans settled in Central Asia itself. Fourthly, the generally low levels of education and training among Central Asian nationalities. Due to this backwardness, Slavs occupied dominant control positions in administrative, security and industrial sectors. In the other spheres it was found that there was shortage of trained personnel; but there was hardly any policy to encourage the local population to overcome this shortage. Decrees issued by the Central Committee in the 1950s and 1960s continued to complain about the failure of Central Asian party organisations to find young, competent officials from the local population and noted the failure of these organisations to adapt their work to the needs of the local situation.

The Russians who occupied the key positions were closely tied to the central party apparatus in Moscow and used their positions in the non-Russian areas to implement central policies. This pattern was strongest in Uzbekistan and Kazakhstan. Important positions like the chairmanship of KGB and others were held exclusively by non-indigenous cardres in Uzbekistan, Tajikistan and Turkmenistan, and only a small proportion of incumbents in Kazakhstan and Kyrgyzstan were indigenous. Thus, while the Russian organisational secretaries were charged with carrying out the regime's policy of promoting Central Asians into responsible positions at the upper and middle levels of the state and party bureaucracies, the Russian chairmen of the KGB were charged with supervising, controlling and removing native cardres. By 1960s, the apparatus of the Communist Party had merged with the state apparatus, creating a party-state. During the final decades of the USSR, the party-state was the only actor in Soviet society that no one could legitimately contest and its authority was supreme. The Party was controlling all the social organisations like Komsomol (youth organisation), various trade unions, women's organisations (Zhentodel), Pioneer (School children's organisation) and the media.

During the Stalin period, the political system was highly centralised; the participation of the general public was very limited. The leadership controlled the Supreme Soviet and had strong hold on the Communist Party. After the death of Stalin, Khrushchev tried to facilitate common masses' participation in the policy-making process and at the administration level by defining the Soviet State as "all people's state". He advocated for the gradual transfer of functions from state to public organisations. As a result, millions of citizens were attracted to part-time work in the Soviets, other governmental agencies and public organisations. In the Brezhnev era, new organisations were designed or created to draw the citizens into public life (e.g., the *druzhiny*). A number of actions were taken that facilitated the access of at least some citizens into the decision-making process.

During the Soviet period, the Communist Party intensively carried out the women's emancipation drive that helped to educate and socialise them to take an active participation in the political process. After promoting their educational development, energetic efforts were made to involve Central Asian women in the political and administrative process. Female delegates were elected to represent their communities in public meetings at local and republican levels. Activists were sent for training to the Communist University, the Turkic School of Soviet and Party Work and other such institutions. In the early 1920s, Central Asian women began to join the Party. In percentage terms participation remained low but the numbers began to increase despite their lack of previous political experience. For example, in Uzbekistan, there were over one thousand Uzbek women Party members by early 1929. In response to Lenin's injunction that more women should be elected to the Soviets, Central Asian women gradually came forward to file their nomination as candidates. By the early 1980s, roughly half of the official working population in Central Asia was female. By the late 1990s, nearly 100 percent women had become literate. At the end of the Soviet period women participated in nearly all aspects of public life. In Uzbekistan, for example, women accounted for 50 percent of those employed by the government, while 45 percent of local deputies to the Soviet were women.

The media groups were working in the purview of the government. Soviet authorities used censorship as a major tool to control information. No official publication or broadcast was free of the Censor Board scrutiny. Every book, article, journal, radio and television script, before publication, was to be submitted to the scrutiny of *Glavlit* (the Chief Administration of Literary and Publishing Affairs), the official censorship agency.

However, the Gorbachev period from the mid-1980s was bringing renaissance at every sphere in the Soviet political system. After coming to power, Gorbachev introduced far-reaching reforms in the political system through his policies of Glasnost and Perestroika, which ushered in a new era of press freedom, political democratisation and decentralisation of decision-making process. It brought about a radical change in Soviet politics and had a profound impact upon social, political and economic system of the country. During this period, the problems of Soviet society like corruption, inefficient economic system, backwardness, clan-dominated political system and heavy bureaucratisation etc. came out into the open. Many social organisations and movements were formed in relation to environmental, ethnic, unemployment, language and religious problems in the Central Asian region. The policy of Glasnost in Central Asia provided the opportunity to the native intelligentsia to reflect on their native history and culture, which was a taboo subject during the earlier period. The relative free flow of information and growth of free press led to the rethinking by the indigenous peoples about their past history and culture. One of the important issues that confronted the Central Asian regions during this period was rampant corruption and involvement of political elites in it. After coming to power, Gorbachev tried to probe the corruption charges levelled against the political leaders and sacked many of them. But by that time the political, economic and social conditions had already deteriorated and many movements and dissident groups sprang up. Their resentments and activities finally led to the disintegration of the USSR.

After independence the Central Asian republics faced numerous problems. The most important problems were: creating a national identity for the Central Asian people, pressure of large number of ethnic Russian minorities in Central Asian republics and problems emerging due to transitional nature of the economy from a command and stateregulated economic system to a market-oriented economy. The Central Asian political elites tried their best to fulfill the needs and aspirations of the people and develop institutional mechanisms to iron out their problems. They also adopted different mobilisation strategies to take on the challenges posed by elements of social mobilisation. However, the experience differed from country to country depending upon the nature of problems posed by social forces. For example, in Tajikistan, structural disequilibrium between weak political institutionalisation and strong social mobilisation led to the breakdown of state authority. In Tajikistan, the regime faced intractable challenges from democrats, Islamic movements and various tribal and clan groups, each trying to take over political power. All the republics had secured their boundaries, territories, and legitimacy during the Soviet period itself. Ethno-national identities were most strongly visible among intellectual elites, party members and the urban population. The rural population continued to identify with traditional *Mahalla* (community), village, residential, kinship, clan, and regional loyalties.

All the Central Asian constitutions in the post-Soviet period characterise their political systems as secular, democratic, legal and social states whose highest values are given to the individuals, their lives, rights and freedoms. The fundamental principles of the activity of the republics are public concerns and political stability. They emphasise the separation of religion and politics. These provisions have been incorporated in their constitutions to keep the radical forces at bay. All the Central Asian constitutions have incorporated the principles of separation of power among the three branches of government to check the hegemonistic tendency on the part of any one apparatus of government. These constitutions, however, have not clearly mentioned the political system as unitary or federal or quasi-federal, but the practice implies that their structures are indeed unitary.

However, in practice, the governmental systems of all the Central Asian countries are closer to a presidential form of government rather than parliamentary. The President is the head of the state in all five republics, and is also the symbol of the unity of people, state power and the guarantor of the Constitution and of individual and citizen rights. The President defines the fundamental directions of internal and external policy of the state and represents the republic within the country and in international forums. The Parliaments of Central Asian states are formally the supreme representative body, exercising legislative functions. According to the constitutional provisions of all Central Asian countries, media and civil society institutions are free to act but within the limits of law.

In the initial period, constitutions in the Central Asian countries provided for clear demarcation of political power between legislature and executive. In course of time, the executive power has been consolidating more power and strong control over legislature through constitutional amendments. The executives and elites are still holding political power since the Soviet period. In the Central Asian political system, the executive branch always dominates over the legislative branch. The President controls all the activities of the state including that of the Parliament. When the laws or other activities of the Parliament have contradicted the power of the President, in that case the President dissolves the Parliament and calls for fresh elections. This regular exercise is very rampant in Kazakhstan and Kyrgyzstan but even in the case of Tajikistan, Uzbekistan and Turkmenistan, the legislative bodies are in complete control of the President. Parliament, being a body of state power and the voice of public interests, bears responsibility to the nation for the quality of laws adopted. It is very difficult for Parliament's functioning under the conditions of an imperfect system of checks and balances, i.e. relating to the legislative, executive and judicial branches of power. Possessing vast authority, the head of the state supersedes and prevails over all the other branches, immobilising their initiatives.

The Presidents of these regions have been trying to monopolise power and to hold power in every way. Authoritarian steps have been taken by the leaders of Tajikistan, Uzbekistan, and Kazakhstan to extend their presidential terms through the holding of referendums rather than Presidential elections. The first country to do so was Turkmenistan, which held a referendum on January 5, 1994, to extend the term of Niyazov's presidency until the year 2002. Uzbekistan held a referendum on March 26, 1995, to extend the President's terms of office until the year 2000. The Uzbek government claimed that 99.3 percent of the voters participated in the referendum and by a majority of 99.6 percent approved the extension of the President's term of office. Except Kyrgyzstan (whose President was ousted by popular protests) and Turkmenistan (whose President expired in office), all the Presidents are still holding power.

The biggest challenge to the political systems of Central Asian states is from the nature of rule of the groups in power. The cornerstones of such rule are networks of patronage underpinning governance, the monopoly of the ruling groups over the main assets, the dominant role of the security sector and a strong leader as a centerpiece of a political regime. Networks are based on the principle of personal loyalty. In Tajikistan and Kyrgyzstan kinship and regionalism are key factors in networks. In Uzbekistan, although power is highly centralised with a strong presidency on the top, the pyramid on which the power rests is not hollow, but consists of a number of pillars. The tension between geographical groups or clans, namely from Tashkent, Samarkand and the Ferghana Valley, define Uzbekistan's politics. In Kazakhstan, influence groups are formed along the principle of personal loyalty and affiliation and interact with each other on the basis of hard, pragmatic interests. These groups are structured in a hierarchy, with Kazakh President Nazarbayev's own group at the top of the pyramid and all groups maintaining links to the President. Political battles happen not for the electorate, but for influence over the head of the state.

All the constitutions provide for a multiparty system. In the democratic system, political parties are the main agents between the state and citizens. These are the chief instruments of political participation in the political process. The functions of political parties are very limited in Turkmenistan, Uzbekistan and Tajikistan. But in the Kyrgyz case, the political atmosphere is liberal, which facilitates a mushroom growth of political movements and political parties. Presently there are more than forty political parties. But in practical terms, there are two groups, one is southern and another is northern, and they are bargaining with each other.

In Kazakhstan, many political parties are functioning, but the government and pro-government political parties are getting more advantages than other political parties in terms of finance and legal matters. Groupism and regroupism is the general phenomena among Kazakhstan's opposition political parties. Many political parties are formed at the time of election, but the frequent changes in the rules and regulations regarding the formation of political parties create hindrances to getting registration as political parties in Central Asia. In the recent constitutional amendment of Kazakhstan, the ethnic minorities are accommodated in the Parliament as minority representatives. In spite of that many political parties in Kazakhstan and Kyrgyzstan have been making consistent efforts to fight against the ruling forces. In many cases, political parties are contesting election as coalitions. Despite the strong government control, political parties are managing to play an intermediaery role between state and citizen. In some countries, political parties have also participated at the policy- making and implementation levels.

The participation of opposition in the Central Asian political process is very limited in Uzbekistan and Turkmenistan due to the strong control of the government. In Kyrgyzstan, many opposition groups are participating in the political process in terms of demonstration, gheraos and other means for demanding constitutional amendment, combating corruption and other causes. In Kazakhstan, opposition political parties formed a coalition and fought against the government. There was some success in Tajikistan during the civil war when the United Tajik opposition group was formed and later given legal recognition to participate in the political system.

In the political process, civil society institutions are playing a very limited role in Turkmenistan, Tajikistan and Uzbekistan. In Uzbekistan, many think tanks emerged, but they are pro-government organisations like the Regional Politics Foundation, Effective Policy Foundation, the Politika Foundation, and the Center for Political Research, whose members are mostly retired officers. After the Andhijan movement, Uzbek authorities tightened the screw both on the civil society institutions and media. It was forbidden by law for more than hundred members to assemble in any particular place. Only recently is the Uzbekistan government taking steps to enhance the role and significance of non-governmental and public institutions.

The development of independent, stable, firm and multi-forum civil society institutions becomes an important constituent of creating a democratic society with a developed market economy. In Kazakhstan and Kyrgyzstan, many civil society organisations are taking part in the political process. In those countries civil society institutions are mostly related to social, economic and environmental issues. In Kazakhstan, more than five thousand NGOs are working and the government is coordinating these NGO networks. Civil society institutions in Central Asia are mainly family enterprises. Apart from these, many independent foreign NGOs have been opening their branches in the Central Asian region like the International Crisis Group, the Institute for War and Peace Reporting, Soros Foundation, James Foundation, Human Right Watch and Organisation for Security and Co-operation in Europe (OSCE). The problem for the growth of civil society institutions is mainly due to the small middle class and lack of finances. Most of the NGOs are working with the help of American grants.

In the case of ethnic minorities, Kazakhstan is more advanced in terms of accommodating the minorities in the Parliament, civil service and other affairs of the state machinery. Mainly Russian and other minority groups are taking part in the election process, policy planning and implementation levels. In Kyrgyzstan, Uzbek minorities are playing a stronger role than other groups. But in Turkmenistan and Tajikistan, the roles of minorities are very limited.

Every country has a constitutionally guaranteed independent mass media. Western media is also active alongside local media and the national media except in Turkmenistan. After the death of former Turkmen President Niyazov, however, electronic media showed various entertainment programmes nationwide. That shows the strong control that he had over media agencies. Many opposition newspapers exist in Kazakhstan and Kyrgyzstan. Most of the media organisations in Central Asia, however, are pro-government because the owners of these media groups are from ruling elites. Opposition media groups are facing lot of problems like financial ones, legal ones, accesses to government information, tax, strong censorship and defamation cases.

In short, political parties, mass media, civil society etc are contributing to the democratisation process in Central Asia despite many constraints and difficulties. The main reason behind the growth in the concentration of a strong executive power with an authoritarian ruler is that traditionally, they have been ruled by a unified (authoritarian) political system rather than a plural (democratic) political system. There is no experience of power sharing among the authorities. After the Soviet disintegration, the economy totally collapsed and most of the political elites thought that the economic system could be improved speedily in an authoritarian system rather than a democratic political system. Central Asian countries are very vulnerable due to the dangers posed by religious fundamentalism, social unrest, clan, regional, and elite conflicts as well as inter-ethnic disharmony. Most of the Presidents of Central Asia are balancing different clans, groups and regions. Political systems in Central Asian countries are not mature. Still they are in the transitional stage. All these factors are responsible to a large extent for the growth of an authoritarian political system. Despite strong constitutional provisions, they have succeeded in keeping their power by maintaining a strong hold of the administration, and by using clan and regional networks.

The growth of a liberal democratic culture in the Central Asian region needs a proper balance of power between legislature, executive and judiciary. One organ should not interfere with other organs of the government. For better political participation, it needs a strong and vibrant civil society, independent media, proper ethnic representation, constructive opposition and a wide space for a multiparty system. Above all, common citizen participation is vital for liberalising the political system and it needs active participation both in the policy making and implementation levels. After the Ukraine crisis in 2014, Central Asian countries shouldfocus more on proper representation of ethnic minorities in the political process and ensure the safety and security of the people.

Index